Property and Politics:
Essays in Later Medieval
English History

Property and Politics: Essays in Later Medieval English History

Edited by Tony Pollard

ALAN SUTTON · Gloucester

ST. MARTIN'S PRESS · New York

1984

First published in Great Britain in 1984
Alan Sutton Publishing Limited
30 Brunswick Road
Gloucester GL1 1JJ

British Library Cataloguing in Publication Data

Property and politics.
   1. Great Britain—History—14th century
   2. Great Britain—History—Lancaster and
   York, 1399—1485   3. Great Britain—
   History—Tudors, 1485–1603
   I. Pollard, A.J.
   942   DA225

   ISBN 0-86299-163-3

First published in the United States of America in 1984
St. Martin's Press, Inc.
175 Fifth Avenue
New York, NY 10010

ISBN 0-312-65173-2

Library of Congress Catalog Card Number 84-40371

Typesetting and origination by
Alan Sutton Publishing Limited.
Photoset Goudy 10/11
Printed in Great Britain.

Contents

List of Abbreviations

AC	*Archaeologia Cantiana*
ADSM	Archives Départmentales de la Seine Maritime, Rouen
AN	Achives Nationales, Paris
BIHR	*Bulletin of the Institute of Historical Research*
BL	British Library, London
BN	Bibliothèque Nationale, Paris
CCR	*Calendar of Close Rolls*
CChR	*Calendar of Charter Rolls*
CFR	*Calendar of Fine Rolls*
CIM	*Calendar of Inquisitions Miscellaneous*
CIPM	*Calendar of Inquisitions Post Mortem*
COD	*Calendar of Ormond Deeds,* 6 vols., ed. E. Curtis (Dublin, 1932–43)
CP	G.E. Cokayne, *The Complete Peerage,* 13 vols., ed. V.H. Gibbs *et al.* (1910–59)
CPR	*Calendar of Patent Rolls*
DKR	*Annual Reports of the Deputy Keeper of the Public Records*
EconHR	*Economic History Review*
EETS	Early English Text Society
EHR	*English Historical Review*
Foedera	*Foedera, Conventiones, Literae et Cujuscunque Generis Acta Publica,* 20 vols., ed T. Rymer (1704–35)
HMC	Historical Manuscripts Commission
NLI	National Library of Ireland, Dublin
PPC	*Proceedings and Ordinances of the Privy Council of England,* 7 vols., ed. N.H. Nicholas (1834–37)
PRO	Public Record Office
PROI	Public Record Office of Ireland
RC	Record Commission
RP	*Rotuli Parliamentorum,* 7 vols. (RC, 1832)

RPC	*Rotulorum Patentium et Clausorum Cancellarie Hibernie Calendarium*, ed. E. Tresham (Irish Record Commission, 1828)
RS	Rolls Series
SR	*Statutes of the Realm*, 11 vols. (RC, 1810–28)
TRHS	*Transactions of the Royal Historical Society*
VCH	*Victoria History of the Counties of England*

Classes of documents in the Public Record Office

Chancery

C1	Early Chancery Proceedings
C47	Miscellanea
C64	Norman Rolls
C66	Patent Rolls
C67	Supplementary Patent Rolls
C139–41	Inquisitions Post Mortem, Series I, Henry VI – Richard III

Court of Common Pleas

CP40	Plea Rolls

Duchy of Lancaster

DL5	Entry Books of Decrees and Orders
DL28	Accounts (Various)
DL29	Ministers' Accounts
DL37	Chancery Rolls
DL42	Miscellaneous Books

Exchequer

E28	Treasury of Receipt, Council and Privy Seal Records
E101	King's Remembrancer, Various Accounts
E122	, Customs Accounts
E163	, Miscellanea
E179	, Subsidy Rolls etc.
E198	, Serjeanties, knights fees etc.
E356	Lord Treasurer's Remembrancer, Customs Accounts
E364	, Foreign Account Rolls
E368	, Memoranda Rolls
E401	Exchequer of Receipt, Receipt Rolls
E403	, Issue Rolls
E404	, Warrants for Issue

Court of King's Bench

KB8	*Baga de Secretis*
KB9	Ancient Indictments
KB27	*Coram Rege* Rolls

Prerogative Court of Canterbury

| PCC | Registered Copies of Wills |

Special Collections

| SC8 | Ancient Petitions |
| SC11 | Rentals and Surveys, Rolls |

Introduction

The essays in this volume were originally presented at a symposium held at the University of Reading in July 1983. The symposium was the third of its kind, following similar meetings at Bristol in 1978 and Swansea in 1979, the proceedings of which were published under the titles of *Patronage, Pedigree and Power in Medieval England*, edited by Charles Ross (1979), and *Patronage, the Crown and the Provinces in Later Medieval England*, edited by Ralph A. Griffiths (1981). As in the earlier meetings, the focus was again on younger scholars, current and recently qualified postgraduage students, who gathered during a sweltering weekend to exchange the results of recent research and progress reports with one another and older colleagues. Although the occasion was a reunion for many of those who had met previously, the research students came from a wide circle of institutions in Britain and the United States. Some of the papers published here were read; others were initially presented as communications. The very nature of the gathering precluded the setting of a specific theme so that, as in the preceding volumes, the subject matter is wide-ranging. However, common ground lay in a shared interest in the world of the property-holding élite of late-medieval England, a reflection of the continuing influence of the late K.B. McFarlane on the direction taken by historical research in recent decades. In effect, this volume offers to the reader variations on the theme of property and politics within the late-medieval ruling class.

The theme of property is nowhere more explicit than in Rowena Archer's synoptic study of a surprisingly neglected topic, the dowager and her rights. In the later middle ages the best years of a (well-born or-wed) woman was her widowhood, when she enjoyed almost complete security in her dower and jointly-enfeoffed lands. The scale of the problem created for her male kinsmen becomes especially apparent in the case of the Mowbray family, no member of which, as either earl of Nottingham or duke of Norfolk, ever enjoyed his full inheritance. In the light of this, the Yorkist kings' well known disregard for the rights of certain prominent dowagers may perhaps reflect a more wide-spread frustration among late-medieval noblemen at their inability to lay their hands on all the estates to which they had an eventual title. To the church, however,

dowager and frustrated kinsman alike were but stewards of the property entrusted
to them by God. The charitable disposal of wealth was, as Peter Fleming points
out, a means towards saving the soul. Nevertheless, to a great many of the
gentry of Kent the provision of obits, the establishment of chantries, the
maintenance of oratories and portable altars, the distribution of alms and the
attention lavished on burial places were means for the public display of wealth
and social superiority. Genuine piety and humility were to be found, but the
majority revealed in their last wills and testaments a proprietary attitude to
religion and a materialistic faith. The possession of property had not only to be
justified in the eyes of God; it had also to be defended in the face of the world.
As canny and worldly-wise man as Sir John Fastolf, despite the care he took, was
hounded by rival claimants to a fifth of his purchases in East Anglia. As
Anthony Smith shows, almost all the claims raked up against Fastolf were
spurious, but nevertheless, because of their political connections, his rivals were
able to force him through time-consuming and expensive litigation and to make
it extremely difficult for him to collect any income from the disputed properties.

Fastolf is the pre-eminent fifteenth-century example of the *nouveau riche*,
having established himself as a man of property in England on the foundations of
his profits of war in France. His earlier career had been as one of those who had
participated in the Lancastrian land settlement in Normandy, further details of
which are elucidated by Robert Massey. Henry V's conquest had created the best
opportunity ever available until the dissolution of the monasteries for the
relatively humble to establish themselves as men of property, albeit French men
of property. For the beneficiaries of the process of settlement, which followed in
the wake of the advancing Lancastrian armies through the Vexin and elsewhere,
were expected to reside on their new estates and contribute to their defence. It
becomes apparent that Henry V set about establishing an Anglo-Norman landed
interest upon much the same basis as the Anglo-Irish community which already
existed in the other Lancastrian 'colony'. And, as Elizabeth Matthew reveals in
her detailed analysis of the financing of the English administration in Ireland, in
his attempt to reduce the burden on the English exchequer, Henry V adopted a
policy there similar to that pursued in Normandy: a policy of encouraging the
Anglo-Irish, through the person of James Butler, earl of Ormond, to pay for
their own defence. In this Lancastrian 'colonial experiment' the settlers in both
Normandy and Ireland, those with vested interests in the colonies' survival,
were to bear the burden themselves.

The creation of a new nobility in one conquest, and the exploitation of an
existing nobility in another, was no radical departure in government. For, as
Bishop Russell of Lincoln wrote later in the century 'the polityk rule of every
region well ordeigned stondithe in the nobles'.[1] Property carried with it
magisterial responsibility and political authority. Russell's maxim was as applic-
able within England as it was overseas, and nowhere more so than in service on
the commission of the peace, for which after 1440 there was a statutory

residential and property qualification restricting membership to those with a clear income from land of above £20 *p.a.* Carol Arnold's analysis of the West Riding bench from 1437 charts the manner in which it became politicized after 1458, its changes in size and composition reflecting the changing fortunes of dynastic factions. What appears to have been a 'broad-bottomed' administration of the 'county' landed interest before 1458, became under the Yorkists and Henry VII, by means of the appointment to the bench of the local stewards of the duchies of Lancaster and York and, increasingly, of knights of the royal household, a body more responsive to the command of the crown. The opportunities offered by a stewardship of the duchy of Lancaster to enhance political authority is taken up and expanded in greater detail by Ian Rowney. William, lord Hastings, he argues, used the resources of the honour of Tutbury, whose steward he was, to buttress his authority in the north midlands. He used these resources, as far as the crown allowed, rather than those of his own property to establish his leadership of local gentry society. It was a question, however, not so much of recruiting an affinity but of moulding himself to the contours of an established gentry society whose leaders were capable of acting independently. In this way he provided a rule which was both political and politic.

Unfortunately, all too often in late-medieval England, especially when the crown was weak, 'the polityk rule of every region' degenerated into factional rule and political conflict. Several contributors to this volume throw light on this innate tendency. Tony Saul explains why two propertied men of a different kind – William Elys and Hugh Fastolf, rich burghers of Great Yarmouth – became targets of the commons in the Good Parliament of 1376. Elys and Fastolf had invested heavily in the East Anglian countryside and had developed close connections with London and the court. Their connections cushioned them against the worst effects of the economic recession on their port, but aroused the hostility of lesser burgesses at Yarmouth and the rival town of Lowestoft who took advantage of the general assault on the crown to settle old scores. With court backing, Elys and Fastolf survived the crisis, though they were to suffer again in 1381. Hugh's nephew, Sir John Fastolf, found himself on the wrong side when factional government took over in East Anglia in the 1440s. Fastolf's foes looked to Suffolk and Scales, and it was their power which enables the likes of Sir Edward Hull to harass him, despite legal judgements in his favour. It was only after York's victory at St Albans in 1455 that Sir John Fastolf was able to turn the tables. Faction also raised its head overseas under Henry VI, where it played a part in undermining his father's 'colonial experiment'. As Robert Massey suggests, it was Bedford who began the process whereby the principal settlers of Lancastrian Normandy and Maine were recruited into noble households: a process, to be intensified under his successors, which led to the distribution of grants of land as mere patronage and the division of the leaders of Anglo-Norman society into factions under the rival dukes of Somerset and York.

The desire to control and exploit this patronage perhaps explains the keenness with which Somerset and York competed for office. In Ireland Henry V's experiment in devolution degenerated in a similar way. In addition to the failing determination of successive governments, the long running feud between the Butler and Talbot families was a contributory cause of collapse, for the patronage and powers that the chief governorship conferred were diverted to factional ends.

Standing apart from this picture of mid-fifteenth century turmoil, as indeed did its subject, is Roger Lovatt's restoration of John Blacman's reminiscences of Henry VI to their rightful place as first-hand evidence of the king's personality. Blacman's work was, it is demonstrated, a genuine if partial recollection written almost certainly before 1485. Henry is cast in the role of a paradigm of contemporary lay piety (just as his father was cast by his biographers in the role of a paradigm of contemporary chivalry). His life is presented to the reader as an exemplar not of bland sanctity, but of the precise, world-weary piety of an imitator of Christ. The king's public vices – his indiscriminate largesse, his reluctance to enforce the full rigour of the law and his erratic attitude to public affairs – are recorded as private virtues. Blacman's purpose, it emerges, was to show that a higher virtue lay in being a bad king. If indeed, as is argued here Henry adopted the role of the 'fool of God', Blacman's reminiscences can help us understand more clearly the political disasters of his reign, the reluctance to depose him and the flourishing cult after his death. Here in this portrait of Henry VI, at the highest level of society, lies the antithesis of that obsession with property and the pursuit of wealth, power and status characteristic of those members of the late-medieval ruling class the dowagers, noblemen, gentry, soldiers, settlers, *parvenus* and burgesses represented elsewhere in this volume.

The contributors to this volume and all the participants in the symposium wish to thank the University of Reading for its hospitality and financial support, especially Anne Curry and her assistants for organising the meeting so efficiently and smoothly. No less a debt of gratitude is owed to Ralph Griffiths and Alan Sutton for their parts in enabling the proceedings to be communicated to a wider audience so speedily.

Teesside Polytechnic   A.J. Pollard

Note

1. *Grants from the Crown during the Reign of Edward V, etc.*, ed. J.G. Nicols (Camden Society, Old Series, LX, 1854), p. xliii.

1

Rich Old Ladies:
The Problem of Late Medieval Dowagers[*]

Rowena E. Archer
University of Oxford

Nevertheless, the apprentices for the most part make good fortunes, some by one means and some by another; but above all, those who happen to be in the good graces of the mistress of the house in which they are domiciliated at the time of the death of the master; because, by the ancient custom of the country, every inheritance is divided into three parts; for the church and funeral expenses, for the wife, and for the children. But the lady takes care to secure a good portion for herself in secret, first, and then the residue being divided into three parts as aforesaid, she, being in possession of what she has robbed, of her own third, and that of her children besides (and if she have no children, the two-thirds belong to her by right), usually in the house who is most pleasing to her, and who was probably not *displeasing* to her in the lifetime of her husband; and in his power she places all her own fortune, as well as that of her children, who are sent away as apprentices into other houses. Then, when the boys are of age, their fortunes are restored to them by their mother's husband, who has enjoyed them for many years, but never to the full amount; and these boys in process of time enact to others the same part that their step-fathers peformed to them. No Englishman can complain of this corrupt practice, it being universal throughout the kingdom; nor does anyone, arrived at years of discretion, find fault with his mother for marrying again during his childhood, because, from very ancient custom, this license has become so sanctioned, that it is not considered any discredit to a woman

---

[*] This paper has sprung from the particular case of the Mowbray family and my own research on the extraordinary succession of dowagers who had to be supported from the Mowbray inheritance.

to marry again every time that she is left a widow, however unsuitable the match may be as to age, rank, and fortune.

I saw, one day, that I with your Magnificence at court, a very handsome young man of about 18 years of age, the brother of the Duke of Suffolk, who, as I understood, had been left very poor, the whole of the paternal inheritance amongst the nobility descending to the eldest son; this youth, I say, was boarded out to a widow of fifty with a fortune, as I was informed, of 50,000 crowns; and this old woman knew how to play her cards so well, that he was content to become her husband, and patiently to waste the flower of his beauty with her, hoping soon to enjoy her great wealth with some handsome young lady.[1]

This somewhat whimsical account of England by an Italian at the court of Henry VII encompasses many of the problems arising from the existence of dowagers at the close of the middle ages. For all his apparent levity, the foreigner showed some grasp of the law relating to dower, the growth of which had been increasingly to the benefit of women; the question of disparagement, previously imposed from without but by this period, rather ironically, often self-imposed; the effect of a woman's mere survival on the inheritances of her children; and the remarkable longevity that some particular individuals exhibited. Taken together, these features made dower one of the commonest and in some cases most destructive of baronial incidents. Though successive generations of historians have observed the effects, often detrimental, of individual dowagers on the lives of particular families, no collective study of dowagers has yet been attempted. This paper is intended as a general survey of the problems as a whole, their development and the failure to find any satisfactory remedy.[2]

From earliest times English law had recognised the need for provision and protection for widows. The Anglo-Saxon law makers included in their codes specific reference to the security of the widow and children of a deceased man. A late-tenth century treatise concerning the betrothal of women indicated that one of the prerequisites of marriage was the man's declaration of what his intended wife should have in the event of his early death, while the record of two marriage settlements of the eleventh century shows that ample provision was made in practice.[3] Anglo-Saxon women seem to have enjoyed a considerable degree of freedom, but feudal restrictions brought a reversal in widows' fortunes. There was no place for the independence of English noble ladies in the immediate post-conquest years. Change triumphed over continuity. It was not until 1100 that the Normans made any direct ruling on the position of dowagers. Henry I's promises in his coronation charter that the widows of his barons would have their dower and their marriage portion and would not be married off against their own will indicated an awareness of abuses in the treatment of surviving dowagers.[4] These were empty promises and in the reign of John the crown's treatment of widows attracted a high degree of notoriety. Extremely high prices were paid for freedom and so many sums were accepted by the crown that there appears to have been a common form for their entry on the fine rolls. Hence, on the Pipe Roll of 1 John, under Berkshire we find, 'Emma, wife of Henry de Montfort: 40 marks for a licence to marry whom she will and to have her dower in peace', and similarly in 12 John, in the same county 'Margaret, who was the wife of Ralf de Summery: 300 marks to have reasonable dower in the lands belonging to the said Ralf, her husband'[5]. Some of these proffers speak very loudly of the insecurity of widows at law and their immense wealth. Hawise, countess of Aumale in her own right, was thrice married. Her second husband, William de Forz, was a Poitevin commander of Richard 1's crusading fleet and a man far beneath her in social rank. Within one month of the death of her third husband, she had paid 5,000 marks for her inheritance, her dower and her freedom.[6]

Until the thirteenth century, a wife's right to a life tenancy in her husband's lands derived from the gift made to her at the church door of lands or chattels or money which her spouse then held, providing it was not in excess of one third of the total value. If she was not specifically dowered in this way, she would receive one third of the lands held by her husband on the day of their marriage. Once she had consented to specific gifts, she could not subsequently sue for more. Thus, she had no rights in property which her husband inherited after the marriage, and where she had accepted chattels or money she was not entitled to any share in her husband's lands.[7] During the thirteenth century the widow's rights were gradually extended and Magna Carta, described as 'one of the first great stages in the emancipation of women'[8] provided some remedy in a clause declaring dower to be chargeable on all the husband's lands. In the main, Magna Carta confirmed existing principles and ideas relating to widows. Upon their husband's death widows were to receive both dower and dowry absolutely free and to be allowed to remain in the principal residence for forty days. Dower was to be assigned from all the property held by her husband on the day of his death, not the day of his marriage. No widow was to be compulsorily remarried, though she was required to seek consent from her lord for any future marriage. With respect to disparagement the barons were especially concerned about how loyal crown supporters, particularly foreigners, had been rewarded by advantageous marriages. John demonstrated that the whim of the monarch was not suppressed at Runnymede. In 1216 Margaret, the widow of Baldwin de Redvers, earl of Devon, was married off to the notorious Faulkes de Bréauté. The latter was eventually exiled in 1224, whereupon Margaret had her marriage annulled and lived as a widow for over twenty years.[9] The 1217 re-issue of Magna Carta set a limitation allowing for the possibility of husbands granting their wives less than one-third at the church door, but by the end of the century widows had become entitled to thirds as a common law right. There was no need for gifts at the church door and none could gainsay her rights. Britton, writing in the time of Edward 1, put it succinctly: ' and because usage of dower is become law, a wife is sufficiently endowed though her husband say nothing[10].'

Basic principles having been established, the law continued, in the main, to work in favour of widows. Inevitably, the law grew more complex as new situations gave rise to the need for new remedies. From an early date, the anomaly of dower must have been self-evident and that, in a general sense, was the first problem which it presented. Dower overrode the feudal interests of the lord. It was always an internal arrangement, the widow holding of her husband's heir, not of her husband's lord.[11] She sued for her dower in the heir's court, though she had long been able, by means of a writ of dower, to carry her case to the king.[12] Even so, her dower was not heritable, no homage was due for it and it was always an irregularity in the feudal system. It is perhaps hardly surprising that the law relating to dower developed piecemeal, and that concessions and admissions were hard won, though in some cases assiduously pursued. In 1274, in a test case between Beatrice, queen of Germany, the widow of Richard, earl of Cornwall, and the heir, Edmund, earl of Cornwall, Beatrice declared, 'for the common benefit of other ladies seeking dower in the future that it would be most dangerous. . .if. . .proofs should willingly, without argument be allowed to keep them from their reasonable dower against the common law of England and the tenor of Magna Carta'.[13] The case revolved around the question of specific dower, in this instance 4,000 marks granted to Beatrice at the church door. The latter invoked the edicts of Magna Carta and the newer rulings on common law dower which entitled her to thirds in all her deceased husband's estates.

Several other legal protections for the widow had received wide recognition by the beginning of the fourteenth century. Only divorce or infidelity could nullify claims to dower. In 1297 John, Lord Greystoke's estranged wife failed in her attempt to sue her former husband for dower. He agreed to resume co-habitation with her in consequence of which her suit was defeated.[14] With respect to child marriages, there was clearly a need for agreement regarding the validity of a mariage contracted by parties under age. Temporal and ecclesiastical law did not always see eye to eye here, particularly when the matter related to wardship and dower. Temporal law chose to ignore the doctrine that marriages under seven were voidable until the parties reached the ages at which they might be consummated — fourteen for boys and twelve for girls. Dower was awarded to nine-year-old widows and Coke declared that he would give dower regardless of the late husband's age, 'all be it he were but four years old'.[15] Alienations of dower could only be made by a husband for his own lifetime. Grants beyond that, or in perpetuity, could only be achieved by fine in the courts in the presence of the consenting wife. Writs of Dower, Entry and Right of Dower were available for widows to sue for recovery of alienated dower.[16] A number of parliamentary petitions show that some widows were ready to go to considerable lengths to preserve the integrity of their dower and that in some cases such measures were the only form of redress. In 1290 Joan de Hansey pleaded for dower in a manor which her husband had sold to the King.[17] The law also protected dower from any diminution arising from the suvival of a second dowager. It was logical enough that the widow of an heir should only receive one third of the two thirds held by her husband, and clearly successive widows fared less well than the senior dowager.[18] Even where parents settled land upon children for their marriage and the father died, leaving a widow, dower was awarded in spite of such arrangements. The property settled by Thomas Mowbray, earl of Nottingham (d. 1399) on his son Thomas and Constance Holand on their bethrothal in 1391 was reduced in 1399 to accommodate the dower of the widow, Elizabeth Fitzalan. The latter was extremely tenacious regarding her dower rights, which affected not only the 1391 settlement, but also those manors which her husband had granted as annuities to his followers for life.[19]

From the end of the thirteenth century, the emphasis on provision for widows moved from dower to jointures. As the latter provided a more immediate benefit and enjoyed a greater security at law, it was their existence which came to be more important and in turn more troublesome in the inheritance of property. Jointure was quite simply that which was held by husband and wife jointly and in survivorship, either by a marriage settlement, a joint purchase or an enfeoffment. In the fourteenth and fifteenth centuries most marriage contracts granted the wife a joint share in part of her husband's lands, the extent of the jointure often representing the importance of the wife. Hence, when Edward 1's granddaughter, Margaret of Brotherton, was married to John, Lord Segrave sometime in the 1330s, Margaret had a jointure in all but three of the Segrave manors.[20] With the increasing use of enfeoffments and conveyances, it became possible for a wife to secure a life interest in her husband's estates – a position which could be realized, and often was realized, to the serious detriment of the heir. The power which this gave to widows did not pass unnoticed. The lords in 1461, when discussing dower with particular reference to the duchess of Bedford, agreed to a provision for her in principle but added the cautionary comment, so that her portion be not too large'.[21]

Clearly then, the best years of a woman's life in the later middle ages were those of her widowhood. Thomas of Stitney, a Bohemian gentleman of the late fourteenth century, recalled his grandmother's comments: 'O good lord, how is it that widows have a greater reward than married folk? How much better and more comfortable an estate we widows have than we had in marriage'.[22] She had emerged from tutelage in her father's household and subjection as a mere appendage of her husband to become *femme sole* and mistress of her own inheritance, if she had one, and of dower and jointure estates which had a virtually unassailable position in the common law. She bore no burden for the maintenance of the heir, nor any responsibility for the debts of her husband in the context of her dower. Neither was her jointure or her dower subject to forfeiture upon re-marriage, and though they might suffer an immediate confiscation if no licence were sought beforehand for such a marriage, they could almost invariably be recovered by payment of a fine.[23]

Only in one area did the law of the period involve severe treatment of widows. Forfeiture for treason never offered protection to dower in late medieval law. Nor in the early fourteenth century did it even protect the wife's own inheritance of her jointure. This is particularly clear in the case of the rebellions against Edward II. John Mowbray's marriage to Alicia de Braose had represented a major step forward in the fortunes of his family. Sole heiress to William de Braose, she brought to her husband the promise of succession to the lordship of Gower and huge estates in Sussex. Immediately following Mowbray's execution after the battle of Boroughbridge, Alicia and their son were imprisoned. The lordship of Gower was granted to Hugh Despenser and Alicia was forced to grant him the reversion of her Sussex inheritance.[24] The law provided no remedy for the widows of contumacious barons and it was only the direct intervention of Edward III that enabled those widowed in the quarrels of his father's reign to recover their inheritances.[25] The distinction between dower and a widow's own inheritance and jointure was carefully and notably drawn in the statute of 1388. There it was admitted, with a commendable degree of logic and humanity, that as rights to inheritance and jointure pre-dated a husband's treason, they should enjoy protection at law.[26] In 1399 the commons petitioned that widows of lords convicted of treason should have dower of their husband's land, but on that occasion the common law was upheld.[27] In spite of this ruling, Henry IV permitted the widows of the earls of Huntingdon and Lord Despenser to sue for their dower notwithstanding the forfeiture of their late husbands. It was in the fifteenth century, with the increasing use of attainder, that heirs could count the survival of mothers and grandmothers a blessing. Perhaps the best known case is that of the Percy earls of Northumberland. In 1461 the Percy estates were saved from immediate extinction by the survival of two dowagers who, though not entitled to their common law dower, were between them holding jointures worth between £1,850 and £1,950 p.a.[28] By and large, however, this was small compensation for the preceding years of continuous obstruction and difficulty presented by the survival of late-medieval dowagers.

As the position of dowagers grew in strength, it became increasingly urgent to protect the heirs of noble estates from abuses to dower lands and to curtail the exploitation of these by dowagers and step-fathers. The law endeavoured to provide remedies for a number of common problems. Excessive dower was probably the least of these. From an early date the crown had made available a writ of Admeasurement of Dower. Where an assignment of dower exceeded one-third of the total estates, the heir, upon coming of age, could sue for recovery.[29] More serious was the danger of waste. The exploitation of dower estates was a special danger when widows re-married. Second husbands, with at best a life interest in dower lands, were often only concerned to make as much as possible from them in the time available. The statute of Gloucester laid down that waste in dower would be punishable with loss of dower and payment of compensation.[30] In some cases, however, even this did not entirely resolve the problem. John, Lord Mowbray, grandfather of the first duke of Norfolk, was married three times. At his death in 1361 he left a son, by his second wife, who was of age. His widow was assigned dower in Bedfordshire and Buckinghamshire which she abused to such an extent that the heir was forced to take action against her. In 1366 he called upon her to show by what right she had prepared to sell or destroy three houses, woods and gardens in the manors of Willington and Haynes. He complained that she had committed waste by destroying the trees, digging up the land and allowing the buildings to fall into decay. Specific mention was made of two courts, two dwellings, four rooms, two kitchens, two granges, various outbuildings, two houses, two dovecots, one chapel and thousands of trees. Elizabeth's defence was decidedly weak: that one dwelling was pulled down as unsafe; another was blown down; and cottages were torn down because the tenants had died of plague. Mowbray reported a loss of 12,000 trees in Sheerhatch wood, something which Elizabeth defended in equally feeble terms, pleading gale damage, need of repair and disease. Mowbray was awarded damages estimated at nearly £1,000. He recovered Sheerhatch wood and a ten acre grove, and was awarded annual payments of £41 payable over twenty years. However, within two years Mowbray was dead, his son was a minor in wardship, and Elizabeth continued to enjoy her dower lands until 1375.[31] For many years there had been considerable risk of permanent alienation. The legislation of Edward 1 concentrated on the defeat of all attempts by life tenants to treat properties as if they were estates in fee. Where dowagers re-married, the second husband and his relatives had difficulty in resisting the temptation to divert dower lands to their own patrimony. The statute of Gloucester went some way towards alleviating this particular problem by enabling an heir to recover dower alienated as soon as the unlawful enfeoffment occurred, whereas previously the heir had been obliged to wait until the dowager's death.[32] In spite of this, the risk remained.

    J.R. Lander suggested that the inclusion in the general livery of his estates to John, fourth duke of Norfolk, of those portions in the hands of dowagers was unusual. It is hard, however, to accept his implication that neither the crown nor the nobility were aware of the risk to estates in dower, and certainly the Mowbrays throughout the fifteenth century had taken special care to include reversions of estates in dower in any conveyances. In 1413 Sir John Grey quitclaimed all his rights in Mowbray property to the Earl Marshal for 5,000 marks. Grey had recently married Mowbray's youthful widowed sister-in-law, Constance Holand, whose interest in Mowbray property was worth at least £400.[33] Earlier in the year both parties had entered recognisances for £1,000 in connection with repairs to the Mowbray manor of Weston by Baldock.[34] The concern over rights raises a number of important points. Firstly, Grey's position was already well prescribed by the common law. Although, by the courtesy of England, Grey would be entitled to hold his wife's own inheritance for life, providing a child capable of inheriting was born to them both, the law of courtesy was not applicable to dower. His interest in the Mowbray estates could not, therefore, extend beyond Constance's lifetime, although as far as the Earl Marshal was concerned this could well be for a protracted period. Constance, as the wife of a condemned traitor, had been treated with some leniency.[35] Mowbray was doubtless aware of the possibility of royal mercy permitting the widows of *traitors* to sue for dower. His inheritance was already burdened with one dower and the agreement in 1413 may represent some attempt by Mowbray to extract a promise from Grey that he would not seek to recover dower. In 1415, before departing for France, John Mowbray included in a general enfeoffment of his estates special mention of the reversion of property held by his mother and Constance.[36] Ultimately, Mowbray fears proved to be well founded. Katherine Nevill, dowager duchess of the second Mowbray duke, secured the reversion of some of the lands of her third husband, John, Viscount Beaumont, for her daugher Joan and – with the Nevill penchant for conveying property to the exclusion of common law heirs – on Joan's second marriage to Lord Berkeley, in 1468, dowered her with some of the Mowbray lands of her own jointure. Joan, however, was not the daughter of either Beaumont or Mowbray, but was the issue of Katherine's second marriage to Sir Thomas Strangeways.[37]

Remedies at law, then, were of limited benefit to the heir. By the fifteenth century protection of dowagers had reached its apogee and this in spite of the known and widely experienced effects of their position. Only the mightiest could undermine the security of widows and even then such things were achieved through a total disregard of the law. In 1447 Eleanor Cobham was barred from any dower, jointure or share in the inheritance or possessions of Humphrey, duke of Gloucester.[38] In 1459 the attainder of the Yorkists in the Coventry parliament specifically excluded the wives of the persons named in the act, but with the notable exception of Alice, in her own right, countess of Salisbury.[39] These two incidents might arguably be described as political expedients, though it is hard to escape completely the suggestion of greed. Certainly no excuse can be made for Edward IV, whose 'shabby and sordid operations' amounted to a flagrant abuse of the law on dower. The widowed countess of Warwick was openly treated 'as though she were now naturally dead' in 1472 in order to benefit Edward's two brothers, and Elizabeth Howard, dowager countess of Oxford was forced to surrender her property to Richard, duke of Gloucester in 1475.[40] Similarly, in appropriating the Mowbray inheritance for his son Richard, duke of York, Edward persuaded the dowager duchess of Norfolk to surrender her dower and jointure in order to increase the estates of her daughter and accept a share in the Mowbray estate which was less than her due.[41]

It is, then, only too apparent that the mere survival of dowagers could and did cause havoc in the normal course of succession. Granted that an early marriage to a child-bride and the premature death of the young groom were frequent occurrences, it is a matter of no surprise to find that virtually every noble family in late medieval England regularly faced the problem of providing for at least one dowager.

Few dowagers ever surrendered their dower interests, though some did co-operate with the heirs over the administration of estates. Mary St Pol, dowager countess of Pembroke, put one of her Essex manors in the hands of her heir, her great great-nephew, John Hastings. Although her Irish lands were also in Pembroke's hands for a few months, mainly on account of her failure to defend them, Mary successfully petitioned the crown for their restoration.[42] Margaret of Brotherton likewise placed some of her estates, notably the lordship of Chepstow and her Irish lands, in the hands of her Hastings son-in-law in an effort to provide for their better administration and defence. Ironically, the arrangement was upset by Hastings's premature death in 1375, only three years later. Margaret not only resumed control of her own estates but also became guardian of the inheritance of her Hastings grandchild.[43] Examples like these are rare, for many solved their difficulties in administering their often very considerable accumulated inheritances by re-marriage. Some doughty widows proved themselves as well able, if not better, at handling their affairs than some of their male peers.[44] Few were as obliging as the dowager countess of Suffolk, Elizabeth Mowbray, and her daughter Katherine, both of whom became nuns and 'ended their lives in prayer and chastity that the earldom should remain to the second brother, Sir William de la Pole, because of the name'.[45]

Some situations were evidently worse than others. If the bride had at least provided an heir, if her jointure was reasonable, and if she survived just long enough to see her child through his minority, following her husband to the grave within a small space, then the consequences were mild, possibly even beneficial, provided she was a caring guardian of her son's inheritance. Examples abound, however, of young widows failing to produce heirs, carrying the estates to second, third, fourth and even fifth husbands, collecting dower and jointure from each and living for forty years. Many of those who did manage to produce heirs also managed to outlive them, depriving them of the full enjoyment of their property. Alice Chaucer was forty-seven years a Montague dowager. She produced no heir and outlived her step-daughter, Alice, countess of Salisbury and her Nevill husband by some ten years.[46] Mary St Pol was for fifty-three years the widow of Aymer de Valence. In three brief years of marriage she had produced no heir and she was still alive when the Hastings line descended from her sister-in-law, Isabel de Valence, was in its fifth and final generation.[47] Joan, Lady Abergavenny, whom Adam of Usk uncharitably described as a 'second Jezabel', was twenty-four years the widow of William Beauchamp, and though she had a son, Richard, earl of Worcester ,she outlived him by thirteen years. She never re-married after Beauchamp's death and she administered a vast estate worth almost £2,000 *p.a.*[48] Elizabeth de Burgh, lady of Clare, probably the best documented of fourteenth-century dowagers and certainly one of the wealthiest, was the youngest of the three co-heiresses of Gilbert de Clare. Her first husband died in 1313 and her third in 1321. For almost forty years thereafter she lived as a widow, managing an estate which, in the late 1320s, produced an estimated £3,000 *p.a.* The first person to benefit from her inheritance was her grand-daughter's husband, Lionel, duke of Clarence.[49]

No study of late medieval dowagers would be complete without special reference to the Nevills. The northern baronage, as their nearest neighbours, were the first to pay the price of alliance with the rising star of the house of Nevill. Increasing prominence, reflected in increasingly eminent husbands for the Nevill girls, spread the awesome consequences to the southern nobility. 'Nevill ladies', observed K.B. McFarlane, 'most of them dowagers, were mostrous tough[50]'. In the first generation the children of Ralph Nevill (d. 1367) and Alice d'Audley included two daughters of considerable durability. Margaret, who was for twenty years a Roos dowager, never produced an heir and carried her Roos interests to the first Percy earl of Northumberland. Her sister, Euphemia, was a Clifford widow for forty-eight years. She was one of a series of Clifford dowagers whose survival was a major factor in the relative obscurity of the Clifford lords. Between 1391 and 1393, no less than three widows had to be provided for out of the estates, and between 1314 and 1436 not a single year passed in which the Clifford estates were free of such burdens.[51] The daughters of Ralph, first earl of Westmorland, maintained and extended the traditions of their female ancestors. The senior daughters, Matilda and Margaret, were for twenty-four years and forty-three years respectively dowagers to the Mauley and Scrope families. Matilda's failure to bear a son or daughter brought to an end the direct Mauley line. Lord Peter had provided her with a life interest in the major part of his estates and made her sole beneficiary of his will.[52] The daughters of Ralph's Beaufort wife proved equally robust. The marriages of Katherine Nevill are without parallel amongst medieval dowagers. At enormous expense, her father had betrothed her to John Mowbray and they were married in the chapel at Raby castle early in 1412, by the abbot of Jervaulx.[53] Short of money in 1415 on account of his preparations for the war in France, Mowbray took time off to travel to Raby in the early summer, seeking payment of 700 marks, the balance outstanding for Katherine's dowry. He managed to extract a derisory £40 from Westmorland and there is no evidence that he ever received the rest. It was a cruel irony indeed, given the extent to which Katherine was to milk the Mowbray estates on her husband's death.[54] Norfolk died in 1432, directing in his will that Katherine, in addition to her dower and jointure, should receive a life interest in his estates.[55] By the 1440s Katherine had married Thomas Strange-ways, a servant of the Norfolk household. He was rapidly followed by a socially more acceptable individual in the person of Viscount Beaumont. It was her marriage to Sir John Woodville, however, a young teenager, when she was certainly in her sixties, that has cemented her reputation as the archetypal medieval dowager; in her own day it was described as *maritagium diabolicum.* Nor must it be forgotten that Katherine had the last laugh, for she survived her young husband by fourteen years and died in 1483.[56] Katherine's death seems to have been anticipated on a number of occasions. As early as 1462, the reversion of estates in Katherine's hands had been granted to William, Lord Hastings, and the following year George, duke of Clarence received a similar grant; but neither of these could match the old duchess in years. More significantly, she had outlived all her Mowbray descendents and by the time of her death was depriving the co-heirs, John Howard and William, Lord Berkeley, of part of their share in the Mowbray inheritance.[58] The longevity of Katherine's sisters produced parallel, if less noteworthy, histories. Anne was twenty years a Stafford widow; Eleanor, who failed to give her Despenser husband an heir, enjoyed his estates for more than fifty years; and Cecily, the youngest, who was Richard, duke of York's widow for thirty-five years, survived both her royal sons. Then, in the following generation, the daughters of Richard Nevill, earl of Salisbury included Alice, who survived Lord FitzHugh for thirty years, outliving her childless son, and Catherine, who was for forty-three years the widow of Lord Harrington and for twenty years, the widow of William, Lord Hastings.

The survival and longevity of medieval women, combined with the dubious activities of some, were often the key to movements within the ranks of the nobility, in particular the swallowing up of one peerage by another, part of that phenomenon of the accumulation of estates in the hands of fewer and fewer men.[59] At the simplest level, this was manifest in the survival of heiresses marrying and carrying their fathers' title elsewhere.[60] At a more complicated level, some ladies were not above dabbling in the succession themselves, mainly through the use of their jointures and life interests. Katherine Nevill has already been observed in such an activity. Mary St Pol, Elizabeth de Burgh and Lady Margaret Beaufort all detached sizeable portions of their estates to endow Cambridge colleges. The most extreme case of meddling must be that of Joan de Burghersh, the wife of John de Mohun, last Mohun lord of Dunster. In 1346 Mohun conveyed his lands to feoffees, with reversion to himself and his heirs male. In 1369, when it was fairly clear that the couple would produce no heir, a fresh settlement was made. A new body of trustees was empowered to dispose of the lands to the pleasure of Lady Mohun. In 1374 Joan arranged to sell the reversion of her Mohun estates to the widowed Lady Elizabeth Luttrell. The latter paid a deposit of £200 and upon Lord Mohun's death the deal was completed for a sum of 5,000 marks.[61] Anticipating trouble from her three dispossessed daughters, Joan sealed all the documents in a chest just before she died and gave them to the prior of Christ Church, Canterbury, instructing him to keep them for Sir Hugh Luttrell, or whoever should succeed her. The dispute which ensued was settled in Sir Hugh's favour in 1406.[62] Two unanswerable questions are of considerable interest: how did Lady Luttrell raise the purchase price and how did Lady Mohun dispose of it? Certainly Joan benefited most from the deal, for she lived for thirty years after the sale. Lady Luttrell predeceased her in 1395 and Lady Mohun closed up Dunster castle, in which she quite clearly had little interest, and moved to London.

While it is true that a great number of family fortunes were made by timely marriages, it should be remembered that the advantages were often slow to accrue and were liable to many diversions on the way. In some cases an untimely old mother could prove to be a blight on her son's fortunes. The triumph of securing such a prize as Anne of Woodstock was doubtless tempered by the fact that her marriage to two successive Staffords left her in control of over half the Stafford inheritance between 1403 and 1438. Her troubled succession to half the Bohun inheritance did not benefit Humphrey Stafford until 1438. Anne was effectively sitting on an annual income which was about three times greater than that which Stafford had inherited from his father.[63]

The difficulties facing the Courtenay earls of Devon in the mid-fifteenth century are in large measure attributable to the fatal combination of a minority and a long-lived dowager. Hugh Courtenay died in 1422 leaving a widow Anne Talbot, whose jointure and dower interests amounted to about two thirds of the Courtenay estates. In examining the distintegration of a Devon affinity based on traditional service to the local earl, Dr Cherry has shown that while the Courtenays were able to parry the intrusion of John Holand, earl of Huntingdon in their sphere, the minority of Earl Hugh's son and the longevity of his mother proved the undoing of the family's ancient place in the county. The minority gave Philip Courtenay of Powderham and Sir William Bonville time to win former Devon men to their affinity. When the young earl came of age, the waste on his own estates by the council set up by his mother, and her longevity, gave him little chance to make good. He had to meet his father's debts from his share of the property and it must have been especially galling to him that her council included associates of Bonville and that she had married John Botreaux, whose family had previously been linked with the senior Courtenays.[64] Certainly some of the financial problems of the fifteenth-century nobility were derived from the burdens of their dowagers. Though the Percies could in some measure count their dowagers an advantage in the 1460s, J.M.W. Bean concluded that 'if we take all sources into account the third earl's financial resources were inferior to those of his father, the second earl. Nevertheless if the third earl had lived to secure the reversion of Percy estates held in dower by his mother his income from land would have exceeded his father's'.[65]

No record survives of contemporary opinion on the existence of dowagers and their effect on succession. The medieval lords by and large probably took a rather fatalistic view of the situation when it arose, mainly because of the frequent recurrence of the problem. Short of extremes, there was nothing to be done except hope for their early demise. There is, however, some suggestion that the subsequent marriages were a source of irritation and that in some very notable cases these had political consequences of the first magnitude.

The battle for freedom to remain unmarried was in essence a struggle for the liberty to marry at will. The opposition to disparagement through a forced second marriage has a curious irony in the propensity of widows for self-disparagement. Most widows did choose to remarry. Some became nuns, though in one or two cases renounced the veil in order to marry again.[66] Others, having run the gamut of several subsequent unions, lived out their last years alone. The *Italian Relation* was wrong in concluding that, however unsuitable a second match might be, a widow suffered no discredit. At the highest levels it was quite clearly the concern of the crown. Since courtesy gave a man a life interest in his wife's estates, second husbands might well replace the tenant-in-chief, though he might be quite inadequate for the rôle. This was more especially the case in the early middle ages, with the emphasis on fulfilling feudal services, but throughout the period the crown upheld the obligation to seek consent for subsequent marriages.[67] A large proportion of the wholesale tax evasion of 1436 has arisen, not only from the estates of widows, but also from the estates in the hands of humble knights and esquires who enjoyed a life interest in the property of wives who had collected thirds or jointures in the noble estates of their first husbands.[68] The crown itself had experienced rebellious females in its own ranks. Joan of Acre, Edward 1's daughter by Eleanor of Castile, was married twice.[69] On the death of her first husband, Gilbert de Clare, Joan married in secret Ralph de Monthermer, a member of Gilbert's household. Edward 1 was not a man to brook such disobediance lightly, especially as he had shortly before given his assent to her marriage to Amadeus of Savoy. On hearing of Joan's illegal union, he confiscated her property and, according to one source, summoned his daughter to answer for her conduct. Joan made the following bold reply: 'it was no disgraceful thing for a great and mighty earl to marry a poor woman in a lawful union and so it was neither blameworthy nor impossible for a countess to advance a capable young man'.[70]

Joan of Acre apart, there were few who defended their marriages to social inferiors with such eloquence. Contemporaries viewed such marriages with active disdain and it must have been an added insult to the heirs to baronies, earldoms and dukedoms to find unsavoury second husbands in control of their inheritances. Neither general disapproval nor heavy fines brought a cessation of the trend. Elizabeth Fitzalan suffered a temporary loss of her dower and incurred a fine of 2,000 marks when, after the death of Thomas Mowbray, in 1399 she married one of his former servants, Sir Robert Goushill. The last instalment had scarcely been paid before Goushill was dead, and by summer 1414 Elizabeth had carried her dower to another knight, Sir Gerard Usflete, whom she also survived.[71] Magaret, Lady Roos, who had been widowed in 1421, had by 1423, as the king's council discovered, 'married herself dishonourably without licence from the king, to Roger Wentworth'. A pardon cost her £1000.[72] Katherine Nevill's second marriage to a knight of Norfolk's household cost the couple a similar sum.[73] Many of these second marriages do seem to have beenn to the servants of a widow's first husband and are highly suggestive of some relationship predating the husband's demise.

That the political implications of unsound marriages could be immense is readily demonstrated. It has recently been said of Katherine Nevill's fourth marriage, to the Woodville youth, that Warwick the Kingmaker 'could reasonably resent the exploitation of his aged aunt' and it may be properly regarded as an additional cause for the breach between Warwick and Edward IV. The latter's own disrespect for propriety had resulted in a disastrous match with that most unsuitable of all widows, Elizabeth Woodville. It was all very well for her to follow family example – her father's marriage to Jacquetta, dowager duchess of Bedford, had been an incongruous union – but for Edward IV it was 'the first major blunder of his political career' and 'ultimately contributed largely to the downfall of the Yorkist dynasty'.[74] The fate of his house was finally sealed by the offspring of a royal widow and an obscure Welsh squire with whom she was infatuated.

In his essay on the magnates, knights and gentry, T.B. Pugh described the dukes of Buckingham and York and the earl of Warwick as the three greatest English landowners in the latter half of Henry VI's reign. He appended a note observing that 'John Mowbray, duke of Norfolk would probably have rivalled the greatest English magnates in the extent of his possessions if the greater part of the Mowbray estates had not been held by his mother, dowager duchess Katherine Nevill'.[75] Pugh was here observing the end, albeit a fairly spectacular end, of a phenomen which had dogged Mowbray expansion since its earliest days, and the family provides a perfect example of the effects which a succession of widows could produce.[76] The first territorial gains made by the Mowbrays in the fourteenth century had been subject to long delays and complications. Roger de Mowbray's wife, Maud de Beauchamp, senior co-heiress of the Beauchamp barony of Bedford, had carried her vaulable inheritance to a second husband, Roger Lestraunge, who died finally in 1311, some thirty years after the division of the barony had been made and after the death of Maud's son and heir. In the next generation, Maud's grandson, John, by his marriage to Alicia de Braose, secured Mowbray rights to all the de Braose lordships; but Alicia, like Maud, re-married and her husband, Robert de Peshalle, delayed the descent of this second acquisition for twenty-seven years after John's death in 1322. Alicia's grandson, John, in addition to the waste committed by his step-mother, Elizabeth, was the first to experience the effects of Margaret of Brotherton's longevity.

Sole surviving heiress of Thomas of Brotherton and widow of John, Lord Segrave, Margaret kept a stranglehold on two estates whose combined annual value in the 1390s was almost £3,000.[77] Her longevity and her Segrave jointure for many years denied the succession of her daughter Elizabeth, her son-in-law, John, Lord Mowbray and their descendants. Margaret was probably born about 1320. By 1384 she had survived her siblings, her two husbands, her niece, her four children and her eldest Mowbray grandson, John, earl of Nottingham. Mowbray estates at this time were probably worth less than half what Margaret enjoyed. Her younger grandson, Thomas, clearly had high hopes of being the first member of his family to benefit from that association. In the last years of Richard II's reign, his grants to his annuitants were made with optimistic promises of additional sums 'when the inheritance shall be increased' or quite bluntly' 'after the death of his grandmother".[78] By the time Margaret did eventually die – aged almost eighty – on 24 March 1399, Mowbray fortunes had already taken a downward turn. Norfolk had been exiled in September 1398 as a result of his quarrel with Henry Bolingbroke, and though Richard II had granted him letters of attorney empowering him to inherit in his absence, the letters were cancelled just four days before Margaret's death.[79] Before the year was out, Mowbray himself was dead, leaving a son Thomas who was a minor and a widow, Elizabeth Fitzalan, who had to be provided for from the estates. The refusal of his son to be reconciled to the Lancastrian régime ended in the execution of the young Thomas in 1405, leaving a second widow, Constance Holand. The heir, Thomas's brother, was a minor. When he came of age in 1413, he was the first adult member of his family to administer the Brotherton and Segrave estates as well as the old Mowbray patrimony since the possibility of inheriting the former had arisen almost seventy years earlier through the marriage of John, Lord Mowbray and Elizabeth de Segrave.

John's legacy was onerous. His estate long bore the burden of two dowagers and such was the family's misfortune that by the time it died out in the male line in 1476, not a single member had ever realized its full potential. Mowbray's mother predeceased him in 1425 but his sister-in-law, Constance, survived until 1437, by which stage John's own widow, Katherine Nevill, was in control of the greater portion of his inheritance. That the burden had severe consequences for John Mowbray iis beyond dispute. In the first place, it curtailed his influence in the shires where his property lay. In Norfolk and Suffolk he was holding seven of the twenty-six manors which had descended to him from Duchess Margaret.[80] Small wonder that it was not in John's lifetime that the family forged close personal links with East Anglia. The Mowbray association with eastern England portrayed by the Paston Letters was not a characteristic of the family activities before the second quarter of the fifteenth century. Secondly, Mowbray's finances were constantly severely over-strained. Whilst he could scarcely consider overall that he was not better off than his forebears, his accounts carry abundant evidence of the inadequacy of the revenues available to meet his expenses. His restoration by Henry V was accompanied by very vigorous campaigning abroad which required very large sums of money, and ambition quickly outran the resources of Mowbray's share of his inheritance.[81] He borrowed where he could and lived always on a diminished estate whose full capacity was never attained. The settlement at his death in favour of his widow left his heir with a hopeless legacy.

TABLE: THE MOWBRAY PEDIGREE

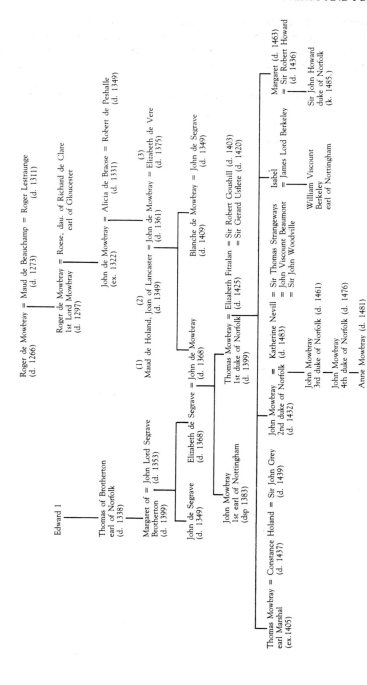

The relative obscurity of the Mowbray family from its first elevation to an earldom in 1377 to its extinction must in some way be attributed to a remarkable run of tough old mothers. Of course, there are other factors to consider which it would be foolhardy to deny, but among baronial incidents there can scarcely have been any other single problem which recurred with the same monotonous regularity and with such unavoidable consequences. Ultimately, there was no solution and many medieval barons would have found sympathy with Horace Walpole's doleful observation of 'a dozen antediluvian dowagers whose carcasses have miraculously resisted the wet'.[82]

Notes

1. *A Relation or rather a true account of the island of England*, ed. C.A. Sneyd (Camden Society, XXVII, 1847), pp. 26–7.
2. K.B. McFarlane, *The Nobility of Later Medieval England* (Oxford, 1973), pp. 65–7, 72–3; C.D. Ross, 'The Yorkshire Baronage, 1399–1435' (Oxford D. Phil thesis, 1953), *passim*; A.J. Pollard, 'The family of Talbot, Lords Talbot and earls of Shrewsbury in the fifteenth century' (Bristol Ph.D. thesis, 1968), pp. 9, 18, 22; L.S. Woodger, 'Henry Bourgchier, earl of Essex and his family, 1408–83' (Oxford D.Phil. thesis, 1974), p. 176; C. Rawcliffe, *The Staffords: Earls of Stafford and Dukes of Buckingham,, 1394–1521* (Cambridge), 1978, pp. 12, 104–5.
3. *English Historical Documents, c. 500–1042*, Vol. 1, ed. D. Whitelock (2nd ed., London, 1979), pp. 393, 403, 445, 463–6, 467–8, 593, 569.
4. Ibid., p. 401.
5. J.C. Holt, *Magna Carta* (Cambridge, 1976), p. 47; *Pipe Roll 1 John*, ed. D.M. Stenton (Pipe Roll Society, XLVIII, London, 1933), 259; *Pipe Roll 12 John* ed. C.F. Slade (Pipe Roll Society, LXIV, London, 1949), p. 103.
6. *CP*, I, pp. 353–4.
7. J. Beames. *A Translation of Glanvill* (London, 1812), Book VI, pp. 112–5; T.F.T. Plucknett, *A Concise History of the Common Law* (5th ed., London, 1956), p. 566; A.B. Simpson, *An Introduction to the History of the Land Law* (Oxford, 1961), p. 65.
8. Holt, *Magna Carta*, p. 46; D.M. Stenton. *The English Woman in History* (New York, 1957), p. 51.
9. *CP*, IV, p. 316.
10. F. Pollock and F.W. Maitland, *A History of English law* (2nd ed., 1898), pp. 11, 421; F.M. Nichols, *Britton* (Oxford, 1865), pp. 11, 236, note a. Gifts of specific dower nevertheless continued to be made. See Aymer de Valence's gift of £2,000 worth of land to his wife, Mary St Pol (*CPR, 1317–21*, pp. 575–6, 596; *1321–24*, p. 12).
11. S.F.C. Milsom, *Historical Foundations of the Common Law* (2nd ed., London, 1981), p. 167.
12. *Glanvill*, Bk. V1, pp. 118–9.
13. *Casus Placitorum and reports of cases in the king's courts, 1272–8*, ed. W.H. Dunham (Selden Society, LX1X, London, 1950), pp. 59–64; F.R. Lewis, 'Beatrice of Falkenburg, 3rd wife of Richard, earl of Cornwall', *EHR*, L11 (1937), 279–82.
14. *CP*, V1, p. 189; Nichols, *Britton*, pp. 11, 237.
15. J. Jackson, *The Formation and Annulment of Marriage* (2nd ed., London, 1969), pp. 26–7.
16. Nichols, *Britton*, pp. 11, 247–8.
17. *RP* I, pp. 61, 403, 405. Some petitions showed the pursuit of dower could be carried too far. The petition of Hawise, widow of Sir Henry Tieys, for instance, was rejected on the reasonable grounds that it had been discovered that she was dead at the time the petition was heard! (*Ibid.*, I, p. 412).
18. Nichols, *Britton*, pp. 11, 245.
19. PRO, E41/202; *CPR, 1401–05*, 110; Berkeley Castle Muniments, General series: general and personal accounts, 20 Edward 1–21. Edward IV (no numbers), Account of John Mowbray's receiver-general, Michaelmas 1414–15 (hereafter Berkeley Castle Acct. 1415), m4. Only two thirds of the manor of West Hatch, granted to Thomas Missenden and his wife for life by Thomas Mowbray (d. 1399), were in the hands of the grantees by 1415. The remaining third was held by Elizabeth Fitzalan. Britton recorded a widow's right to be endowed of any lands due to the heir on the death of a life tenant, though only of an express establishment of dower, not common law dower (Nichols, *Britton*, pp. 11, 239).
20. *CIPM*, X, pp. 103–09; McFarlane, *Nobility*, p. 66.
21. W.H. Dunham, *The Fane Fragment of the 1461 Lord's Jornal* (Yale University Historical

Publications, XLV, New Haven, Connecticut, 1935), p. 9. See BL, Harleian Charter, 54.1.9, for the marriage settlement between William de la Pole and Alice Chaucer which made a very large conveyance of property to both parties jointly.

22. F.R.H. DuBoulay, *An Age of Ambition: English Society in the Late Medieval Ages* (London, 1970), p. 108.

23. *RP*, I, p. 463: a widow's petition for discharge of a fine incurred by her husband and for its charge on her son's estate. Nichols, *Britton*, pp. 11, 253; T.F.T. Plucknett, *Legislation of Edward I* (Oxford, 1949), p. 121.

24. R.E. Archer, 'The Mowbrays; earls of Nottingham and dukes of Norfolk to 1432' (Oxford D.Phil. thesis, 1984), pp. 10–13; *CCR, 1318–23*, p. 659; *CPR 1321–24*, p. 426.

25. *RP*, II, p. 6.

26. C.D. Ross, 'Forfeiture for treason in the reign of Richard II', *EHR*, LXXI (1956), 567.

27. *RP*, lll, p. 440.

28. J.R. Lander, *Crown and Nobility, 1450–1509* (London, 1976), p. 150.

29. *Glanvill*, Bk. Vl, p. 113.

30. Whitelock *English Historical Documents*, p. 417, clause 5.

31. *VCH Bedfordshire*, III, p. 263; *CIPM*, XII, pp. 380–86.

32. Plucknett, *Legislation*, p. 123.

33. *CPR, 1399–1401*, p. 402; *1401–05*, p. 110; PRO, CP40/612, m66; Lander, *Crown and Nobility* p. 111n.

34. *CCR, 1409–13*, p. 434.

35. Constance was Henry IV's niece. After the Earl Marshal's execution she had been confirmed in some of the Mowbray's Norfolk estates and continued to enjoy her jointure (*CPR, 1405–08*, p. 38; *1401–05*, 110).

36. *CPR, 1413–16*, 319. John, Lord Clifford's enfeoffment in 1415 similarly included mention of dower estates. The Cliffords, like the Mowbray lords, had long suffered from a remarkable line of tough dowagers and were no doubt acutely aware of the problems (*CPR, 1413–16*, p. 320; C.D. Ross, 'Yorkshire Baronage', pp. 276–80).

37. *CPR, 1461–67*, p. 179; *1467–77*, p. 107.

38. *RP*, V, p. 135.

39. *Ibid.*, p. 350.

40. C.D. Ross, *Edward IV* (London, 1974), pp. 248, 336, 190–1.

41. *RP*, Vl, p. 169.

42. *CPR, 1374–77*, p. 287; *1370–74*, pp. 89–90, 186.

43. *CCR, 1374–77*, p. 333; *CFR, 1369–77*, p. 321; *CPR, 1374–77*, p. 396.

44. Owing to limitations of space, the administration of dower estates cannot be dealt with here. It seems on the whole that, apart from the loss of estates through dower, many heirs could at least be content with the administrative efforts of their mothers. A number of the latter have earned considerable reputations for ruthlessness in this direction, amply making up for any disability thought to derive from their position as women. (R.R. Davies, 'Baronial Accounts, incomes and arrears in the later middle ages', *Econ. HR*, 2nd series, XXI [1968], pp. 215–6, 218, 221, 227). Surviving dowager accounts indicate that business was as usual (PRO, SC11/816, valor of the estates of Anne, countess of Stafford; SC11/25, valor of Joan, Lady Abergavenny; SC11/799, 801, valors of Lady Elizabeth de Burgh; BL Add. MS., 34122A, accounts of Isabel de la Pole, Lady Morley; BL Egerton Roll, 8779, compotus of the receiver-general of Alice, duchess of Suffolk).

45. BL, Add. MS, 14409, f230. Elizabeth de Montford, Lady Montague renounced her dower in certain lands in Somerset in 1320, though she did not die until 1354, after the death of her son, the earl of Salisbury (*CIPM*, Vl, p. 142).

46. *CP*, Xl, p. 395.

47. H. Jenkinson, 'Mary de Sancto Paulo, foundress of Pembroke college, Cambridge', *Archaeologia*, LXVI (1914–15), 402–446.

48. CP, I, p. 26; *Chronicon Adae de Usk*, ed. E.M. Thompson (2nd ed., London, 1904), p. 63; PRO, SC11/25.
49. C.A. Musgrave, 'Household administration in the fourteenth century with special reference to the household of Elizabeth de Burgh, lady of Clare' (London MA thesis, 1923); PRO, SC11/799.
50. McFarlane, *Nobility*, p. 163.
51. Ross, 'Yorkshire Baronage', pp. 129–131, 275–6.
52. *Ibid.*, pp. 314–6, 241–2.
53. CPR, 1408–13, 307; *Testamenta Eboracensia*, III, ed. J. Raine (Surtees Society, XLV, 1865), p. 321.
54. Berkeley Castle Acct 1415, m8, 17.
55. *The Register of Henry Chichele, Archbishop of Canterbury, 1414–43*, II, ed. E.F. Jacob and H.C. Johnson (Canterbury and York Society, XLII, 1938), pp. 473–5.
56. BL, Harleian MS. 433, fo 117v.
57. CPR, 1461–67, 104, 141, 178–9, 227, 428; 1467–76, 19, 107.
58. R. Virgoe, 'The recovery of the Howards in East Anglia', in *Wealth and Power in Tudor England:* Essays presented to S.T. Bindoff, ed. E.W. Ives, R.J. Knecht, J.J. Scarisbrick (London, 1978).
59. McFarlane, *Nobility*, p. 59.
60. CP, V, p. 753–75, listing persons summoned to parliament in right of their wives. Women were usually deemed incapable of bearing a title above the rank of baron. The creation of Margaret of Brotherton as duchess of Norfolk in her own right in 1397 was, in peerage terms, a considerable honour.
61 R.G.K.A. Mertes, 'The secular noble household in medieval England, 1350–1550', (Edinburgh Ph.D. thesis, 1981), p. 53, seems to have thought that a sum of 200 marks represented the total purchase price, but see H.C. Maxwell-Lyte, *A History of Dunster*, I (London, 1909), pp. 50–53. The sum was paid for her jointure in Dunster, Minehead, Kilton and Carhampton, not for her dower lands which she could not possibly have alienated.
62. *Ibid.*, 57, 84. The manor court at Kilton, Somerset, was held in 1402 in the names of Elizabeth, wife of William, earl of Salisbury and Edward, earl of Rutland, daughter and one of the sons-in-law of Lady Mohun, and 'others'. The similar court of 1400 was held in the name of Lady Mohun (Somerset Record Office, DD/L P24/4). I am indebted to Dr. R.W. Dunning for the above information.
63. Rawcliffe, *The Staffords*, p. 18.
64. M. Cherry, 'The struggle for power in mid-fifteenth-century Devon', in *Patronage, the Crown and the Provinces in later medieval England*, ed. R.A. Griffiths (Gloucester, 1981), pp. 123–40.
65. J.M.W. Bean, *The Estates of the Percy Family, 1416–1537* (Oxford, 1958), p. 85.
66. Elizabeth of Juliers, countess of Kent, broke a vow of chastity at Waverley Abbey by marrying Eustace D'Aubrecicout. She survived her first husband by fifty-nine years, by which time the Holand line of the earls of Kent had failed (CP, VII, p. 149). Katherine Grandison, countess of Salisbury made a vow of chastity and had dower in the estates of William Montague (*Ibid.*, XI, pp. 387–8).
67. RP, II, pp. 260. This ruling was unheld in 1354 and the penalties of forfeiture were re-stated.
68. C.D. Ross and T.B. Pugh, 'The English baronage and the income tax of 1436', BIHR, XXV (1953), 1–28.
69. Joan had been bethrothed to Herman, son of the king of Germany, but he had fallen through the ice while skating and died in 1282 before the marriage could be solemnised. (CP, V. p. 708).
70. CPR, 1292–1301, pp. 243, 288; *Johannis de Trokelowe chronica et annales*, ed. H.T. Riley (RS, 1886), 27.
71. CPR, 1399–1401, pp. 541, 544–5; CCR, 1399–1402, pp. 381–2; CFR, 1399–1405, pp. 130, 134; PRO, E401/623, 21 October; 626, 5 May; 627, 19 October; 630, 21 May; CCR, 1402–05, pp. 209–11; CPR, 1413–16, p. 209.

72. PPC, III, p. 149.
73. CPR, 1441–46, p. 61.
74. Ross, Edward IV, pp. 85, 87.
75. T.B. Pugh, 'The magnates, knights and gentry', in Fifteenth century England: Studies in politics and society, 1399–1509 ed. S.B. Chrimes, C.D. Ross and R.A. Griffiths (Manchester, 1972), p. 105.
76. The following account is based on my own research: R.E. Archer, 'The Mowbrays', Passim.
77. College of Arms MS, Arundel 49.
78. CPR, 1399–1401, pp. 193, 28.
79. RP, III, p. 372; CFR, 1391–99, p. 296.
80. Berkeley Castle Acct. 1415, m.1–5.
81. Berkeley Castle Acct. 1415, m.8. In 1415 Mowbray borrowed 1,000 marks from his uncle, Thomas Fitzalan. At the most conservative estimate, costs over and above wages amounted to £1,000 for items exclusively connected with the earl's preparations for war.
82. Quoted by McFarlane, Nobility, p. 65.

2

Charity, Faith, and the Gentry of Kent
1422–1529

P.W. Fleming
University College of Swansea

Probably less than two per cent of the total population of fifteenth and early-sixteenth-century Kent was of gentle rank. Gentry society in the county can be divided into two broad groups, consisting on the one hand of the parish gentry, and on the other of the county gentry. The parish gentry comprised mainly gentlemen who held only one or two manors and whose landed income was less than £20 *per annum*. Their social and landed significance was for the most part limited to their own parish, and although they played little or no part in the governance of their county, they accounted for over two thirds of the total number of gentry. The county families had interests throughout Kent and often in other counties too. They supplied the senior personnel of the county administration, and many held important positions in central government. Within this group of about one hundred county families was an *élite* of approximately twenty families with annual landed incomes well in excess of £40; in the absence of dominant magnate influence, it was they who enjoyed hegemony in county society. The county gentry were mainly knights or esquires, and of long-standing in the shire.[1]

A characteristic of Kent society was the clannish nature of many families. The typical clan family consisted of several distantly related branches of widely differing rank. Thus, within the same parish there could reside gentlemen, yeomen, and husbandmen, all bearing the same name and all in one way or another related. This was probably the result both of the stability of residence of many families within the county, which gave ample time for the development of cadet branches and of the gavelkind system, a partible inheritance custom which allowed those cadet branches to remain in the same locality along with the senior line, but with an ever-decreasing share of the patrimony. Many gentry families held land by gavelkind tenure well into the Tudor period.[2] This paper, based on a sample of 200 wills, outlines the more important aspects of the religious life of these gentry, and attempts to relate their attitudes to faith and charity to some of their other preoccupations.[3]

In the middle ages the rich man was regarded as but the steward of wealth entrusted to him by God. These 'ryche men whyche arn Goddis revys and Goddis baylys' were consequently obliged to dispose of their wealth in a pious and charitable manner, or else imperil their immortal souls.[4] The will was the prime instrument by means of which that obligation was discharged, and so was esteemed as a document of considerable religious significance. By the same token, to die intestate was regarded as sinful.[5] That these ideas were current in fifteenth-century Kent is shown by the preamble to the will of 1490 made by Robert Ballard, a gentleman of Greenwich: 'entendyng . . . not to departe out of this lyfe intestate make and ordeyne this my present Testament of my mevible goodes the which oure lord god hath lent me'.[6]

Debt was a misuse of God-given wealth, and the thought of dying with debts unpaid was particularly abhorrent to the propertied classes, especially since at that period the debtor's liability died with him. Dying without providing for the payment of debts was therefore tantamount to theft, and would not go unpunished in the life to come:

> Yet some wyll suffer hys dettes unpayd tobe
> And dye and Ieopard hys soule rather than he
> Wyll any of hys landes mynysh and empayre
> That shuld after hys deth come to hys heyre[7]

In many wills the first clause to be included, after the committal of the testator's body and soul, was along the lines of *volo primo et principaliter quod debita mea plenarie sint soluta*.[8] In some cases, the prospect of Divine Judgement did not entirely overcome business-like discretion, and certain testators took pains to add that specific instances of indebtedness had first to be proved before any recompense would be made. Thus, in her will of 1464 Joan Mareys ordered the payment of all her debts, 'the whiche of right may be proved'.[9] Katherine Haute had another kind of debt to pay: by her will of 1493 she left 40s. to Walter Oliphaunt, 'in recompense of a dede that my husband dyd to hym'.[10]

Most wills contained some form of provision for prayers for the dead, thereby demonstrating the widespread acceptance of the concept of *purgatio*, and the concomitant belief in the efficacy of intercessionary prayers.[11] Prayers for the dead usually took the form of masses said at the time of burial, followed thirty days later by the commemorative 'month's mind' service, and then by the anniversary *obit*. These were often supplemented by further annual *obits*, or by the foundation of a chantry, which provided daily or weekly masses to the memory of the deceased, either for a limited period or in perpetuity. Some testators showed a particular familiarity with the details of the liturgy, and were very discerning in their choice of services. For example, in 1490 Robert Ballard asked for an *obit* to be said on 18 July every year, 'doyng one Even, Placebo & Dirige Solempnely by note . . . In which prayeres I put my singular confidence for the wele of oure soules.'.[12]

The priest was not always regarded as the sole intermediary between God and man: prayers could also be solicited from the laity. Funeral inscriptions often asked for prayers from passers-by. The usual form for these requests was followed on the tombstone of Sir William Scott, who died in 1524: 'Of your Charite, pray for the sowle of Sir William Scot, knight'[13]. Such a device was merely a request for prayers; gifts and bequests put the recipient under an actual obligation. Robert Ballard ordered that three months' wages were to be paid to his servants, so that they might 'pray the more especially for my soule', while by his will of 1479 John Green esquire requested 'that my broder Holgrave and my suster his wiff each of them have some tokyn forto pray for me' – an early example of a *memento mori*.[14] In both of these wills, however, provision was also made for at least one priest to pray for the testator, and the role of the priest as intercessor seems to have remained unquestioned.

There was a tendency to restrict the number of named recipients of prayers to a small group comprising only close family and friends.[15] Such a restricted provision neglected one's duty to remember those others – friends, kinsmen and benefactors – who were also deserving of prayers, and so all-embracing formulae were often appended, such as 'Myne Auncetores and frendes' or, more generously, *animabus omnium fidelium defunctorum*.[16] Sometimes there were pangs of 'death-bed' conscience to contend with: Sir John Fyneaux provided for the appointment of a private chaplain for his widow, part of whose duties were to include praying for those 'unknowen to whom I am Bounde afore god to make restitucion unto in discharge of my conscience yf they were knowen'.[17]

These prayers were said in return for bequests of money, goods, or land alienated in mortmain. In theory these endowments were unconditional gifts, given out of pure charity: the priest was put under no obligation by them, save only that which arose from a feeling of gratitude towards his benefactor, a feeling that naturally would have led him to show a proper concern for that man's soul. The justification for this practice was the doctrine that good works should accompany the Sacrament:

> This Sacrament helpeth nat yt a-lone,
> But devoute offrynges also echone;
> Alle that we offre at the messe,
> Alle oure Saluacyon hyt ys;[18]

In these terms the practice could be condoned, but if there was any hint of a contractual arrangement then it came perilously close to simony. Occasionally the terms of a bequest suggest that the testator hoped for, rather than expected, a spiritual return on his money: by his will of 1490 Robert Ballard bequeathed one mark to the church of the Temple in London's Fleet street, 'to thentent that it may please the maister there to pray for my soule'.[19] Usually, however, the testator was more direct: *Al freres austynes de Rye pour tenir mon obit et anniversarie xl s.*[20] It was a proprietory attitude that prevailed: the testator regarded himself as the purchaser, the priest as the vendor, and his own spiritual welfare as the commodity.

As well as the usual funeral, 'month's mind', and anniversary services, the health of the soul could be further safeguarded by the establishment of additional *obits* and chantries, either for a limited period or in perpetuity. An example of a perpetual *obit* is to be found in the will of 1494 made by William Brent, a gentleman of Charing: he requested that his executors establish a perpetual *obit* for his soul in Charing church; this was to be financed by an annual rent of 10s. from a meadow adjacent to his manor house, and part of the rent was to be used to provide alms at each service.[21] The prayer foundation established by Roger Clitherow, an esquire of Ash, near Sandwich, was of a limited duration: a chaplain was to receive all the profits from the Clitherow manor of Nelmes, together with an annual rent of 15s. from a tenement in Sandwich, in return for which he was to celebrate mass in the parish church of Ash for the souls of Roger, his wife, and his parents for twenty years, after which time the manor and rent were to revert to Eleanor, Roger's daughter.[22]

The establishment of long-term or perpetual prayer foundations necessitated a constant source of income; this could be provided either by the alienation of land or, as was the case with the two examples quoted above, by rents from lands held in trust. The latter was by far the most common method, since the alienation of land to the church – alienation in mortmain – was only possible by special licence from the king, which did not come cheaply.[23] This legal impediment could largely be avoided by granting land to a group of feoffees who had the power to co-opt new members, and who were authorised to use the profits for the support of one or more cantarists.[24] The details of such an arrangement are to be found in the will of John Cobbes, a gentleman of Newchurch who made his will in 1472. He ordered his feoffees to make over certain of his Newchurch lands to twenty-four 'of the worship fullest and trustiest and most wysest of the parish of Newchirche and of the contry adjoynaunt . . . to thentent yat they shall morteys a Chauntrie of iiii priests to singe in the chirche of Newchurch, and none other place, takyng every priest xii marcs by ye yere'; in addition, a treasurer or bursar was to be appointed, and every Michaelmas he was to render account to these trustees in the church of Newchurch.[25] Most trustees were appointed on such an *ad hoc* basis, but in 1466 James Dreyland took the unusual step of entrusting the administration of the *obit* which he founded for the souls of his parents to the mayor and commonalty of Faversham.[26]

Prayer foundations served a social, as well as a spiritual purpose. They lent prestige to the family of their founder, and so it is no surprise that there should have been a relationship between rank and the frequency with which prayer foundations were established, as the following table shows:

	Knights	Esquires	Gentlemen
% of testators who established perpetual prayer foundations:	0	21.3	9.6
% of testators who established limited prayer foundations:	52.3	29.3	45.1[27]

Most of the testators who established perpetual foundations were of armigerous rank; it is perhaps surprising that none were knights. The families of most of the knightly testators had long been prominent in Kentish society, and so it is likely that in most of these families chantry foundations had already been made, in which case it was only necessary for the knight to add his name to the chantry-priest's bede-roll. Stress was laid on the desirability of providing a large number of prayers immediately on the soul entering purgatory, and so the knights' emphasis on limited prayer foundations probably reflects a desire to provide a 'booster' to the family chantry in order to ease their initial period *in purgatio*.[28] The enthusiasm shown by esquires for perpetual chantries and *obits* may suggest that such foundations were regarded as status-symbols. Such considerations were probably not so important to those of knightly rank, whose status had been publicly recognised by their knighthoods; for lesser families, on the other hand, the prestige of a perpetual prayer foundation would have been welcomed as a means of displaying a rank that in some cases had only recently been acquired. The esquires' concentration of their resources on perpetual foundations probably accounts for their seeming reluctance to participate in the establishment of limited prayer foundations. In contrast, the gentlemen were very active in this latter activity. Naturally enough, limited prayer foundations were likely to have been less expensive than their perpetual counterparts, and thus more attractive to gentry of lesser means. At least one gentleman aimed too high in his provision for prayers. John Denys, a gentleman of Ickham, attempted to found a perpetual chantry of one chaplain, but the endowment – consisting of an unspecified number of tenements, 38 acres of land and a rent of 4s. – proved insufficient to maintain a priest, and in 1483 Archbishop Bourgchier had to appoint the rector of Ickham to administer the property so that Denys's bequest could at last be used in some way for the health of his soul.[29]

Attitudes to personal salvation did not remain static. There seems to have been less emphasis placed on prayer towards the end of our period, with a decline in the number of testators who made detailed prayer provisions, and an increasing number whose only provision was a request for their executors to attend to the health of their soul:[30]

	1422–80	1481–1529
% of testators making detailed prayer provision:	10.0	5.3
% of testators making no specific prayer provision:	7.1	13.0

This trend was accompanied by a substantial fall in the number of perpetual prayer foundations established during the latter half of the period:

	1422–80	1481–1529
% of testators who established perpetual prayer foundations:	20.0	10.7

Perpetual prayer foundations were expensive; consequently, few gentlemen could afford them. A less expensive – but also less prestigious – way of acquiring similar spiritual benefits was through membership of a religious gild. A gild was formed by local laymen, usually to maintain a perpetual chantry for its members.[31] The membership of these gilds was predominantly non-gentle, but three of our sample of testators – all gentlemen – left bequests to gilds, indicating that they were members.[32] One of these three was James Dering of Lyminge, who left a measure of barley to each of five gilds.[33] Another was Robert Cobbes, who left a cow to the Brotherhood of Our lady in Newchurch, on condition that they 'will putt their money of the same broderyeld in to a stokke for to encrease, if not I bequeth to the said brotheryeld v s.'. Cobbes seems to have had little confidence in the financial expertise of his fellow gild-members, and wished to instill some of his own business acumen into their dealings.[34] In 1491 Robert Gore of Maidstone – our third testator – left a bequest to the gild of *Corpus Christi* in Maidstone church; this gild had been founded forty-six years previously by two local gentlemen, Robert Est and Richard Barbour. The royal licence for the foundation describes its organisation and function in some detail. The 'Gild and Chantry of the most precious body of Jesus Christ of Maidstone' was to be perpetual, and its members could be of both sexes; its purpose was to support a chaplain to sing daily in the collegiate church of All Saints, Maidstone, for the good estate of the king and the gild members and for their souls after death. The gild was to be incorporated, with two wardens, its own seal, and the power to plead before a court of law, and it could acquire lands up to the annual value of £20.[35] Gild membership shows a readiness to co-operate both with other gentry and with those of lesser rank; consequently, joint enterprises such as gilds strengthened the bonds between the gentle and the non-gentle within the parish community.

The nature of the available evidence tends to put great emphasis on those aspects of religious practice which dealt with the care of the soul after death, but it is unlikely that many gentry only turned their thoughts heavenward when death seemed imminent. Religion pervaded daily life, and there is little to suggest that the vast majority of the gentry did not take their religion very seriously. For instance, there was a fairly busy commerce between Kent and Rome for the purpose of securing indulgences. Between 1427 and 1483 at least seven Kentish gentry received papal indults allowing them to choose their own confessors, six received plenary indulgences, and three were granted indults to hear mass before daybreak.[36] In 1479 Sir John Scott was excused from fasting in Lent on account of ill-health, but his indulgence made it clear that this was only on condition that he did other works of piety in compensation, as directed by his confessor.[37] While all of these indulgences were sought as a means of easing the burdens of religious observance, the fact that they were sought at all shows that those burdens were taken seriously.

Portable altars were by far the most common subjects for papal indulgences: between 1429 and 1475 nineteen gentry received indults to have them.[38] A licensed and consecrated portable altar enabled its owner to hear mass outside the walls of a church and so, while the altar itself would have been useful on long journeys, it is likely that its real attraction lay in the opportunity it afforded to hear mass in the privacy of one's own chamber. In all likelihood, therefore, an indulgence for the purpose of owning a portable altar served the same purpose as a licence to maintain a private chapel. Licences for private chapels for the hearing of mass in one's own chambers were granted by the archbishop of Canterbury. The hearing of private mass without a licence was one of several accusations made against Roger Harlakynden, a gentleman of Woodchurch, by his fellow parishioners during Archbishop Warham's visitation of All Saints Church, Woodchurch, in 1511; it was claimed that Harlakynden, 'a common oppressor of his neighbours whom none loveth', brought regular clergy into his house to sing in his oratory without authority. He claimed that he had only done this when he was sick, in which circumstance, he maintained, he had a perfect right to do so; the archbishop does not seem to have taken the matter any further.[39]

Both portable altars and private chapels were probably regarded as status-symbols. From all the available evidence, it seems that few – if any – knightly families did not possess a private chapel or retain a private chaplain, while the incidence of both diminished markedly further down the gentry hierarchy. Chapel-owning testators can be identified by their bequests of vestments and other chapel equipment: in 1471 Sir Thomas Cobham left to the church of Stonebridge in Kent, 'my litill paire Organes standing within the chapell of my castell of Starbough and myne old masse booke noted therto'.[40] In addition, some testators mentioned their family chaplain, sometimes by name. The following table has been compiled from this evidence, and shows the relationship between rank and chapel-owning and priest-retaining:

	Knights	Esquires	Gentlemen
% of testators who owned chapels or retained priests:	38.0	12.0	4.8

Private chapels could often be quite richly appointed: after leaving most of his 'stuffe that longith unto my chapell of Repton' to his son, Sir John Fogge was still able to give his wife two silver basins, a silver cross, a set of velvet vestments, and a second mass book, among other things from this same chapel.[41]

Only rarely are relics to be found in the possession of the Kentish gentry; it may be that these objects were becoming less popular or, conversely, it may be that they were seldom given away because they were so highly prized, and therefore do not tend to appear in wills. Only two testators mentioned relics. In 1430 Richard Poynings of Sandwich, the son of Robert, Lord Poynings, left a portion of the True Cross to his wife, after whose death it was to go to a local church, where it was to remain *imperpetuum*; this last condition, which was often made in connection with precious gifts, suggests that he thought the church authorities might at some time be tempted to sell the relic in return for ready cash. Poynings's veneration of the sacred object did not prevent him from asking that a piece of it be broken off and given to his step-son: *Volo quod . . . Willelmus de Arundel, filius dicte uxoris mee, habeat unam peciam dicte pecis Sancti Crucis sibi et heredes suis imperpetuum.*[42] William Haute, an esquire of Bishopsbourne, seems to have had a particular fondness for such things: by his will of 1462 he bequeathed a piece of stone on which the Archangel Gabriel stood during the Annunciation to his parish church of Bishopsbourne, where it was to stand before the image of the Virgin, and he also left a bone of St. Bartholomew to the church of Waltham, which was dedicated to the saint.[43] In Haute's case at least, the matching of gift to recipient was evidently made with some care. One object which cannot exactly be described as a relic, but which was still invested with special – indeed, with magical – powers, was the *anum aurem cum saphro quam est bonus et salubris ad oculos* that John Kelsham left to the Carmelites of Lossenham. No doubt the friars' devout lucubrations made such a gift most welcome.[44]

The pilgrimage was the most adventurous expression of piety and religious enthusiasm, in theory at least. Although such travels were waning in popularity during the fifteenth century, four of the sample group of testators made provision for them by proxy, and at least three of these seem to have been in fulfilment of promises to go in person. In her will of 1437, Agnes Appleton expressed her wish that two pilgrimages were to be completed, one to the shrine at Walsingham in Norfolk, and the other to Becket's tomb in Canterbury.[45] Two of the Culpepers, Nicholas and Sir Thomas – the sons of Sir Thomas Culpeper of Bayhall, who died in 1428 – also provided for pilgrimages to Canterbury and Walsingham.[46] The pilgrimage to be undertaken by the terms of Sir John Scott's will was a much more ambitious affair, for he instructed William, his chaplain, to make offerings for him at St. Peter's in Rome. In this case it would seem that the priest had intended to go anyway, and Sir John was merely asking to be included in his prayers when he arrived, and that he should complete his pilgrimage within a certain time. In return, and after having satisfied Sir John's son that he had in fact made the trip, William was to receive £10 and accommodation as the family chaplain.[47]

Sir Richard Guildford was not content merely to go on pilgrimage by proxy; rather did he set out himself in 1506 – when he was probably in his fifties – on that most arduous of all pilgrimages, the journey to the Holy Land. His will, made the day before he embarked for Normandy, is taken up almost entirely with the settlement of his property on his heirs. Doubtless Sir Richard considered the pilgrimage itself to be a sufficiently demonstrative – not to mention expensive – expression of his piety, and he did not feel it necessary to include any charitable provisions in his will.[48] Accompanying Sir Richard on his journey was his chaplain, who took the unusual step of recording their travels, in a work entitled 'The Pylgrymage of Sir Richard Guylforde'.[49] Unfortunately, what could have been a most revealing account of Sir Richard's character amounts to little more than a conventional travelogue, and the author makes mention of his master but once, and then only to record Sir Richard's death and burial on Mount Sion. The book is as much a testament to its author's wanderlust as to his piety, and shows that the desire to see distant lands still motivated pilgrims over a century after the Wife of Bath had 'passed many a straunge streem'.

The impulse behind most medieval charity was not primarily philanphropic; rather was it concern for personal salvation, the same impulse that motivated prayer provisions. 'Men don mest comounly her elmesse in hope to ben thankyd & rewardyd therfor at the laste dom[50]'. The doctrine of Holy Poverty was extended not only to mendicants and other religious, but also to those who had not chosen to be paupers through devotion to God, but who had been forced into that condition by misfortune. Consequently, it was believed that the salvation of the poor was reasonably well-assured if they bore their lot with patience, but the rich depended for their salvation on the use of their wealth in pious and charitable acts. In short, the poor had been created so that the rich might prove their charity.[51] The notion that the great gulf between rich and poor was divinely ordained assuaged the rich man's guilt, while by stressing the degree to which the lesser ranks were dependent on him, it actually strengthened his position in society.[52]

Most alms took the form of cash or food donations given at special distributions or as part of requiem services. The poor were often present at funerals, clad in black gowns and bearing torches round the coffin.[53] The practice of giving alms indiscriminately at funerals would have drawn large crowds of paupers. Sometimes wills specified that the poor at the service were to be 'honest' or of 'good conversation', but the demand for such qualifications was by no means universal, and the prospect of funeral alms may well have attracted large numbers of vagabonds and professional beggars. Certainly, few could have been so naive as to imagine that such a host attended the funeral simply through affection or respect for the deceased. Most alms were given for the benefit of the donor rather than the recipient: by their presence at funerals, paupers testified to the deceased's wealth and munificence – thus adding to his family's prestige – while their cheaply-bought prayers eased his soul's passage through purgatory. The doctrine of Holy Poverty was even extended to prisoners. Charity to prisoners was a symbolic act of faith, since Christ himself had once suffered incarceration. At the Day of Judgement God will say to the charitable: 'Y was in prisoun and ye visytedyn me, & that ye dedyn to the leste of myn ye dedyn it to me'.[54] This symbolism is implicit in the annual gift of alms to each prisoner of Maidstone gaol which William Bettenham established, for the appointed day of the alms-giving was to be Good Friday.[55]

Although these occasional deeds of charity gave temporary relief to certain individuals, they probably made little impact on the general level of poverty. Alms-houses and hospitals, where relief of a long-term nature could be found, were of greater utility in alleviating suffering, but donations to such institutions are only rarely to be found. By his will of 1486, Roger Brent, a gentleman of Canterbury, gave a messuage to that town's mayor and his successors on condition that they built a poor-house and maintained it in perpetuity.[56] Another alms-house was founded at Dartford in 1453 by John Bamburgh and William Rotherley, two local gentlemen.[57] John Roberts, a gentleman of Cranbrook, was especially munificent in this regard, and founded two alms-houses by his will of 1460: one was to be in Cranbrook, and the other in Goudhurst, three miles to the north. They were to be financed from the profits of Roberts's Sussex manor of Deringdale. Each establishment was to house seven poor men, who were each to receive an annuity of one mark. In addition, one mark was to be provided annually to each house for repairs. The election of the alms-folk was to be left to his heirs, who were to choose them from among the local poor, 'and in esspecially of my Kynnesmen if any of hem have nede thereof'.[58] The only testator who gave to a hospital was John Ellis: by his will of 1467, he left 8d. to the inmates of Bedlam, which by that time was already a home for the insane.[59] It would appear that support for such regular forms of relief was uncommon, but because of the nature of the evidence, it is possible that much alms-giving has gone unrecorded. By his will of 1473, John Thornbury requested that 'dame Philippa my doughter have an oversight that myn Almes folke in Faversham have their almes that I have left unto them', which suggests that these 'Almes folke' had been supported by Thornbury on a regular basis during his lifetime.[60]

Traditional attitudes to charity may have been changing in the fifteenth and early sixteenth centuries. There are signs of a movement against indiscriminate alms-giving in favour of donations to certain well-defined groups, especially to the parish poor, as the following table shows:

	1422–80	1481–1529
% of testators giving indiscriminate alms:	18.5	11.5
% of testators giving alms to parish poor:	8.5	13.8

Some testators in the latter half of our period went so far as to state that their alms were not to be given indiscriminately, but only to local paupers. Thus, in her will of 1516 Joan Frognal, the widow of Thomas Frognal esquire of Buckland, desired her executors to 'geve nor deale in doole for me at my burieng nor monethes day in manner in money, brede, drynke or offerwise other than I have appoynted and assigned in the seid parisshes of Tenham and Lynstied'.[61] This increasing particularity about the uses to which their alms were to be put may indicate that the gentry were becoming more concerned about the actual condition of the poor. Pauperism was a growing problem in early Tudor England, and the increasing numbers of poor probably impinged on the consciousness of the gentry to a greater extend than in the past. It is likely, therefore, that the gentry were beginning to view charity as a predominantly philanphropic activity, rather than as a kind of eschatological insurance, and were turning their gaze from an imagined purgatory to the actual suffering that lay all around them.[62]

Testators of knightly rank were especially particular in their choice of recipients of alms:

	Knights	Esquires	Gentlemen
% of testators giving indiscriminate alms:	14.2	21.3	8.6
% of testators giving alms to parish poor:	38.0	6.6	10.5

It is likely that knights, above both other gentry ranks, saw themselves as the leaders of their local community, especially in the absence of strong magnate influence. This apparent concern for the parish poor may therefore be evidence of the greater gentry's paternalistic attitude toward their lesser neighbours. If this were so, it is unlikely to have been a wholly altruistic paternalism: the more dependent the parish became on their lord of the manor, the more his influence in the locality was enhanced.

Provision for the repair of roads and bridges was regarded as an act of charity. In the early 1520s the ploughman in *Gentleness and Nobility* praised merchants for their generosity in the following terms:

> Many be good and worshipful also,
> And many charitable dedis they do,
> Byld Churchys and amend the hyeways,
> Make almyshowsys and help many decays.[63]

This view of road-repair as a charitable activity was shared by the Kentish gentry: in 1466 James Dreyland gave instructions for a road to be repaired 'to the pleasure of God and profet and ease of the cuntre'.[64] In these bequests, it was usually the practice to specify a particular local bridge or stretch of road. For example, in 1519 William Brockhill left £4 to amend 'the Evill and comberous wayes bitwene Oldrumeney and Lyde', and another £4 for the road from John Frebody's door to the stile at Appledore Court, the Brockhill family seat.[65] This was the only area of charity in which gentlemen predominated, as the following table shows:

	Knights	Esquires	Gentlemen
% of testators giving to road and bridge repair:	4.7	8.0	14.4

Gentlemen – mostly among the parish gentry – would in general have had more restricted horizons than the greater gentry of county-wide significance and so, compared with these county gentry, they would have spent relatively more time travelling within their own immediate locality. Their munificence in this regard was probably prompted by an irksome familiarity with local 'Evill and comberous wayes'.

The frequency with which testators provided for church building, repair, and adornment declined during our period: half of the testators who made their wills between 1422 and 1480 made provision for these purposes, but only one third did so in the period 1481 – 1529. The momentum behind the fourteenth-and early-fifteenth-century rebuilding seems to have largely spent itself by the later fifteenth century, at least as far as the gentry of Kent are concerned. It may be that there was little left to be done by this time, and would-be benefactors had to be content for the most part merely with repairing and adorning what had already been built; on the other hand, this trend may have resulted from declining enthusiasm for ecclesiastical aggrandizement. Most bequests to the fabric of ecclesiastical buildings were directed to parish churches; Nicholas Culpeper's donation towards the building of Combwell priory was a rare example of a bequest to building work in a regular establishment.[66]

In most provisions for church building and repair, the donation is simply 'to the fabric' or 'to the work', with little other comment as to its intended use. Such bequests give no indication that the testator was particularly well-acquainted with the needs of the church in question. In a small number of wills testators display a detailed knowledge of the particular needs of the recipient church, implying close ties with that church and previous discussion with its vicar or church warden. One of the most munificent church benefactors among our sample was John Pympe, an esquire of Nettlestead. He not only provided a rood-screen for Nettlestead church, but also made provision for the church roof to be leaded, its floor to be tiled, canopies to be provided for the altars, additions made to the belfry, and a 'faire litell porche of stone' to be built at the south door – a porch which still stands as testimony to Pympe's charity. Pympe knew exactly what he wanted: the canopies above the altars were to be fan-vaulted, the screen was to be built in a manner which did not block the light from the windows, and was to be constructed 'wit the Fairrest borde that canne be made of okes growing in the maner of Nettlestead'. The terms of his bequest show that he had a real concern for the practical needs of his fellow-parishioners and was not merely giving his gift as a salve to his conscience.[67]

The relationship between rank and the frequency with which testators left bequests for church building and maintenance is shown by the following table:

	Knights	Esquires	Gentlemen
% of testators giving to the church fabric:	28.5	42.6	39.4

The relative scarcity of knightly bequests is probably explained by their more common ownership of private chapels, which made them less dependent on their parish church. Private chapels were sometimes more richly appointed than the local church: the chapel which William Horne built at Horne's Place in Appledore in the fourteenth century still stands, and architecturally it is far superior to any of the surrounding churches.[68]

As one would expect in an age of monastic decline, the religious orders attracted a decreasing number of gifts and requests for prayers and burial, and it was the older orders which fared the worst. The following table shows this trend:

	1422–80	1481–1529
% of testators supporting mendicant establishments:	24.2	16.6
% of testators supporting non-mendicant establishments:	28.5	10.7

The popularity of the friars, who espoused a more personal and informal pattern of worship, did not decline so rapidly, and two reforming movements – those of the Observants and Carthusians – were relatively popular; five bequests were made to the Carthusian Charterhouse in London, and one was made to their Surrey house at Sheen. The Observant friars in Greenwich and Canterbury, whose houses had only been founded in 1482 and 1496 respectively, between them received seven bequests. The relative popularity of the friars may be judged by the fact that, including the Observants, there were only nine mendicant houses in Kent, compared with the Benedictines and non-mendicant Augustinians, for example, who between them had twelve

Kentish houses.[69] When asking for prayers, it was fairly common for testators to specify that the cantarists were to be friars, a condition not found with regard to members of other orders.

Support for the religious orders was greater among the higher ranks of the gentry, as the following table shows:

	Knights	Esquires	Gentlemen
% of testators supporting mendicants:	33.3	26.6	11.3
% of testators supporting non-mendicants:	33.3	24.0	8.6

Families of long-standing in the county – for the most part those of county prominence – may have developed a tradition of patronizing a particular house, a tradition that had been formed in an age of enthusiasm for the religious orders and which persisted even when that enthusiasm had declined among the lesser ranks. In addition, it may be that the support of monasteries was regarded as one of the customary duties of the greater gentry, and so the county families, wishing to be seen to act in a manner befitting their station, felt obliged to maintain their support for the orders.[70]

Some gentry went further than merely giving gifts to the orders and entered into formal associations with them as *confratres*. A *confrater* warranted special inclusion in the prayers of the house, and at his death he was prayed for as one of the order. Such an association often involved a tacit understanding that the *confrater* would don the habit of the order when death seemed imminent.[71] It was widely believed that to die in a religious habit – especially the habit of a mendicant order – would confer special benefits on the soul.[72] In return for these privileges, a legacy was naturally expected. In 1501 John Isaac gave lands in Chartham and a tenement in Northgate to the prior and convent of the Augustinian house of St. Gregory in Canterbury; from the profits of this property the monks were to keep a fifty-year *obit* for his soul, and in addition they were to receive him into their community as a *confrater*. The deed of gift details the spiritual benefits that would accrue to Isaac: his name would be registered on the roll of those brothers for whom an annual mass and *dirige* were to be said, for 'as long as the place standys'.[73] Both examples of *confratres* in our sample of testators had chosen to be associated with the new reforming movements. In 1493 Sir John Guildford requested that a trental (a set of thirty masses) was to be sung for his soul and for the souls of his parents in the Carthusian Charterhouse in London, 'to whom I am a brother'.[74] In 1434 John Kelsham, an esquire of Headcorn, left 100s. to his fellow brothers in the Observant house of Sheen in Surrey.[75] Neither of these testators wished to be buried in these houses, however, but instead preferred their own parish church. John Isaac's place of burial is unknown.

Most gentry were buried within a few miles of their principal residence. Of the few gentry who asked for burial outside Kent, most asked for a London burial and were themselves of London origin. For example, both Richard Lee, an esquire of Rochester, and his son of the same name, who was a gentleman of Maidstone and who died in 1525, were buried in the church of St. Steven in Walbrook, London. They were the son and grandson of Sir Richard Lee, an alderman of London who died in 1472 and who lies buried in the same church.[76] The following table shows the burial sites chosen by those testators who named a desired place of interment within Kent:

	Knights	Esquires	Gentlemen
Mendicant houses:	9.5	1.3	3.8
Non-Mendicant houses:	.7	1.3	2.8
Cathedrals:	9.5	1.3	0.9
Parish churches:	76.2	96.1	92.4

The relative popularity of the friars is again shown by these figures but it is the parish church which emerges as by far the most usual place of interment.

A sense of hierarchy extended even to the grave, and many testators asked to be buried in a manner 'most covinable and honest for my degree'.[77] Twenty-eight per cent of gentlemen or their wives, and eight per cent of esquires asked for burial in the churchyard, but of the rest the chosen place of burial was within the body of the church, which was a more prestigious resting-place. More prestigious still was a position near the high altar: twenty-two per cent of knights and twenty-one per cent of esquires requested burial in this area, but so did eighteen per cent of gentlemen. The location of the burial site had a spiritual as well as a social significance. The mass was believed to have had a near-magical efficacy for the souls of those buried close to the spot where it was celebrated. Consequently, burial near the altar was additionally sought-after as a further insurance against damnation. The high altar was the centre of an area of sanctity that enveloped the church and its precinct, but there were other places of special significance. John Pympe and Sir John Guildford both asked to be buried near the Easter sepulchre. The latter testator requested burial 'wher the ressurection of our lord is made': the celebration of Christ's resurrection symbolised the promise of individual spiritual re-birth into God's grace.[78] The tomb of Joan Mareys in Sheldwich church expresses a similar anticipation of spiritual re-birth: it depicts her rising from her funeral shroud, bearing a heart to represent her soul, which an inscription asks to be brought to eternal life. Such a resurrection motif was unusual in the fifteenth century, and did not become common in England for another two hundred years.[79]

Familial sentiment played its part in determining where testators asked to be buried. Thirty-seven testators asked to be interred near the tomb of a relative; their choice is shown below:

Burial requested beside:	Father	Mother	Spouse	Children	Uncle	Ancestors
No. of testators:	9	1	22	2	1	2

No testator asked to be buried next to a brother or sister. These figures show a predominantly patrilineal family feeling. According to this evidence, bonds of familial sentiment ran from parent to child and between husband and wife, and generally did not extend to siblings or other collateral relatives.[80] To judge by the evidence of surviving tombs, it seems that most couples were buried together, but often in the same church as the husband's father. Since many gentry families were of long-standing in the county, such burial traditions often led to several generations of a particular family being buried in the same church, parts of which consequently came to resemble family mausolea.[81] Needless to say, such a burial pattern strengthened the identification of a gentry family with its local parish church. The church was the focus of parish life, and such an association enhanced the family's proprietorial claims on their locality.

Testators often made detailed provision for the construction of their tombs. One gentleman, Robert Cheeseman of Lewisham, tells us why: 'And there to be made a tombe over me to thentent to have me in a bettyr memorye'.[82] The presence of imposing family tombs in the parish church stressed the family's venerable status, thus reinforcing its position in local society.[83] John Pympe's will includes the exact wording he wished to be placed on his tomb; it amounts to no less than an account of his lineage stretching back five generations, together with a plea for Christ to have mercy on the souls of those named. Not content with this, and in part payment for his benefactions to his burial church of Nettlestead, he requested that there be inserted into the blank spaces of the windows in the nave the arms of members of the St. Leger, Cheyne, and Guildford families, and he asked of his executors 'that a knoleche be sought howe alliaunce of Sellinger, Cheyne and Pympe came first in by mariage', and that this too be shown by armorial glass. His executors did not need to look far in the case of the St. Leger alliance, for his father, also called John, had married Phillipa St. Leger. The Guildfords were also close relatives by marriage: the testator's sister was the wife of Sir Richard Guildford. The relationship between the Pympes and the Cheynes has not been discovered, however. The Cheynes, St. Legers, and Guildfords were of great prominence in Kent – of greater prominence than the Pympes – and so it was natural for John Pympe to wish his family's connections with them to be proclaimed in glass, even if one of those connections may perhaps have been the product of wishful thinking.[84]

Towards the end of our period, there appears a new element in burial provisions: seven testators, the first of whom made his will in 1482, gave no preferred site for interment, but merely asked for 'my body to be buried where it shall please god for hit to dispose'.[85] Another, related trend was the expression on the part of some testators of a reaction against excessive funeral pomp. In 1472 Cecily Kyriel, the widow of Sir Thomas Kyriel of Sarrecourt in Thanet, requested that her executors *non faciant illo modo circa sepultarum corporis mei nec in die Anniversarii mei aliquos pomporas expensis.*[86] An extreme example of the kind of extravagence of which Cecily Kyriel would have disapproved is provided by the funeral arrangements made by Thomas Bulkley, a gentleman of Sandwich who made his will in 1490. In this will he asked that his body be carried from Sandwich in procession, accompanied by friars, four priests and a clerk, with children riding and singing by their side and with eight torches to light them when they passed through a town; this was to continue all the way to Canterbury, and from there to Bulkley's chosen place of burial in Woolwich, where they were to be met by sixteen poor men from London bearing tapers and torches.[87] Apart from indulging the medieval tendency to externalise emotions and present them in the form of pageantry, such displays once again glorified the individual and his family, while the impressive spectacle they presented would have helped to fix the memory of the deceased firmly in the minds of those who might feel disposed to pray for him, especially if the funeral was attended by an alms-dole.

Cecily Kyriels's unease at such manifestations of personal and family pride was shared by several other testators. In 1493 Sir John Guildford wished 'my out beryng to be made not pomposely . . . Also I will that at my yeres mynde be leyde on me a playne stone and noo tumbe', while in his will of 1525 Sir John Fyneaux asked that at his funeral 'all pompes and vayne glories be sett apart'.[88] This new note of humility sometimes sat uneasily with a lingering desire for commemoration: immediately after his request for a simple tomb, Sir John Guildford added that the 'playne stone' was to be inscribed 'with suche epitaphis as by me or myne executors shalbe devised'.

Each of the three gentry ranks had different approaches to charity and faith, suggesting that behind these nominal distinctions lay significant differences in life-style and outlook. These differences were particularly apparent between the county and the parish gentry. Two considerations dominated the gentry's attitude to religion: characteristically, one was spiritual – the need to save their souls – and the other was secular – the desire to promote themselves and their kin through displays of wealth and munificence. In many respects, theirs was a materialistic faith: prayers were a form of currency in a transaction between man and God; physical objects, such as relics, were esteemed by some, and the treatment of the corpse was generally regarded as of great importance. their inner faith was manifested outwardly through ceremony and symbolism. Certain religious practices served to strengthen their position in society, by emphasising their role as patrons and leaders of their local communities. No great division was perceived between the sacred and profane, and the gentry did not hesitate to promote their temporal interests through the medium of the church: the spiritual and temporal interpenetrated to a far greater extent than they do today.

The gentry showed great concern to perpetuate the family name, and even at the point of death the family was uppermost in their mind. The perpetuation of the family name ensured a kind of temporal immortality. The gentry were acutely aware of their own individual mortality, but the establishment of perpetual foundations implies a belief that the social organisation which allowed those foundations to flourish would always exist. This belief in an unchanging *status quo* was soon to be shattered, and the first signs of an impending change of attitude are apparent among the gentry of Kent in the decades preceeding the Reformation. They seem to have been moving towards a more personal, less institutionalized form of worship, with less emphasis on prayers and funeral ceremonies, a decline in support for the religious orders, and the beginnings of a new attitude towards charity. However, it must be stressed that these attitudes were only to be found among a minority of gentry: for most, it was the older forms of religious thought and practice which held sway.

Notes

In the manner of a medieval testator, I wish first of all to acknowledge a debt: my thanks are due to Professor R.A. Griffiths, who kindly read an early draft of this essay.

1.   The sources used to estimate the average wealth of the three gentry ranks are as follows: inquisitions *post mortem* from 1422 to 1509 (PRO, C139–141; *CIPM*, 2nd series, vols. I–III); returns of the fifteenths and tenths for the reign of Henry VI (PRO, E179/124/93, 9, 110, 114); returns of the 1431 subsidy (*Inquisitions and assessments relating to Feudal Aids; with other analogous documents preserved in the Public Record Office A.D. 1284–1431*, vol. III, pp. 56–81); returns of the 1450 subsidy (PRO, E179/124/218); returns for 1457–8 and 1503–4 of those persons in Kent holding 40 or more librates of land, and returns of 1502–5 of those who were fined for not accepting knighthood (PRO, E198/4/16, 20–22); and the list of Kentish gentry composed in 1501–2, which gives the yearly income of twenty of the hundred gentry listed (BL, Harleian MS. 6166/97). This last document was probably made in preparation for the distraints of 1502–5. It has also been used to calculate the relative proportions of the three ranks, together with pardons taken out by Kentish gentry between 1422 and 1509 (PRO, C67 37[a]–55, together with those pardons found on the Patent Rolls); and a list of Kentish gentry compiled as a result of an heraldic visitation, probably conducted soon after 1499 (BL, Cotton Faustina MS. Eii, printed in *AC* XI [1877], 394–7). P. Clark, *English Provincial Society from the Reformation to the Revolution* (Sussex, 1977), p. 6, estimates the population of Kent in 1500 as about 85,000, rising to 130,000 a century later; W.K. Jordan, 'Social Institutions in Kent 1480–1660', *Essays in Kentish History*, ed. M. Roake and J. Whyman (London, 1973), estimates the county's population in 1570 as around 140,000, implying a somewhat higher estimate than Clark's for the end of the fifteenth century. There were probably less than 250 gentry families in Kent at any one time.

2.   *VCH, Kent*, III, 324 ff.; F. Hull, 'The Customal of Kent', *AC*, LXXII (1958), 148; W.S. Holdsworth, *A History of English Law* (3rd ed., London, 1925), III, p. 260; henceforth cited as *English Law*. Partible inheritance was found elsewhere in England, but nowhere so prominent as in Kent: G.C. Homans, 'Partible Inheritance of Villagers' Holdings', *Econ. HR*, VIII (1937–8), 48 ff.

3.   The wills made by Kentish gentry between 1422 and 1529 were proved before the Canterbury Prerogative, Consistory, and Archdeaconry courts of probate. The wills of most gentry testators were proved before the Prerogative court, the senior court of the three. Wills proved before the other two courts were mainly of non-gentle testators, but some gentlemen and a few of higher rank did have their wills proved there. M.L. Zell, 'Fifteenth and Sixteenth Century wills as Historical Sources', *Archives*, XIV (1979–80), 67–74, provides a useful discussion of the subject. Prerogative court will registers are preserved in the Public Record Office as PCC; Archdeaconry and Consistory court will registers in the Kent Archives Office as PRC. Some Prerogative court wills are transcribed in *The Register of Henry Chichele*, II, ed. E.F. Jacob and H.C. Johnson (Canterbury and York Society, XLII, 1938); henceforth cited as *Chichele*. For the purpose of statistical analysis, the period has been divided into two sections: 1422–80, and 1481–1529. The number of wills in each section is respectively 70 and 130. Of the 200 wills, 21 were made by knights, 75 by esquires and 104 by gentlemen or their wives. 'Will', as used in this essay, denotes both the *testamentum*, dealing mainly with chattels, and the *ultima voluntas*, which deals mainly with the disposition of lands.

4.   *Dives and Pauper*, Vol I, part ii, ed. P.H. Barnum (EETS, Original Series, 275, repr. Oxford, 1980), ix:xvi; henceforth cited as *Dives*. For the notion of stewardship, see P. Ariès, *The Hour of our Death* (English ed., London, 1981), pp. 195–6; henceforth cited as *Hour*. See also W.K. Jordan, *Philanthropy in England, 1480–1660* (London, 1959), p. 152; J.A.F. Thompson, 'Piety

and Charity in Late Medieval London', *Journal of Ecclesiastical History*, XVI (1965), 194; and S. Thrupp, *The Merchant Class of Medieval London* (Chicago, 1948), pp. 174ff. For another contemporary expression of the idea, see Everyman, 11. 161–7 (*Everyman and Medieval Miracle Plays*, ed. A.C. Cawley [London, 1956], p. 211).

5.   *English Law*, III, p. 535. In theory, the intestate were denied burial in consecrated ground: *Hour*, p. 189
6.   PCC 19 Horne.
7.   *Gentleness and Nobility*, II, ed. A.C. Partridge and F.P. Wilson (Malone Society, Oxford, 1949–50), pp. 705–8; henceforth cited as *Gentleness*. For the legal position of debtors, see *English Law*, III, pp. 418–9.
8.   PCC 2 Wattys.
9.   PCC 9 Godyn. See also the wills of Sir John Fyneaux, 1525 (PCC 1, Porche), and Elizabeth Alfegh, 1502 (PCC 17, Blamyr).
10. PCC 4 Vox.
11. *Hour*, pp. 107, 153–4, 462–7; J.C. Dickinson, *An Ecclesiastical History of England: The Later Middle Ages* (London, 1979), pp. 16–17. The few wills which do not contain specific prayer provisions are in the main very short, and often made when the testator was so close to death that he only had time to make the most basic provisions. For example, the will of Nicholas Sibill, made in 1464, begins with the statement that he was so close to death that he could not wait for a scribe and so made an oral will in the presence of at least two witnesses (PCC 9 Godyn).
12. PCC 19 Horne. Another example is provided by the will of John Chamberlain, 1474 (PRC 17/2/373); and see D.M. Owen, *Church and Society in Medieval Lincolnshire* (Lincoln, 1971), p. 103, for details of services.
13. J.R. Scott, *Memorials of the Family of Scott of Scott's Hall* (London, 1876), p. 43.
14. PCC 25 Ayloffe; PCC 15 Logge.
15. Sir John Fyneaux's provision for prayers for his late wife's first husband was most exceptional in this respect (PCC 1 Porche).
16. From wills of, respectively, William Appulderfield, 1482 (PRC 32/3/181), and John Chamberlain, 1474 (PRC 17/2/373).
17. PCC 1 Porche. John Alfegh, a gentleman of Chiddingstone who made his will in 1488, had similar feelings of guilt: he ordered prayers for 'the soules of all tho that I have takyn eny Fee reward or Benefyte of unrecompensid or deservid' (PCC 18 Milles).
18. *Robert of Brunne's 'handlyng Synne'*, Part I, ed. F.J. Furnival (EETS Original Series 119, London, 1901), W. 10711–14. See also *Dives*, vol. I, part ii, vii:xxi–xxii; and B. Manning, *The People's Faith in the Age of Wyclif* (2nd ed., Cambridge 1975), p. 74.
19. PCC 19 Horne.
20. From the will of Sir Thomas Culpeper of Bayhall, 1428 (*Chichele*, II, pp. 382–6).
21. PCC 32 Vox.
22. AC, XXXIV (1920), 58.
23. K.L. Wood-Legh, *Perpetual Chantries in Britain* (Cambridge, 1965), p. 48. Alienation of land to the church – under whose 'dead hand' it would forever remain – denied the king a potential source of revenue; consequently, legal restrictions were placed on such alienations, such as the 1391 statute of Mortmain. In his will of 1465, Thomas Ballard made provision for the establishment of a chantry but also provided for alternative acts of piety in the event of Edward IV denying him a licence to alienate land in mortmain (PCC 14 Godyn).
24. S. Raban, *Mortmain Legislation and the English Church* (Cambridge, 1982), pp. 114–8; A. Gooder, 'Mortmain and the Local Historian', *The Local Historian*, IX (1971), 391.
25. AC, XIII (1880), 462. This understandable emphasis on the rectitude of the trustees was common; for example, an *obit* which Sir John Fogge established by his will of 1490 was to be administered by four of 'the most trystiest and discrete dwellars in the . . . parisshe of Esshetysford (Ashford)' (PRC 32/3/280).
26. PCC 18 Godyn.

27. The tables given in this essay are based on the sample of 200 wills. Unless otherwise stated, the figures represent percentages of testators within each rank or two sub-periods.
28. The Culpepers, for example, had enjoyed the use of a chantry since at least 1329, when Sir John Culpeper founded a chantry chapel in Pembury churchyard: A. Hussey, 'Chapels in Kent', AC, XXIX (1911), 217ff. The desirability of having prayers immediately after death is stressed in Dives, vol. I, part ii, vii:xxi.
29. Registrum Thome Bourgchier Cantuariensis Archiepiscopi, A.D. 1454–1486 ed. F.R.H. DuBoulay (Canterbury and York Society LIV, 1957), p. 59.
30. For an example of detailed prayer provision, see the will of Robert Ballard, cited above, p.
31. T. Smith, English Gilds (EETS, Original Series, XL, 2nd ed., Oxford, 1963), pp. xlix ff.; H.F. Westlake, The Parish Gilds of Medieval England (London, 1919), passim.
32. Sir John Fogge of Ashford intended to found a gild during his lifetime, but his participation in Buckingham's rebellion in 1483 and his subsequent fall from grace ended such ambitions. See AC, LXXV (1961), 122; The Itinerary of John Leland in or about the years 1535–1543, Parts VII and VIII, ed. L.T. Smith (London, 1909), p. 38.
33. James Dering made his will in 1497: PRC 32/4/154 . Membership of several gilds at one time was not uncommon.
34. PCC 25. For stocks, see H.F. Westlake, Parish Gilds, p. 61.
35. Robert Gore's will: PRC 32/3/298. Est and Barbour's licence: CPR, 1441–46, p. 361.
36. These indulgences are recorded in Calender of Entries in the Papal Registers relating to Great Britain and Ireland: Papal Letters.
37. Ibid., 1471–84, p. 660.
38. For example, ibid., 1427–47, pp. 310–11: grant to William Swan of Southfleet and Joan and Elizabeth his sisters of an indult to have a portable altar, on which they may have mass celebrated.
39. AC, XIV (1882), 350–1.
40. PCC 2 Wattys.
41. Sir John's will of 1490 (PRC 32/3/280). Repton was one of his two principal seats, the other one being at Ashford.
42. J.T. Rosenthal, The Purchase of Paradise (London, 1972), pp. 87–8. For Poynings's will, see PCC 14 Luffenam.
43. PRC 32/2/79.
44. PCC 16 Luffenam. Saphires are accredited with such properties in the late-fifteenth-century Peterborough Lapidary. See English Medieval Lapidaries, ed. J. Evans and M.S. Serjeantson (EETS Original Series, 190, London, 1933), p. 101.
45. PCC 25 Luffenam.
46. Chichele, II, pp. 539–40, 382–6.
47. PCC 15 Logge. The priest could have obtained a certificate or some other form of souvenir from St. Peter's to prove that he had been there: Hour, p. 72.
48. PCC 28 Fetiplace.
49. Edited by Sir Henry Ellis (Camden Society, Old Series LI, London, 1850). The Guildfords were blessed with unusually literate chaplains: Sir John Guildford's will of 1497 asked for a priest to 'syng for Mathewes soule somtyme my clerke and wrote my boke of Gowir' (PCC 29 Dogett).
50. Dives, II, ix:xiv.
51. G.R. Owst, Literature and Pulpit in Medieval England (Cambridge, 1933), pp. 560–2.
52. The Book of the Knight of La Tour-Landry, ed. T. Wright (EETS, Original Series XXXIII, 2nd ed., New York, 1969), ch. XX, LXXXVII. CII; Peter Idley's Instructions to his Son, Book I, ed. C. d'Everlyn (London, 1935), 11. 1037–8, 1043; J.A.F. Thompson, Ecclesiastical History, p. 194; S. Thrupp, Merchant Class, p. 179.
53. By his will of 1474, John Chamberlain arranged for alms to be given at his anniversary obit (PRC 11/2/373). In 1519 William Brockhill provided for the presence of 13 paupers with black

gowns and torches at his funeral, 'month's mind' and *obit* (PCC 25 Ayloffe). Robert Ballard requested black gowns to be made for the poor at his *obit* (PCC 19 Horne).

54. *Dives*, II, ix:xiv.
55. PRC 32/3/361.
56. PCC 5 Milles.
57. CPR, *1452–61*, p. 114; and Hussey, 'Chapels in Kent', pp. 217ff.
58. PCC 22 Stokton. Another gentleman with poor relatives was John Alfegh of Chiddingston, who in his will of 1488 ordered that money be provided for 'Pour Maydens mariagis of my Kynne' (PCC 18 Milles).
59. PCC 24 Godyn. For Bedlam, see D. Knowles and R. N. Hadcock, *Medieval Religious Houses: England and Wales* (London, 1971), p. 286. We know of no case of insanity in the Ellis family.
60. PCC 12 Wattys.
61. PRC 17/13/89.
62. A more specific allocation of alms was also an increasingly common feature in the wills of the Yorkshire gentry after 1450: M.G.A. Vale, *Piety, Charity, and Literacy among the Yorkshire Gentry, 1370–1480* (Borthwick Institute Papers, L, 1976), pp. 26–7. For the increase in pauperism, see L. Stone, 'Social Mobility in England, 1500–1700', *Past and Present*, XXXIII (1966), 23–4.
63. *Gentleness*, ll. 671–4.
64. PCC 18 Godyn.
65. PCC 25 Ayloffe.
66. *Chichele*, II, pp. 539.
67. PCC 2 Horne.
68. J. Newman, *The Buildings of England: West Kent and the Weald* (London, 1969), p. 127.
69. For the Observants and Carthusians, see Knowles and Hadcock, *Religious Houses*, 30–7, 42–5, 133, 230; for the popularity of the friars, see Vale, *Piety*, p. 20; B. Manning, *People's Faith*, p. 122.
70. The more traditional forms of religious benefaction tended to survive among the nobility: Rosenthal, *Paradise*, pp. 102ff.
71. D. Knowles, *The Monastic Orders in England* (2nd ed., Cambridge, 1966), pp. 475–9.
72. *Ibid.*, and K. Thomas, *Religion and the Decline of Magic* (London, 1971), p. 35; B. Manning, *People's Faith*, p. 122n.
73. BL, Harleian Charters, MS 78/I/17.
74. PCC 29 Dogett.
75. PCC 16 Luffenam.
76. PCC 15 Porche; J.C. Wedgwood, *History of Parliament: Biographies* (London, 1936), pp. 530–1; S. Thrupp, *Merchant Class*, p. 353; for the pardons of Richard Lee II and III; see PRO C67 49, 51, 55.
77. From the will of Sir Thomas Cobham, 1471 (PCC 2 Wattys).
78. Pympe's will, PCC 2 Horne; Sir John's, PCC 29 Dogett.
79. J. Newman, *The Buildings of England: North East and East Kent* (London, 1969), p. 443. This hopeful expectation is echoed in Joan's will of 1464, which begins with the committal of her soul: 'that when it departeth from my body it may be received into the cite of heven as thow hast promysed Abraham and his issue' (PCC 9 Godyn).
80. The same pattern was to be found among the nobility: Rosenthal, *Paradise*, p. 17.
81. See the Lees, above, p. . St. Mary's church in Brabourne contains the tombs of three members of the Scott family who died between 1433 and 1524, together with the tomb of Elizabeth Poynings, the daughter of Sir John Scott and the wife of Sir Edward Poynings, the lord deputy of Ireland: Newman, *North East and East Kent* p. 151. The chancel of St. Mary's church in Cobham, Kent, contains the tombs of sixteen Cobhams and Brooks (the family that inherited the Cobham title) or their close relatives (*ibid.*, pp. 219–20).
82. His will was made in 1498 (PCC 20 Horne).

83. In the seventeenth century, one Kentish knight, Sir Edward Dering of Pluckley, went so far as to construct several pseudo-ancestral brasses in Pluckley church, with the intention of supporting his grandiose – and totally false – claims to royal kinship: J. H. Round, *Peerage and Pedigree*, vol.II (London, 1910), pp. 110–6.
84. PCC 2 Horne.
85. The testators were Sir John Fyneaux (1525, PCC 1 Porche); Valentine Petit (1485, PCC 36 Milles); Sir Edward Poynings (1521, PCC 21 Maynwaryng); John Roger (1524, PCC 24 Bodfelde); Ralph St. Leger (1517, PCC 22 Ayloffe); William Appulderfield (1482, PRC 32/3/181); and Richard Brode (1521, PCC 38 Bodfelde).
86. PCC 9 Wattys.
87. PCC 27 Milles.
88. PCC 29 Dogett; PCC 1 Porche.

3

Litigation and Politics:
Sir John Fastolf's defence of his English property

Anthony Smith
University of Oxford

A late medieval English landowner forced to defend his property at law faced a daunting prospect. The rules governing descent of property were complicated and the processes of the common law courts were tortuous and expensive. Much was to be feared, as well as hoped, from the capacity of lords, whether by influence or intimidation, to control the country's legal institutions in the interests of themselves and their dependents. One particularly well-documented example of such a landowner is Sir John Fastolf.

Sir John Fastolf (1380–1459) was frequently involved in legal disputes. Many of these were over relatively minor issues, but some were of great importance because they concerned valuable properties he had bought in East Anglia and were challenges to both his financial wellbeing and his reputation. These acquisitions were Beighton and Bradwell (together worth £35 per annum), Titchwell (£20 per annum), Fritton (valued at £25 per annum), and a rent of £16 13s. 4d. paid annually by Hickling Priory. An understanding of the issues involved in these four lawsuits and their progress through the courts is possible from private letters, account rolls, and notes and drafts written by Fastolf's servants and lawyers, as well as from the records of the royal courts. It may be inferred from this evidence that Fastolf fought no other lawsuit in England for property of this kind. One further serious disagreement, regarding the manor of Dedham in Essex (worth about £80 per annum), did occur but it did not reach the courts. These five major disputes, four of which gave rise to litigation, concerned only a fifth of all the properties Fastolf bought in England with the profit of his service in France. There were another twenty acquisitions which caused him very little, or no, discernible trouble.[1]

Care in buying helped Fastolf to escape litigation. Most often Fastolf bought land directly from, or by the mediation of, very reliable men. They were relatives, military colleagues, senior estate officials or legal counsellors. Beighton and Bradwell, for example, were acquired from Sir Hugh Fastolf, a close relative and comrade-in-arms of Sir John Fastolf: Fritton and Titchwell were bought on the responsible advice of retained local lawyers and gentlemen councillors who had direct knowledge of these properties.[2] Risks were reduced by following a policy of limiting purchases to the East Anglian region which the servants and lawyers knew best. Fastolf's councillers examined the legal circumstances of a property with some care before buying it; at least once, unhappiness about a vendor's title did much to persuade them to abandon plans to buy a manor.[3] The councillors also took pains to collect as much relevant documentary evidence as possible, both during and after a transaction. They did this even when there was no threat of litigation to encourage their industry.[4] Such evidence was mostly stored in a central archive at Caister Castle, as can be seen from Fastolf's order, given in 1446 shortly before he began litigation in the Court of Common Pleas against Hickling Priory, that deeds relating to Hickling should be brought to London from the tower at Caister.[5] All this suggests that Fastolf took reasonable care when buying land, with the result that relatively few of his acquisitions were afflicted by serious disputes.

The paucity of important lawsuits explains why litigation did not reduce very greatly the profitability of Fastolf's investment in land. By 1445 Fastolf had spent £13,855 on land worth £780 *per annum*. This brought him a return of five and a half per cent *per annum* on his investment. His total legal expenses, including losses of revenue when his opponents occupied his possessions, were about £1,650. If this total is added to the amount of money spent on land, it only reduces Fastolf's return to five per cent *per annum*, a figure which K.B. McFarlane thought was a standard rate of return in the fifteenth century[6]. If the purchase of land was considered simply as a financial investment, (which, of course, it was not), Fastolf had done extremely well. As ownership of land conveyed status and power as well as income, Fastolf's investment was remarkably successful. His experience shows that heavy spending on land was not necessarily accompanied by ruinous litigation in defence of the investment for, as a consequence of the small number of lawsuits he fought, his expenditure on litigation was tiny compared with that on land.

Fastolf's investment should have been more profitable than it was. He was most unfortunate in facing litigation over Hickling, Beighton and Bradwell because care had been taken when buying them and the evidence of the title deeds and claims made in court shows that Fastolf's titles to them were sound. Hickling Priory's arguments to justify non-payment of a rent to Fastolf were easily refuted. The rent issued from the manor of Hickling Netherhall, which had been divided into thirds in the fourteenth century, each third finally being acquired by Hickling Priory. In order to obtain one of these portions, which belonged to Sir Lewis Clifford, the priory was obliged to pay a £16 13s 4d rent annually to Clifford, his heirs and his assigns. Fastolf became Clifford's assign when he bought the rent in 1428.[8] In the 1440s Hickling Priory made three important claims about this matter: these were that the obligation to pay had ceased on Clifford's death, that Hickling Netherhall had never been divided into thirds, and that if a rent were payable it was not from Clifford's portion of the manor. These claims were not only all demonstrably false but also mutually inconsistent. Once this was made clear in Common Pleas by Fastolf's lawyers, the priory could only resort, as it did with some success, to a series of delaying tactics.[9] Philip Wentworth's claims regarding Beighton and Bradwell were as groundless as Hickling Priory's regarding the rent. He alleged that Fastolf had illegally disseised Sir Hugh Fastolf of the two manors, an allegation which was easily refuted. In reality Bradwell had been conveyed to Fastolf by Sir Hugh's feoffees after Sir Hugh's death. This fact accounts for Wentworth's subsequent claim that Fastolf had merely possessed a joint interest in Bradwell with others whom he had disseised. It was true that Fastolf had been one of Sir Hugh's feoffees, but the sale of Bradwell had nevertheless been agreed by Sir Hugh before he died.[10] Sir Hugh's manor of Levington, to which Wentworth never referred, had similarly been acquired by Fastolf after Sir Hugh's death, with the assent of Hugh's feoffees.[11] Wentworth also appears never to have known about a claim made to Beighton by the mayor of Norwich, soon after Fastolf had bought the manor from Sir Hugh in 1415. Not that this challenge indicated any weakness in Fastolf's or Sir Hugh's title to Beighton. It was almost certainly based upon a forgery. Sir Hugh, furthermore, agreed to help Fastolf resist the mayor, which he would not have done had he been in dispute with Fastolf on his own account over Beighton.[12] Wentworth, it is plain, was very poorly informed about the history of the three manors which Fastolf had acquired from Sir Hugh; his case was very weak, and it was not the result of any lack of caution on Fastolf's part.

The dispute over Titchwell was different from the ones so far discussed. This was because Fastolf's opponent, Edward Hull, at least had a plausible legal claim to the property through his wife's ancestors. Yet, as P. S. Lewis pointed out, Hull's arguments involved quite as much guesswork as did Fastolf's defence. Neither man had a watertight case. Moreover, since Hull's challenge rested mainly on an obscure entail dating as far back as 1270, it is perhaps an exaggeration to say that Fastolf acted rashly when he bought Titchwell; he was most unfortunate to be troubled for it at all.[13] By contrast, Fastolf bought Fritton fully aware that two unresolved disagreements concerning it were in existence. His decision was a calculated risk taken because the price was favourable and because his counsellors thought that his title would be superior to claims put forward by Gilbert Debenham. Debenham was a feoffee to the use of William Lawney, who had owned Fritton. When Lawney sold Fritton to a vintner named John Pekker, Debenham refused to surrender his rights to the manor and continued to claim an estate in it. To complicate matters, Lawney, probably with encouragement from Debenham, asserted that he had conveyed Fritton to Pekker not in fee simple, as Pekker sold it to Fastolf, but for a term of years.[14] Fastolf, however, believed that Debenham's action was not justifiable and could be corrected by the chancellor: he also supposed that Pekker was telling the truth about the status of Fritton, otherwise he would not have bought the manor from him. His gamble was successful: these disputes involved him in only a brief appearance before the justices of assize in Suffolk and, in 1441, before the chancellor in chancery, while the manor, and the revenue from it, never left his hands.[15] It is obvious from these cases that it was not simply sensible buying and the possession of sound titles that averted troublesome litigation, and the reverse that caused it. Other considerations, such as the exercise of lordship and political power by magnates, played an important part in litigation too.

Lordship sometimes helped and sometimes hindered Fastolf's litigation. An early instance of the advantages to be derived from lordship occurred in 1415. During this year a challenge from the mayor of Norwich to Fastolf's title to Beighton, a manor close to Norwich, was quickly thwarted when Humphrey, duke of Gloucester, and Thomas, earl of Dorset, were named as Fastolf's feoffees and the manor was occupied by Fastolf and other squires from the household of his lord, Thomas, duke of Clarence.[16] At this time Clarence was probably very concerned to defend the interests of his best soldiers. The lord to whom Fastolf usually turned was the duke of Norfolk. The favour of John, duke of Norfolk, was certainly important in ending conflict over the manor of Fritton: both Fastolf and his adversary, Gilbert Debenham, were Norfolk's men and, once their dispute had reached the chancery in 1441, Norfolk apparently intervened to impose a settlement in Fastolf's favour. Norfolk probably supported Fastolf because Fastolf's title was better than Debenham's, but it is also likely that he considered Fastolf's friendship more valuable than Debenham's because the latter was of inferior wealth and status and was notorious for his unruly behaviour.[17] In 1450 Fastolf was confident that Norfolk's good lordship would help him in all his lawsuits, especially since Norfolk was a commissioner of oyer and terminer for East Anglia. With reference to the duke, Fastolf wrote that his servant Thomas Howes 'or John Bernay or onye othyr of my lerned councell may meoffe unto him and I doubt not but he wode gefe you audience'. Fastolf planned to ride from London to East Anglia to wait upon Norfolk, feeling that his presence there with the duke would hasten the redress of his grievances.[18] Norfolk gave considerable support to Fastolf in the dispute with Philip Wentworth during the 1450s: for example, when Wentworth sued Thomas Howes, Fastolf's servant was lodged in the duke's household to deter Wentworth and to persuade the sheriff and jury to do all they could on Howes's behalf. Two surviving letters of 1455 from Fastolf to Norfolk beg most humbly for the continuation of the duke's support against Wentworth in East Anglia, 'this contré wher ye be prynce and souereyne next owre souereyne lord'. It was

Fastolf's misfortune that Norfolk's power never matched the status attributed to him, in either the 1440s or the 1450s.[19] Thomas, Lord Scales's lordship, which always acted against Fastolf's interests regarding Hickling Priory, went unchecked by Norfolk. On one occasion, in 1451, Bishop Lyhert of Norwich told Fastolf, who had hoped to see episcopal discipline exercised over the offending priory, that he was unable to act because Scales had instructed him not to meddle in the affair. Even when, in July 1455, Fastolf secured a writ of distress *per omnia bona et catalla* directed against the priory, his hopes were dashed by Scales. In the preceding May the prior had delivered his evidences to Scales, who subsequently occupied Hickling himself to prevent the execution of Fastolf's writ.[20] Thus, Fastolf's litigation provides evidence of the capacity of fifteenth-century lords to defend the interests of their dependents much more cheaply and effectively than their dependents could defend themselves in the royal courts. Lordship, however, was never entirely divorced from the political conditions in which it was put to use.

The political background to Fastolf's litigation is evident in the origins of the disputes which troubled him most. These disputes all began in the 1440s when Fastolf, and those magnates (most notably the dukes of Gloucester, York, and Norfolk) who regarded him with favour, were excluded from political influence by a faction which the duke of Suffolk dominated. Indeed, with the exception of that regarding Hickling, which began in 1444, the disputes erupted between 1447 and 1449, when Suffolk's power was at its height. In one draft of a petition to Henry VI, Fastolf explicitly attributed the unlawful disseisins of his property at Beighton, Bradwell, Titchwell, Hickling and Dedham to the ill-will of the officers and servants of the king's chief minister.[21] However, disseisin in Suffolk's name occurred only at Dedham; elsewhere it happened in the name of Sir Edward Hull, Sir Philip Wentworth, and the prior of Hickling. In other words, Fastolf's petition asserted that the losses these men caused him were imposed by means of Suffolk's influence with the king and his control over East Anglia. The circumstances under which the lawsuits involving these men arose certainly suggest that this was the case.

Sir Edward Hull, who challenged Fastolf over Titchwell in October 1448, was an influential courtier. He was appointed constable of Bordeaux in 1442 and held important positions in Queen Margaret's household. Hull alleged that Titchwell ought technically to be in royal hands; he was thus able to hold the manor at farm from the crown on advantageous financial terms whilst he sought to prove in the courts that his wife had a title to it by descent which invalidated Fastolf's purchase. The inquest by which Hull did this was, Fastolf believed, forged by the deputy escheator, John Dalling, on instructions from the escheator, Thomas Sherneborne. The escheator received counsel from the duke of Suffolk's legal servant, John Heydon, and from William Willy, who also laboured the jury of inquisition. Willy was known to Fastolf because he had, in partnership with John Heydon and Sir Thomas Tuddenham, maintained

Fastolf's opponents in a dispute during January 1447.[22] By 1449, moreover, Willy held Titchwell on lease from Sir Edward Hull. Obviously much of the impetus in this dispute was provided by Suffolk's East Anglian adherents, who cooperated with corrupt royal officials. One of these, Dalling, was also involved in Philip Wentworth's challenge to Fastolf during 1449. The other, Sherneborne, was in the Queen's household and was, together with Philip Wentworth, an associate of Edmund Clere, esquire of the king's household.[23] Since Hull himself held neither lands nor offices in East Anglia, assistance from men of this kind was invaluable to him. What made their support readily available was Hull's prominence at court and, more important, the duke of Suffolk's favour, which Hull evidently enjoyed, for he became a feoffee of the duchy of Lancaster in November 1443. As Dr. G.L. Harriss has shown, control of the duchy's offices and revenues was most important in the rise to power of Sufolk and his court party after 1437.[24] The circumstances of Hull's claim to Titchwell also afford evidence of Suffolk's favour, since such men as Heydon and Willy would not have acted contrary to the duke's will. Fastolf was correct to suppose that Suffolk was very important in the outbreak of a dispute which, between 1448 and 1455, cost him £20 of annual income and substantial legal expenses.

Philip Wentworth's claim to Beighton and Bradwell was only possible because the king granted to Robert Constable, Wentworth's brother-in-law and ally, the wardship and marriage of Thomas Fastolf, notwithstanding Sir John Fastolf's complaint that Thomas's father had appointed him as guardian (to use the boy's inheritance for the 'most advayle' of his mother and his sister's marriage) and that Thomas's mother was imprisoned in the Fleet 'undre duresse' to force her to hand her son over to Robert Constable.[25] This Thomas was the grandson of Sir Hugh Fastolf, from whom Sir John had acquired Beighton and Bradwell. Having gained control over Thomas Fastolf's inheritance, Wentworth organised illegal inquisitions which, in the suummer of 1449, found that Beighton and Bradwell were rightfully a part of that inheritance. By traversing the inquests, Fastolf prevented the manors from entering Wentworth's hands, but he was obliged to farm them from the crown for three and five years respectively, thereby incurring substantial legal expenses and loss of revenue.[26] The men who conducted Wentworth's business were John Ulveston (a lawyer and steward of the duke of Suffolk in the county of Suffolk) and John Andrew (one of Suffolk's councillors), who were counselled by John Heydon, Suffolk's notorious legal adviser.[27] In addition to the connection between Wentworth and Suffolk's servants, Wentworth's own intimate connection with the court can be established. Wentworth was a member of Queen Margaret's household and a feoffee of Edmund Clere, who was an esquire of the king's household from Norfolk. As well as representing Suffolk in parliament in 1447 and 1449, Wentworth acted as sheriff of Norfolk and Suffolk during 1447–48. Undoubtedly the combination of Suffolk's power in East Anglia, his dominance at court, and his control over royal patronage afforded Wentworth an excellent opportunity to challenge Fastolf.

The dispute with Hickling Priory began earlier than, and in a different manner from, the disputes over Titchwell, Beighton and Bradwell. The priory paid regularly and without complaint a rent of twenty-five marks from the time Fastolf bought it in 1428 until May 1444, when it was withheld. On 30 October 1444, Fastolf entered Hickling Priory's manor of Palling and removed three horses worth twelve marks.[28] This was unwise, for Fastolf's legal counsellors, William Wangford and William Jenney, had advised him that the terms on which he held the rent did not permit him to distrain for it, although he could recover it, together with arrears, damages and costs, by assize or by a writ of entry in the court of Common Pleas.[9] Plainly, in October 1444 Fastolf did not expect the opposition which ensued, but by 1452 he was certain that, through malice towards him and in anticipation of gain, the duke of Suffolk's associates had advised the priory to default. Suffolk's involvement in this dispute is evident. In 1447, during litigation in Common Pleas between Fastolf and the priory, John Heydon spoke cleverly in the priory's defence, even thought he was not acting as its attorney. When Fastolf wished to examine useful documents possessed by the Benedictine nuns of Redlingfield, Suffolk prevented him from seeing them. Redlingfield, lying in Hartismere hundred (Suffolk) near Eye and holding land from the honour of Eye, was well within Suffolk's sphere of territorial influence. Its fourteenth-century benefactor, Sir William Kerdiston, was an ancestor of Sir Thomas Kerdiston, who was closely connected with Suffolk during the 1440s.[30] Similarly, Fastolf was unable to see or have summoned into court documents possessed by Lord Saye and Sele which, he was informed by John Vampage, attorney-general in the court of Common Pleas, were relevant to the case. In view of Saye and Sele's association with Suffolk in the governing régime, this failure is hardly surprising. Fastolf was also opposed by Thomas, Lord Scales, lord of Hickling manor and the priory's patron, who, in addition to having personal grievances against Fastolf, was allied with Suffolk by about 1447.[31] There can be little doubt that it was Suffolk, and those over whom he had influence, who opposed Fastolf in his dispute with Hickling Priory and stopped Fastolf recovering his rent by proceedings in Common Pleas when the legal arguments were distinctly in his favour.

Thus, during the time that Suffolk enjoyed political power, East Anglian officials, members of the royal households, and men in Suffolk's employment and affinity caused Fastolf serious losses and expense by forcing him to engage in major lawsuits. Over the same period there were other disputes and incidents, involving less litigation and smaller losses, in which Fastolf's interests were attacked by men of this kind. Suffolk's importance in these disputes was considerable. Indeed, he was party to a number of them. In February 1437 Suffolk persuaded Henry VI to grant him the wardship and marriage of Anne, daughter and heiress of Sir Robert Harling, even though Harling's property was in the hands of feoffees and the girl not the king's to grant. Fastolf, the most important of the feoffees, was obliged to buy the wardship, and a disagreement with Suffolk regarding payment soon resulted.[32] During 1441 another dispute occurred when Fastolf was wrongly accused of having defaulted on payments for the purchase (in 1434) from Suffolk of the manors of Cotton and Wickham Skeith. Following this, Suffolk's officers made distraints on the properties, injustices which Fastolf keenly wished to see punished by the commissioners of oyer and terminer appointed in the summer of 1450, after the duke's death.[33] Suffolk was indirectly responsible for other abuses of which Fastolf complained in 1450. Persistent attempts by Sir Thomas Tuddenham and John Heydon to disseise 'my lord Cromewell of a knyghten service' in Saxthorpe cost, according to Fastolf, £20 *per annum* 'yn approwement of my chattell'. Tuddenham claimed that Saxthorpe was held of the manor of Hethersett in the honour of Richmond, which was in the crown's possession and controlled by Suffolk's servants, whereas it was in fact held of Cromwell's manor of Tattershall. Fastolf and his tenants suffered similar problems in a part of the manor of Blickling which was held of Richmond honour.[34] More serious were the losses arising from exploitation of the duchy of Lancaster by Suffolk and his men. Amercements were wrongfully levied and distraints taken on Fastolf's officers and tenants at Blickling by Thomas Fowler and the officers of the hundred of South Erpingham, which was part of the duchy: and the duchy steward, John Heydon, ignored a writ commanding cancellation of the amercements. Fastolf's bailiffs underwent harassment, and his shepherd was driven from his service. One of Suffolk's own councillors, Robert Brampton, gentleman, illegally occupied lands rented by Fastolf at Blickling and would not move.[35] The insignificant men, like Thomas Fowler, John Dynne, yeoman, and Robert Brampton, who were responsible for these and similar injuries to Fastolf's interests, dominated East Anglia by taking service as Suffolk's councillors and officers and by holding offices, in the gift of the crown, to which Suffolk was able to appoint them. Fastolf's inability to resist these men testifies to the political power attained by Suffolk and the abuse of it which he was prepared to tolerate.

Suffolk was responsible for illegal actions of this kind in two ways. On the one hand, he failed properly to supervise men, in particular Sir Thomas Tuddenham and John Heydon, who acted in his and Henry VI's name; on the other hand, he set such men a poor example, as is clear from his dispute with Fastolf over Dedham. Suffolk's officers occupied Fastolf's two manors there early in 1447, by which time the duke's power as chief minister was practically unassailable. Their action could not be justified in law: even though Dedham had once been granted by Richard II to the first de la Pole earl of Suffolk, Fastolf's title to the property was perfectly sound. The first earl had lost Dedham when his political career ended in ruin, and it was in Archbishop Roger Walden's hands when the second earl restored the family fortunes early in Henry IV's reign. The second earl had confirmed Walden's title by quitclaim. Fastolf bought Dedham legitimately from men who had been granted remainder rights by Roger Walden's brother and heir, John Walden. All this was well known at the time Suffolk took the property from Fastolf. The weakness of Suffolk's legal position is evident from the rapidity with which Fastolf recovered Dedham following Suffolk's fall in January 1450. On 16 February John Stafford, archbishop of Canterbury,, and Walter Lyhert, bishop of Norwich, the arbitrators presiding over the case, acting on the advice of Chief Justice Fortescue and Justice Yelverton, awarded the property to him.[36] Yet during the preceding three years Fastolf had been unable to gain any redress at all. Not surprisingly, he had made no attempt to challenge Suffolk at common law or by means of a suit in chancery. Instead he had sought a private settlement by negotiation with Suffolk, making offers which were extremely favourable to the duke. He had proposed that the dispute should be decided by arbitrators. If they found for Suffolk, he would seek only compensation for his investments at Dedham (principally the building there of a new mill valued at £31 *per annum*). Were his own title established, he would pay Suffolk £100 just to have secure possession of his own lands. This offer having been rejected, Fastolf had made another: he would give Suffolk's eight-year-old son the manor of Dedham Overhall and sell Dedham Netherhall to Suffolk 'after the valew and rate of XX yeer and so he shuld best by that moyen have his gode lordship and the wey of peese'. This meant that Fastolf was prepared to offer Suffolk for £200 property which had cost him £1,160, hardly an advantageous settlement. Fastolf had even appealed to Suffolk's sense of honour, informing him that his settlement of this unjust disseisin would be 'for hys worship and trouth' because men would think it 'extortionately doon that onye man shuld be sterid to depart from hys good by that meene'. One of Fastolf's main aims in this negotiation was to prevent further trouble, for he knew that Suffolk also coveted his valuable manor at Hellesdon. Here, and at nearby Drayton, harassment by Suffolk's officers had caused Fastolf financial losses since 1440. Only the duke's fall seems to have saved Fastolf from losing Hellesdon, a property to which Suffolk had no title whatsoever. The attraction of Hellesdon and Dedham for Suffolk was their high annual values, which Fastolf had enhanced by spending considerable sums on improvements.[37] In just three years Suffolk's action cost Fastolf over 300 marks in income from Dedham.[38] For as long as the duke held power, there was nothing Fastolf could do in this case, as in numerous others. It is little wonder that he so keenly sought Suffolk's 'gode lordship' and the 'wey of peese'.

Fastolf was encouraged by the fall of the duke of Suffolk and the consequent disarray in which the duke's adherents found themselves. The recovery of Dedham was a result of Suffolk's disgrace and, for much of 1450, Fastolf hoped to gain compensation for losses of revenue and damages at Dedham and elsewhere caused by Suffolk's officials and councillors. In March 1450, before Suffolk had left England, Fastolf already planned to present a bill to parliament, listing losses, reckoned to be 5,000 marks, at their hands.[39] He probably hoped that the members of the commons who had shown the duke such hostility would look favourably on him. The bill was never presented, possibly because it took many months to prepare, but throughout 1450 Fastolf continued to insist that a comprehensive, accurate list of losses and expenses incurred since 1437 should be drawn up, mentioning every offence committed against him by Suffolk's officials and councillors. In September, encouraged by his own rise to political importance in the wake of Cade's rebellion, Fastolf intended to place his grievances before the king's council.[40] During the autumn of 1450 the possibility of presenting a bill before parliament was still being considered and Fastolf was ready to allow the justices of the peace to deal with some cases involving Suffolk's servants. However, Fastolf increasingly directed his attention towards achieving a favourable settlement by the commissioners of oyer and terminer appointed for Norfolk and Suffolk (1 August) and the city of Norwich (1 November), amongst whom were some of his most powerful allies: the duke of Norfolk, the earl of Oxford and Justice William Yelverton were named in both commissions and Ralph, Lord Cromwell sat with them on the commission for Norwich. Between September 1450 and May 1451 Fastolf used the oyer and terminer sessions mainly to pursue Suffolk's officers and councillors. Apart from John Ulveston and John Andrew, who were indicted for the assistance they had given to Philip Wentworth, no one was prosecuted before the commissioners for his part in the disputes over Hickling, Bradwell, Beighton and Titchwell, though Fastolf did consider indicting William Willy and others on 13 January 1451 at Lynn for what they had done to help Sir Edward Hull to gain possession of Titchwell.[41] Presumably Fastolf thought that the favourable conditions following Suffolk's disgrace would enable him to settle these disputes without such measures, as seemed possible in the disagreement with Hickling Priory. Once Suffolk was dead, Fastolf expected that he would be able to obtain copies of the valuable documents owned by the nuns of Redlingfield: 'seth it ys soo the world ys changed gretely over it was y pray you and charge you parson, labour ye. . .so as I may come by a copy of theyr evidens', he wrote in May to his servant, Thomas Howes. The copies were available early in August. Undoubtedly they helped Fastolf's cause, for he reached agreement with Lord Scales, now Hickling Priory's principal supporter, before the end of August.[42] This success, and the ca he held power.

Unfortunately for Fastolf, the removal of Suffolk's malign influence did not bring the many resounding victories in legal matters that he had expected. He received no compensation regarding Dedham; the prosecutions of Suffolk's servants and associates in the oyer and terminer sessions were frustrating and disappointing; and little progress was made in the disputes with Wentworth, Hull, and Hickling Priory. Lord Scales, for instance, abandoned his agreement with Fastolf and was once more supporting the priory by November 1450. He opposed Fastolf's efforts to have the case settled through a special assize, and he subsequently thwarted all Fastolf's attempts to make the priory pay the rent. In addition, Scales defended Suffolk's affinity when the oyer and terminer commissioners met at Lynn in January 1451 and Walsingham in May 1451; Scales was assisted in this by the judge John Prisot, who was a fellow commissioner.[43] Scales's decisive exercise of lordship was possible owing to changes in national politics during late 1450 and 1451. He allied himself to the new court party, led by Edmund Beaufort, duke of Somerset, hich emerged when York failed to find a place in the ruling régime after the disturbances of 1450. Somerset exercised power through the royal households and the surviving members of Suffolk's régime and affinity, including Lord Scales; Scales enhanced his own power by sustaining, and thereby gaining the support of, Suffolk's East Anglian associates. These political changes altered the favourable circumstances which followed Suffolk's fall and prevented Fastolf from making much headway against the duke's adherents or in the disputes over Hickling, Titchwell, Beighton and Bradwell.

Political conditions similar to the favourable ones of 1450 occurred once more during Fastolf's life. The political power wielded by Fastolf's lord, Richard, duke of York, after his victory in May 1455 at St. Albans, where the duke of Somerset was killed, led Fastolf to hope for a quick settlement of the disputes over Hickling, Bradwell and Beighton. He knew that only York's influence could overcome enemies who had enjoyed the favour of Somerset and Queen Margaret. It was political change that Fastolf referred to when, one week after St. Albans, he wrote that 'as the woorld goth nowe' success in his litigation was to be expected.[44] He was quickly proved right. In March 1455 Fastolf and Hickling Priory had agreed to arbitration in their disagreement, but the priory had swiftly allowed the arrangement to founder. Encouraged by St. Albans to return to the common law, Fastolf immediately gained a favourable verdict in Common Pleas, something which was never forthcoming whilst Suffolk was in power; and a writ enabling him to distrain for the rent and arrears was available in July 1455.[45] Similarly, in the year following St. Albans, Fastolf came as close as he ever did to defeating Wentworth utterly. Fastolf's servant William Barker thought that the outlook for Wentworth after the battle was dismal. He reported in June that Wentworth had abandoned the king's standard at St. Albans and dared not enter Henry VI's presence. The duke of Norfolk was threatening to hang Wentworth.[46] Heavy expenditure on litigation regarding Wentworth during Trinity term 1455 well illustrates Fastolf's optimism at this time. An important result of this activity was the final recovery of Beighton from the crown, for judgement was given during Trinity term 1455 in Fastolf's favour respecting his traverse of the 1449 inquest on Beighton. On 21 June 1455, moreover, the treasurer ordered that all the profits of the wardship of Thomas Fastolf should rightfully be delivered to Sir John Fastolf. These successes were followed by others. During two parliamentary sessions of 1455 the lords in parliament gave favourable consideration to a bill of complaint against Wentworth submitted by Fastolf: they were told by Chief Justice Fortescue that, owing to Wentworth's untruthfulness, there was no validity in a verdict, given early in 1453, by which Fastolf's traverse of the 1449 Bradwell inquisition was rejected and the manor was awarded to the king.[47] In February 1456 Fastolf persuaded Wentworth to accept arbitration of their differences respecting the wardship of Thomas Fastolf, and as late as May 1456 a petition from Wentworth on the status of Bradwell was sharply criticised by the exchequer barons.[48] This gratifying progress owed much to the help Fastolf received from York's colleagues, Thomas Bourgchier, the chancellor, and Henry Bourgchier, the treasurer. Only the political manoeuvres of mid-1456, in which a faction surrounding Queen Margaret attained power at York's expense, prevented Fastolf from forcing a final settlement on Wentworth. There was also a connection between York's political success and Fastolf's decisive victory in the Titchwell dispute, even if Sir Edward Hull's death at Castillon in 1453 had reduced the opposition that Fastolf faced. Money was first spent on litigation designed to disprove the crown's right to Titchwell in Michaelmas 1454. This was when York still held power during his first protectorate. Crucial proceedings were started in chancery on 15 May 1455: York's victory a week later must have contributed to their success and the final imposition of a settlement in Fastolf's favour during Michaelmas 1455.[49] York's supremacy was not maintained sufficiently long for Fastolf to conclude every dispute. Yet the recovery of Beighton and Titchwell, and the progress made regarding Hickling and the other matters between Fastolf and Wentworth, leave no doubts as to the consequences of York's ascendancy for Fastolf's litigation.

Despite the value to Fastolf of the properties in dispute and the social status and political power of his opponents, neither Fastolf nor his opponents resorted to violence to advance their interests. It is true that after arbitrators had awarded Dedham to Fastolf in 1450 Suffolk's servants caused serious damage to the property before leaving it. John Waryn (Suffolk's steward) and John Squire (his chaplain) damagingly attacked the mill, mill dam and streams, in the company of some of the duke's affinity in the area, principally John Bukk, who did damage valued at £20, and John Cole. Bukk was parson of Stratford St. Mary (a village owned by Suffolk) and Cole came from Stoke by Nayland: these are places close to Dedham on the Suffolk side of the River Stour. Fastolf regarded Bukk and Cole as longstanding enemies: they had unlawfully fished his waters and taken twenty-four of his swans and cygnets since 1447. Having obtained information from loyal tenants at Dedham, Fastolf proposed, in December 1450, to indict all these men before the commissioners of oyer and terminer in Suffolk. Although Squire, who was hated for his association with the duke, had been murdered in the summer by men from Suffolk and was beyond retribution, Fastolf's lawyers did prepare evidence against Waryn which was apparently never used, for Waryn, Bukk and Cole seem to have escaped prosecution.[50] Dedham was, of course, an unusual case because Suffolk was not a typical opponent and because the greatest damage was done there after Dedham had been awarded to Fastolf, rather than as a means of advancing a cause still in the courts by using pressure outside them. Intimidation was a method adopted by Suffolk's officials, servants and councillors to enrich themselves during the duke's ascendancy but, at least where Fastolf's interests were concerned, unlawful distraints and harassment by threats and by malicious lawsuits rather than overt physical violence were the forms it took. Indeed, the usual burdens that Fastolf's legal disputes brought to his tenants were financial ones coupled with the disruption of everyday life. Fastolf's litigation with Philip Wentworth during the 1450s, for instance, produced incidents like that in October 1454 when Fastolf's and Wentworth's representatives tried simultaneously to hold court at Nacton, a part of Thomas Fastolf's inheritance. At another of Thomas's properties one man acted as farmer for Sir John Fastolf while a different man acted for Wentworth who, moreover, was trying to sue Fastolf's man for trespass. Elsewhere Fastolf found it necessary to distrain on a farmer who would not enter an obligation to him after being threatened by Philip Wentworth.[51] Yet actions such as forcible entries, where force of arms was alleged in indictments, appear from private letters to have been conducted peacefully. The only hints of physical violence in Fastolf's important lawsuits were the rumour of riotous behaviour by Henry, son of Philip Wentworth, at Cotton in 1456 and Philip Wentworth's unsuccessful attempt to abduct Thomas Fastolf in June 1454 after Fastolf had bought the wardship and marriage from the crown. Since Fastolf sought the duke of Norfolk's support for complaints about Henry Wentworth's behaviour, there may have been substance to the rumour about him, but his father's action was evidently not violent, even though he rode with an armed company.[52] Thus, the evidence of Fastolf's litigation gives scarcely any support, other than the Dedham episode, for the view that legal disputes went hand in hand with physical violence and vandalism amongst the landowning classes of fifteenth-century England.

Indeed, there were a number of peaceful procedures available to a wealthy and well-connected litigant besides protracted suits in the common law courts. During 1450 Fastolf expected quick, favourable results from the justices of the peace and from the commissioners of oyer and terminer, though this was almost exclusively in minor matters, not in the more important litigation against Hull, Wentworth and Hickling Priory. Fastolf's lawyers suggested proceeding against Hickling by special assize, a method which was tried in 1450. The priory was once again the target when, in 1451, Fastolf petitioned Chancellor Kemp for an impartial commission of inquiry into the dispute.[53] On several occasions Fastolf had petitions heard by the chancellor, whose equitable jurisdiction he sought. This procedure was used in the lawsuits over Fritton and Hickling: it was also adopted in several other disagreements, mainly involving contracts. One petition, of 1451 or 1452, was rather unusual, for in it Fastolf complained to the chancellor about rumours current in East Anglia which stated that Thomas Daniel, esquire, had affirmed that he possessed documents, sealed by Fastolf, proving that he was Fastolf's heir and entitled to inherit his property. Fastolf asserted that he had given no such documents to Daniel and had no intention of doing so. He complained that Daniel's behaviour was a 'noisome grete vexacion and trouble' to his feoffees and executors, and he requested the chancellor to examine Daniel and recommend a form of action that could be taken against him. This petition reflects the interest men showed in Fastolf's great wealth as, without an heir, he approached death. The chancellor often heard petitions dealing with uses; indirectly Fastolf's petition concerned one but the advantage of this procedure was the opportunity it gave Fastolf publicly to deny the rumours and to make an example of Daniel, if Daniel had really acted as the rumours alleged.[54] Besides petitioning the chancellor, it was possible to bring grievances before the royal council and parliament. Fastolf planned to use the former procedure against Suffolk's councillors and servants in 1450. He thought that the parliamentary session of 9–31 July 1455, which was Yorkist in sympathy, would treat his legal disputes fairly, and he was prepared to attend it. He presented a bill of complaint regarding Sir Philip Wentworth in this session, though not in person.[55] Clearly one way to avoid the delays and frustrations of the common law courts was to have recourse to other courts which dealt with disputed issues more quickly and straightforwardly.

There were also less formal methods of trying to find settlements. One way was to obtain the help of a lord in ending a dispute. The duke of Norfolk, for example, was able to halt the dispute over Fritton; Fastolf evidently hoped the duke would be able to do the same for his disagreements with Philip Wentworth on several occasions in 1455 and 1456. In some circumstances an ecclesiastical lord might be expected to exercise influence of this kind: Fastolf certainly wanted Bishop Lyhert of Norwich to use his authority to bring the dispute with Hickling Priory to an end. Another method was private arbitration, which Fastolf regarded as an attractive option. In May 1451 he offered to accept the ruling of Bishop Bourgchier of Ely and whomever the prior of Hickling should name, and in March 1455 he agreed with the prior to refer their disagreement to the common lawyers John Paston and John Fyncham, sergeant, for settlement. According to the 1455 agreement, contentious issues were to be decided by Archbishop Bourgchier and Bishop Lyhert on the advice of any two justices except the chief justices.[56] These arbitrations were proposed at times when, although circumstances were not favourable to Fastolf, there was some prospect of negotiating an acceptable solution. Fastolf also undertook arbitration when no such prospect existed. One example of this is the offer made to Suffolk before 1450 regarding Dedham; another is the two approaches made to Sir Edward Hull and Thomas Wake in connection with Titchwell in mid-1451. These approaches echoed the one made by Fastolf to Suffolk in their appeal to his opponents' sense of honour: according to one draft proposal, Fastolf 'knowyth well that (his opponents Edward Hull and Thomas Wake). . .bee men of worshyp and of concience and supposith that they wold desyre no manys goode but that they hafe ryghtfull title untoo . . .' As with Fastolf's offer to Suffolk, this attempt to persuade his opponents was fruitless.[57] Arbitration was also appropriate when success was expected, as in the dispute over Dedham early in 1450, when Suffolk had lost power, and the one with Philip Wentworth in February 1456. The choice of arbitrators was apparently not determined by the importance of a dispute or the likelihood of settling it. Fastolf preferred to have reliable men of high status, whether laymen (like Lords Cromwell and

Beauchamp, whom Fastolf named in the offer made to Sir Edward Hull in 1451), or ecclesiastics (like Bishop Bourgchier, named in the Hickling dispute in 1451), to act on his behalf. He was not unwilling to propose courtiers and royal councillors as arbitrators, even in cases as minor as those involving a few tenements in Southwark. On one occasion the ruling of the steward and treasurer of the royal household was sought; on another the arbitrators proposed by Fastolf included Lords Cromwell, Sudeley, Beauchamp, Stourton and St. Amand.[58] Yet arbitration was sometimes left to ordinary common lawyers acting alone. The common law counsellors, of course, were always on hand to give advice throughout the negotiations involved in any arbitration, for, although the procedure more nearly resembled diplomacy than litigation, their skills were invaluable. There is no evidence that civil lawyers, whose training was possibly more appropriate, were specially employed by Fastolf for these arbitrations. In spite of Fastolf's liking for arbitration, it cannot be concluded that he found it a more successful method than any other for resolving disputes about property.

Sir John Fastolf's experience suggests that ruinous litigation was not a necessary consequence of heavy investment in land. Fastolf bought land carefully and was well informed about the purchases he made. Consequently, he was troubled by only a few serious challenges. These came from men whose strength derived from political power possessed by themselves and their overlords rather than from an armoury of title deeds and clever legal arguments. William, duke of Suffolk, in particular, used his political power to enrich his servants and friends at Fastolf's expense. The opposition of Thomas, Lord Scales, who enjoyed the support of the court during the 1450s, also caused Fastolf great annoyance. Political power determined the outcome of Fastolf's disputes. Neither Fastolf nor his opponents were inclined to use overt violence in their conduct of litigation, but they were prepared to try many different peaceful means, of which arbitration was the most important, to negotiate settlements.

Notes

1. I am much obliged to the President and Fellows of Magdalen College, Oxford, who have generously given me permission to cite documents owned by Magdalen College. These documents formed the basis of my D. Phil. thesis, 'Aspects of the Career of Sir John Fastolf, 1380–1459' (Oxford, 1982).
2. Smith, 'Fastolf', pp. 15–16, 27–29.
3. Smith 'Fastolf', pp. 30–31: the manor was Stapleford.
4. Care was taken with the deeds relating to property in Gorleston that was bought in 1434 (Fastolf Papers 9: Foreign Expenses); certain evidences relating to Hellesdon were acquired two years after the manor itself (F.P. 9: Deliveries of Money).
5. Magdalen Ms., H. 67.
6. K.B. McFarlane, *The Nobility of Later Medieval England* (Oxford, 1973), p. 57.
7. Magdalen Ms., H. 80 and 87, 106; F.P. 29.
8. Magdalen Ms., H. 90.
9. Magdalen Ms., H. 109; Smith, 'Fastolf', pp. 196–199.
10. Magdalen Ms., F.P. 48; BL, Add. Ms. 39848, Antiquarian Collections, no. 184. Wentworth's amended claim is referred to in BL, Add. Ms. 39848, no. 243.
11. Magdalen Ms., C.P. 3/32; B. 111.
12. Magdalen Ms., B. 30; B. 101; Smith, 'Fastolf', p. 208.
13. P. S. Lewis, 'Sir John Fastolf's Lawsuit over Titchwell, 1448–1455', *Historical Journal*, I (1958), 1–20.
14. Magdalen Ms., C. 13; C. 80; and PRO, C1/7/134.
15. Magdalen Ms., F.P. 32, 56; PRO, C1/11/214.
16. Magdalen Ms., B. 31; B. 101.
17. Smith, 'Fastolf', pp. 183, 188. On Debenham's notoriety, see W. I. Haward, 'Gilbert Debenham: a medieval rascal in real life', *History*, XIII (1929), 300–14.
18. BL, Add. MS. 39848, no. 253.
19. *Paston Letters and Papers of the Fifteenth Century*, ed. N. Davis (2 vols., Oxford, 1971 and 1976), II, no. 511; *The Paston Letters, A.D. 1422–1509*, ed. J. Gairdner (6 vols., London, 1904), III, pp. 19–21; Davis, *Paston Letters*, I, no. 51 (whence the quotation)
20. Magdalen Ms., H. 89; Davis, *Paston Letters*, II, no. 560.
21. Gairdner, *Paston Letters*, III, p. 65.
22. Lewis, 'Fastolf's Lawsuit', pp. 7–8; for the dispute of January 1447, see PRO,, KB 9/272, m. 3.
23. BL, Add. MS. 39848, no. 237 (Dalling); Smith, 'Fastolf', pp. 206–7 (Sherneborne).
24. Lewis, 'Fastolf's Lawsuit', 4; G. L. Harriss, 'The Finances of the Royal Household, 1437–60', (Oxford D. Phil. thesis, 1953), pp. 37, 39, 40, 44, 51.
25. Magdalen Ms., F.P. 48, 49.
26. The Bradwell inquest was held on 14 April at Needham Market (F.P. 49), the Beighton inquest at Norwich Shirehouse on 14 June (Briggs and Boyton 24); Smith, 'Fastolf', p. 205.
27. Magdalen Ms., F.P. 49; BL, Add. MS. 34888, fo. 48; Heydon's role is noted in F.P. 42. Also see Smith, 'Fastolf', pp. 206–7.
28. Magdalen Ms., F.P. 9, 14; H. 157 (7) and (8); H. 137.
29. Magdalen Ms., H. 71.
30. Magdalen Ms., H. 132 and 141 (1452); H. 96 (Heydon); BL, Add. MS. 39848, no. 229 (Suffolk); for the Kerdistons, see Smith, 'Fastolf', pp. 194, 195.
31. Magdalen Ms., H. 155 (Saye and Sele); for Scales, see Smith, 'Fastolf', pp. 195, 203–4; H. 104 is a letter from Scales's to Fastolf which shows that Scales felt wronged by Fastolf, who had had one of Scales's servants outlawed.
32. Magdalen Ms., F.P. 17; PRO, C1/15/331, 335; Davis, *Paston Letters*, II, nos. 554, 555.

33. Magdalen Ms., F.P. 9, 10, 11, 13, 16, 20, 23; BL, Add. MS. 39848, nos. 245, 253.
34. Smith, 'Fastolf', pp. 153–154; BL, Add. MS. 34888, fo. 49.
35. BL, Add. MSS. 43488, fo. 15; 39848, no. 225. John Heydon held several duchy offices, including (from 1443) the stewardship of Norfolk, Suffolk and Cambridgeshire, this in partnership with Sir Thomas Tuddenham: R. Somerville, *History of the Duchy of Lancaster* , I (London, 1953), pp. 425, 430, 453, 594.
36. For Dedham, see Smith, 'Fastolf', pp. 126–131; Magdalen Ms., F.P. 1 contains notes about the descent of Dedham and the proposals Fastolf made to Suffolk.
37. For Hellesdon, see Smith, 'Fastolf', pp. 131–135. Losses there are mentioned in BL, Add. MS. 39848, no. 229. A new mill had been built at Dedham; improvements at Hellesdon are recorded in receivers' accounts (Smith, 'Fastolf', pp. 35–6).
38. Gairdner, *Paston Letters*, III, p. 56.
39. BL, Add. MS. 39848, no. 225; for the sum of 5,000 marks, see Gairdner, *Paston Letters*, III, pp. 56–57.
40. BL, Add. Ms. 39848, nos. 223, 253, 245; on Fastolf's political importance, see Smith, 'Fastolf', pp. 121–2, 144.
41. Ulveston and Andrew were indicted at Beccles on 7 December 1450 (PRO, KB, 9/267, m. 20);
    for Willy, see Lewis, 'Fastolf's Lawsuit', 17.
42. BL, Add. MS. 39848, nos. 223, 224, 277.
43. Davis, *Paston Letters*, II, nos. 471, 472 (Lynn); BL, Add. MS. 34888, fo. 68 (Walsingham).
44. Davis, *Paston Letters*, II, nos. 520, 523.
45. Magdalen Ms., H. 152; Davis, *Paston Letters*, II, nos. 554, 560; Magdalen Ms., F.P. 42.
46. Gairdner, *Paston Letters*, III, pp. 32–33.
47. Magdalen Ms., F.P. 42; Davis, *Paston Letters*, II, no. 526; BL, Add. MS. 39848, no. 31; for the lords in parliament, see Davis, *Paston Letters*, II, nos. 536, 569.
48. Davis, *Paston Letters*, II, nos. 537, 548.
49. Lewis, 'Fastolf's Lawsuit', 19.
50. Smith, 'Fastolf, pp. 128–129.
51. Davis, *Paston Letters*, II, nos. 508, 551.
52. Davis, *Paston Letters*, II, nos. 569, 570; distraints were made at Cotton (F.P. 42).
53. BL, Add. MS. 39848, no. 230; Magdalen Ms., H. 99.
54. PRO., C1/19/115.
55. Davis, *Paston Letters*, II, nos. 529, 530.
56. Magdalen Ms., H.107; H. 152.
57. Lewis, 'Fastolf's Lawsuit', pp. 17–18.
58. Magdalen Ms., Southwark 201.

4

The Land Settlement in Lancastrian Normandy

Robert Massey
University of Liverpool

On 17 August 1450 James Gresham wrote to his master, John Paston I, with news of their attempt to have Lord Moleyns evicted from the Paston manor of Gresham, which Moleyns had seized by force some eighteen months previously.[1] Two days later, a note was appended to the letter reporting 'that Shirburgh is goon and we haue not now a foote of lond in Normandie', and Calais itself was thought to be under threat.[2] Paston was well aware of the abiding concern at the progress of the war of his patron Sir John Fastolf, whose firm views on the best strategy and tactics to be adopted were the product of long experience as a soldier, household official, *conseiller* and, not least, as a landholder.[3] John Paston's father, William, had formerly been involved in an aggravated dispute with Walter Aslake, another returning Norman landowner, concerning the advowson of Sprowston church, an action which was eventually brought to arbitration in 1428.[4]

Land was a valuable commodity to the Pastons, and although they themselves did not participate in the French wars, the family formed part of a Norfolk gentry society with a keen interest in the acquisition of territory on both sides of the channel. Not the least of the consequences of a reconquest which must have appeared as sudden and bewildering to contemporaries was the loss of land and of any further opportunity for its acquisition. For French lands which had belonged to successive English kings by legal right, as they had claimed, had been distributed to loyal subjects in considerable quantity from the early months of Henry V's conquest until the final years of the Lancastrian occupation. The speed of the military defeat and the scale of the territorial losses suffered by the English between 1448 and 1450 were recognised as a dramatic reversal of fortunes which effectively brought to an end one phase of the Anglo-French war.

It is now accepted that a settlement based upon land lay at the very heart of the military conquest and subsequent occupation of Normandy and northern France.[5] The intention of this paper is to discuss three questions which have recently been raised concerning the extent and nature of this settlement. First, there are uncertainties about the amount of land and urban property available for redistribution and about the number of beneficiaries.[6] Secondly, the demands of military service and the problem of absenteeism raise doubts about the effective role of Englishmen as long-term resident owners and managers of land.[7] Thirdly, the recent stimulus to studies of patronage and connection within fifteenth-century society has made it necessary to relate some of the questions currently being asked about obligation and service to the situation in France.[8] An attempt to discuss these problems must therefore try to set out the scale and distribution of the settlement, to assess its permanence and flexibility, and to reach some preliminary conclusions about the nature of the ties which bound men together at different stages of the war.

In its turn, the land settlement provided the essential foundation for the establishment of an Anglo-French society within northern France. The ownership of land affords a means of access to the study of certain social and occupational groups whose membership, expectations and commitment to the Lancastrian cause can be better understood by an analysis of the lands they held, their distribution, value and method of tenure. The relationship between the garrison soldier and the ownership of local fiefs, between those of the rank of esquire and the holding of both office and lands, and between the knight or military commander and more extensive estates scattered across several *bailliages* can tell us something about the *mentalité* of a society at war, even if we remain a long way from 'une sociologie de la guerre'.[9] In addition, case studies of areas of relatively dense settlement, such as that in the Vexin Normand between February 1419 and August 1422 and that in Rouen between 1422 and 1436, reveal the impact of a concentrated occupation of a small geographical area by settlers of different rank.

Sources for the land settlement begin with official records of the grants themselves, kept in roll or register form.[10] The Norman Rolls for the period 1417–22 (in the Public Record Office) and the registers of the *Trésor des Chartes* (in the Archives Nationales) for the years 1422–36 provide key information. This is supplemented, and continued for the post-1436 period, by invaluable evidence contained in the Collection Lenoir: delays for the performance of feudal services owed; copies of grants for almost the entire period of the occupation; *informations* in great detail of the estates of individual landholders, all contribute towards our knowledge of the settlers and the lands in their possession.[11] Legal records, too, are of great benefit in exposing the means of administration employed for conquered lands. Pride of place goes to the proceedings of the Paris *Parlement*, which throw light on the constitutional and political implications of the occupation,[12] whilst at a local level the registers of the *tabellionnage* at Rouen and Caen are a fruitful source of information for the purchase, rent and sale of properties and for the extent of English integration in urban society.[13] National manuscript collections, including the additional charters at the British Library, the nouvelles acquisitions françaises at the Bibliothèque Nationale and series P at the Archives Nationales, yield biographical and financial material in addition to details of the system of land tenure and the effects of prolonged warfare upon that system.

The printed calendars give a comprehensive summary of the contents of the Norman Rolls, but the brevity of the standard entries does mask salient features of the occupation.[14] For the rural settlement, the exclusion of both the estimated value of granted lands and the obligation to provide men either for the royal armies or for the defence of the lands in question is regretable,[15] while the conciseness of entries referring to the urban settlement excludes details of the properties themselves, their location, rents and the performance of the *guet* and other duties.[16] A similar degree of caution is needed in approaching the longer extracts taken from the same source by Bréquigny,[17] which vary from useful transcripts *in extenso* to complete omissions and errors.[18] For the later period, the documentation is less complete, and after 1436 the copies made by Lenoir are the only source for grants themselves, though much can be gleaned from references to land tenure in delays for the performance of duties owed and from allusions in titles and forms of address. Lenoir's express concern was to compile material for a projected history of Normandy, which may help to explain why so few grants in Maine were recorded by comparison with those for the duchy itself; one suspects that Maine and the *pays de conquête* fell beyond the pale of his interests.

The confiscation and redistribution to Englishmen of conquered estates was a logical extension of Henry V's claim to Normandy, its land and its people.[19] The inhabitants of the duchy could either swear allegiance to their new lord and enjoy the lands and properties which they had held before 1 August 1417, the date of the English landing at Touques, or forfeit their lands and moveable goods to the crown as absentees or rebels, as some were uncompromisingly described. This inherently feudal idea of conquest and punishment, reward and obligation, and binding by oath of fealty, effectively underpinned the early years of the land settlement. On the French side, many landowners chose to stay and have their submission duly recorded.[20] Amongst the English, the first to be rewarded were the military commanders and great captains, whose leadership and commitment to the royal cause earned them potentially profitable, strategic lordships on the frontiers of the occupation. On 1 April 1418 Sir John Cheyne was granted the barony of La Haye-du-Puits in the Cotentin to the value of 1,500 *écus* per year,[21] and shortly afterwards the lordship of Bricqueville-sur-Mer was given to the earl of Huntingdon as a direct reward for his active participation in the naval and military successes of the early years of Henry's reign.[22] The priority which lay behind these first grants was the defence of territories gained, and to that end the knights and magnates who secured the most prestigious awards were expected to provide from their landed revenues either a specified number of men-at-arms and archers for the royal armies, or, in more exposed positions, a force sufficient to defend their *caput* and its surrounding area. If rewards were made available to match the status of their recipients, then the obligations incumbent upon more eminent owners were correspondingly high and had some bearing on the net revenues which lands might yield.

How were grants issued? The complexities of the grant-making process permit only cautious remarks. Almost all the awards made by Henry V bore the note of warranty *per ipsum regem*, indicating that a petition had been approved by the king in person and handed directly to the chancellor for issue. The handful of grants made by writ of privy seal, again probably the result of petitions, cannot be distinguished by content or date from immediate royal warrants; the two processes, it has been observed, went on side by side.[23] It is likely, therefore, that the written petition was the essential preliminary to the granting of lands and urban properties and that the king himself received petitions brought to him at Caen, Rouen and Vernon and wherever he made camp.[24] Mistakes were inevitably made. Within nine days the lordship of Tosny, on the opposite bank of the Seine to Les Andelys, was given first to Henry Warryn and then to John Eston in similar terms.[25] Repeated attempts were made by the crown to determine which lands belonged to Normans who had sworn allegiance to Henry V, which to named rebels and absentees, and which owed revenues as demesne lands, in order to avoid just such problems.[26] Moreover, the registration of this information was vital to the effective administration of a settlement which was intended to be as just as the conditions of war would allow and respectful of local customary practices. The personal involvement of the king in the distribution of his newly-won landed patronage testifies to the importance attached to conquered territory from the earliest date in the occupation.

The fall of Rouen on 19 January 1419 brought the first turning-point in the land settlement. From that date, the distribution of Norman fiefs on a large scale can be seen as one basic element within a long-term policy of occupation and settlement. Almost without exception grants were issued in fee tail, a sign of the royal intention to inculcate a sense of responsibility into the minds of men taking up the opportunities which military conquest had made available. To equate landed revenue with the traditional gains of war derived from looting and plunder is to misunderstand the intentions which lay behind the Lancastrian settlement. The king's aim was rather to establish a permanent English presence on French soil which would give *de facto* recognition to those claims which were so carefully disseminated on his behalf, a presence which relegated the pursuit of quick profit at the expense of the indigenous population to a position subordinate to the broader needs of the occupation.

The geography of the settlement was partly dictated by the requirements of defence, which made the acquisition of local strongpoints desirable, and partly by the movements of the field armies. Grants of land tended to follow in the wake of the advancing forces, but occasionally comprised territories which had not already been brought into the English obedience. On 1 July 1418 the duke of Exeter was awarded the valuable *comté* of Harcourt which lay on the eastern frontier of the conquest, as it then stood, together with the castle and lordship of Lillebonne, which remained in French hands until after the capture of Rouen.[27] Such grants were uncommon, though, and it was more typical to find the pattern of land allocation reflecting the presence nearby of the major field armies. This helps to explain the relatively dense settlement in the *bailliage* of the Caux and in the Vexin Normand after 1 February 1419, as large numbers of men were assembled for the reduction of upper Normandy and marshalled against the strongholds of the Seine valley below Rouen. Between that date and 31 August 1422, some twenty-one Englishmen received a total of thirty-one fiefs for which a specific location can be found within the Vexin Normand; the total rises to at least forty-two men if all grants which include the *bailliage* of Gisors are aggregated. This above-average concentration of grants owed much to the presence of military and civilian personnel engaged in the sieges of Gisors and of Château-Gaillard, and a further stimulus was provided by the presence of the king at nearby Vernon during April and much of May 1419, two of the busiest months for the distribution of lands.[28]

The beneficiaries of the Vexin settlement included Sir Walter Hungerford, who was granted the lordship of Tourny,[29] and Sir Henry Noon, who was given lands at Heuqueville and Pont-Saint-Pierre north-west of Les Andelys.[30] It is not surprising to find men of knightly rank acquiring landed interests in the Vexin as elsewhere: Sir John Baskerville was another, taking up lands in at least three *bailliages*, including that of Gisors.[31] In numerical terms, however, it was men drawn from the middle ranks of society and often designated 'armiger' or 'escuier' who derived maximum benefit from the confisaction and re-allocation of lands during this period. This broad category encompassed both grantees of quite humble status, some of whom were probably men-at-arms serving in local garrisons, as well as men who practised the same profession but who, by dint of ability, opportunity or favourable connection, played a more prominent role in the war. The correlation between the value of granted lands and the status of their recipient can at best be only approximate, but it does provide a useful guide to the standing of these middling men in relation to their contemporaries.

Richard Abraham, esquire, received lands worth up to 400 *écus* per year,[32] and like Thomas Tyringham he was to supply one man-at-arms and three archers for the royal armies.[33] Roger Ingerland was to do the same and assist in the defence of Vernon, the nearest garrison town to his lordship of Aveny, whenever such service was required.[34] John Wenlock, esquire, later constable of Vernon, took over lands to the value of 600 *livres tournois* in 1421 which had formerly belonged to a fellow-countryman by royal grant.[35] It was upon men such as these that the success of the English occupation depended, for they acted as landowners and as office-holders in the civilian and military administration. The grant to Richard Wydeville of the lordship of Dangu[36] was soon followed by his appointment as *bailli* of Gisors and later of Chaumont;[37] but the close relationship between land tenure and the holding of office indicates that there was more than convenience of location at stake. The constancy of this relationship suggests an affinity of interest between the attractions of office to the settler intent on pursuing a career in France and the crown's need for loyal, able men to carry out its wishes. The use of local landholders to exercise the king's authority would therefore involve a two-fold commitment to the Lancastrian cause.

Settlers were present in every *bailliage* of Normandy by August 1422. Some areas proved more popular than others: the fertile *bocage* lands of the Cotentin peninsula were attractive, whilst the *pays de Caux*, the Vexin Normand and the region of Caen and Bayeux became well-peopled with incoming Englishmen. Some of their number spilled across the traditional frontier of Normandy marked by the river Epte and moved into what became known as the *pays de conquête*.[38] Renewed impetus came in June 1424 with the grant to the regent Bedford of the duchy of Anjou and *comté* of Maine, *pourveu toutefuoies que notre dit oncle le Regent les conquerra et mettra en notre obiessance et subjeccion*.[39] The obligation to conquer granted estates was by no means typical,[40] and may well reflect the intention of the *grand conseil* to unite Bedford's desire to possess lands commensurate with his status in France with their own declared intention of capturing the support of those Frenchmen of uncertain allegiance, whose adherence to the treaty of Troyes might be secured by the prospect of newly-conquered territory. The *conseillers* may have had doubts, too, about the nature of Bedford's authority in France in the absence of a written commission setting out his rights, for in practice grants were made by letters patent issued in the king's name, occasionally with the advice of the *grand conseil* but more often with the advice of Bedford alone.

The great victory of Verneuil on 17 August 1424 paved the way for the expansion of the occupation into Maine and Anjou, and whilst lands were still in plentiful supply within Normandy, the extension of the frontiers of the armed conquest to the south and west served both to increase opportunities and to heighten expectations.[41] Success in battle attracted new men to the land settlement and galvanized existing landholders into augmenting their current holdings. As the area of northern France under Anglo-Burgundian control reached its territorial limits in 1429, so the boundaries of the land settlement were pushed forward as a response. It was by means of frontier grants to the campaign commanders that English landed interests were reorientated south-wards and away from Normandy, with other settlers following in their lee. Thomas Montagu, earl of Salisbury added the lordship of Courville-sur-Eure west of Chartres to already substantial holdings in November 1425, and in the same month he received a rent of 100 *livres tournois* from lands at Longny-au-

Perche.[42] The Vexin landholder Sir Thomas Chetwood was given lands in June 1428 which came under the jurisdiction of the *prévôt* of Paris, whilst further south in the *bailliage* of Chartres lay estates which Thomas Barneby, esquire, acquired in the same year.[43]

The question, then, arises of how effective these transactions were in practice. For military defeat pushed back the frontiers of the occupation as surely as success had advanced them, and for the likes of the *bailli* of Evreux, Richard Waller, who was given lands on the outskirts of Orléans in September 1428, there was simply no time to enjoy potential revenues.[44] The ownership of land was not conducive to the rapid accumulation of income, and the brevity of tenure of certain territories rendered some grants ineffective, or at best short-lived. This reversal of fortunes destroyed the confidence and dynamism of Bedford's earlier settlement, and although grants were still made after 1429, they were fewer in number, perhaps the first demonstration of a reluctance to take up available opportunities.

After the fall of Paris in April 1436, the English administration in Rouen continued to redistribute land to men of all ranks. There has been a tendency to regard the military and diplomatic reversals of the period 1429–36 as disastrous to the Lancastrian cause in France, marking the beginning of a slow but relentless decline in the exercise of political authority which culminated in the loss of initiative and will to continue the struggle, something which was characterised by the lack of resistance to the swift advances of the French armies between 1448 and 1450. Such a view owes more to the reasoning of hindsight than to contemporary reality. The prospects for the future of Lancastrian France did not necessarily look bleak in 1436. The ending of the Burgundian alliance and the loss of Paris were serious matters indeed, but a defensible occupation based upon the duchy of Normandy was certainly a practical proposition. In spite of the array of problems facing soldiers and settlers, the gains made during an occupation which had lasted for over fifteen years were thought to be worth protecting and defending. If the future did not exactly look rosy for profit-seekers and profit-takers, then at least those men who had secured or sought their livelihood with more modest revenues might contemplate the preservation of the balance of power as it then stood without undue concern for their safety.

An active period of grant-making in the years 1436 and 1437 provided a relative increase in numbers compared with Bedford's final years, but in the following years the harsh economic conditions which occasioned a widespread decline in seigneurial revenues and in land values probably caused demand for land to fall away.[45] For all the difficulties and hardships involved in its tenure after 1436, however, land was too precious a resource to be judged purely in financial terms. It was not given up lightly, nor was it distributed carelessly. On 29 August 1437 William Awmoney was given a small grant in the *prévôté* of Chaumont to the value of thirty *livres tournois*, and for life only.[46] Two weeks later the *chambre des comptes* requested of the local royal officials a comprehensive declaration, not only of the revenues of the lands in question but also their location, means of tenure, services owed and monies payable to others.[47] Even life-grants of little value on paper were viewed by donor and recipient with respect in a litigious age, and the Rouen *chambre* was a jealous guardian of the crown's rights regardless of the vagaries of war and the economy which might affect incoming revenues in the short term. The persistent interest shown in the region of Maine and Alençon also serves as a reminder that landholders had a faith in the maintenance of the existing frontiers to which their own presence bore testimony.[48] If many of the grants in Maine were of little value, then the same could be said of lands further north. It was precisely these small tenants who could least afford the loss of livelihood brought about by the cession of Maine in 1448.[49] The surrender of the *comté* revealed a difference between the perception of the war and settlement held by the king and certain members of his council in London and the realities of the occupation as viewed from Normandy.

Settlement within the towns of Normandy and northern France played an integral role in the Lancastrian occupation. The distribution of houses, properties and rents in considerable quantity at Harfleur, Caen and especially Rouen began in September 1417 and continued at varying speeds until the French reconquest.[50] Elsewhere, Lancastrians abroad became established in much smaller numbers in the ports of Cherbourg,[51] Honfleur,[52] and Dieppe.[53] In Paris, Bedford rewarded men who had seen distinguished service as army commanders, administrators and household officials with *hôtels* befitting their status. Prominent among those given property were a number of itinerant men whose duties made frequent visits to the Anglo-Burgundian capital necessary.[54] Rouen, on the other hand, attracted a thriving colony of merchants primarily engaged in the supply and provisioning of the royal armies, and also a number of tradesmen and retail traders. The evidence suggests that in all these towns men took over properties suitable for their specialist needs, houses whose location and construction were suited to particular functions. It was surely not by coincidence, for example, that the barber Roger Mot was granted properties in Harfleur which included the house of Guillaume de Mount, also a barber.[55]

The attractions of Rouen were manifold: it was the ducal capital and principal administrative centre, the seat of an archbishop and a port with a lively and bustling trade along the Seine to Paris and to England. By 1420 English merchants were making an impression on the commercial life of the city. Thomas Bonneville, already holding property by royal grant in Caen and Harfleur, rented a house in the parish of St. Martin from Robin Alorge, 'bourgeois de Rouen',[56] whilst the London merchant Thomas Markby took over the right to claim a specific revenue from vessels travelling along the Seine.[57] Participation in wholesale and retail trade in its turn helped to foster a commitment to the maintenance of the conquest, and the ready accessibility of houses for rent or purchase made integration with the urban community possible and desirable.

Soldiers, too, were willing to move out of their garrisons in order to take up properties in Rouen, among them Roger Rowen, esquire, who rented from Robert Berkeroft in 1422 a house with a garden and trees distinguished by its sign of a helm.[58] The resourceful Berkeroft retained a room and a stable for four horses for his own use whenever he chose to visit. Four years later, he and his French wife again rented out this property, situated in the parish of St. Laurent.[59] The London barber Robert Regnart and his German wife also held a share in the *hôtel*, which they sold, along with some other property nearby, to Thierry du Bosc.[60] As the effective capital of Lancastrian France after 1436, Rouen was also the home of the senior personnel of the *chambre des comptes* who, like William Miles, seemed to prefer residence in the north-western parishes of the city,[61] and of the royal secretaries Ralph Parker and John Profoot, who bought houses in 1440 and 1443 respectively.[62] Although certain parishes and streets were undoubtedly preferred to others, the distribution of settlers within larger towns suggests that a proximity to the institutions of government was a more cogent consideration in the choice of location than a concern for collective security. The transition in the status of Rouen from that of a besieged, conquered city to that of the principal seat of Lancastrian authority was achieved with the support of a settlement aimed at integration and participation with native Frenchmen in urban life.

The supply of rural lands and urban properties was matched by a healthy demand which, although fluctuating according to prevailing economic conditions and the fortunes of war, was sufficient to ensure not only a settlement on a large scale but also one which came to embrace many elements of contemporary society. These settlers were not transient men. Some clearly did not perform the services which they owed or abandoned their estates. Yet many others were prepared to put down roots in France, and soldiers afford a good example. The Vexin landholders provide important evidence of the relationship between garrison service and land tenure. Richard Abraham, esquire, was appointed captain of Étrépagny in 1424,[63] and by 1434 he had almost surrounded his original lordship of Saint Martin with further holdings which he had acquired.[64] Thomas Tyringham was granted several delays for services due on lands held since 1419, including one as late as 1445, although these and other lands in the *bailliage* of Gisors had been reported in September 1443 as being of no value because of the war.[65] Roger Ingerland served as a mounted lance in the garrison at Vernon in 1423, and again in 1436 and 1437;[66] the following year he was accorded a delay for the valuation of those lands granted to him by Henry V.[67] Finally, John Wenlock, esquire, who was given Vexin lands in 1421, was *contrôleur* of the garrison at Gisors in 1431.[68] This was probably the same man who enjoyed a long and chequered career as councillor to the duke of York, member of the royal household, and M.P. for Bedfordshire.[69]

It clearly made good sense to acquire lands close to a garrison base, where their upkeep and defence might be more easily managed, but this pattern of tenure and service was only one of several which obtained in northern France. Personal mobility was such that absence from fiefs and properties held was unavoidable, and the services demanded by the crown or individual patrons could militate against a fixed, static settlement. Rather can one sometimes identify geographical areas frequented by known office-holders and soldiers into which their major activities fell, including landownership.

In the bountiful distribution of lands which followed the battle of Verneuil, soldiers were rewarded with grants which made specific reference to their presence on the great day. Among the lands which became available for re-allocation were those belonging to the large numbers of Frenchmen slain on the battlefield, and those confiscated from men who had renounced their allegiance to the treaty of Troyes prior to the battle. As a result, the settlement was able to embrace ordinary men and to fulfil the expectations which armed success had raised. At least thirty-two archers were rewarded,[70] including Thomas Kyreby, who was given the fief of St.-Jean-de-Livet south of Lisieux, *afin qu'il ait mieux de quoi avoir la vie et estat de lui sa femme et ses enfans.*[71] Kyreby and his French wife and family settled in this area of Normandy, receiving two further awards before purchasing Saint-Jean in perpetuity, whereas his previous grants had been made for life or at the king's pleasure. Archers were no less willing than other social and occupational groups to make new homes for themselves, support their families and earn their livelihood on French soil. John Regnault and John Preston were both given small grants in 1425, and each was accorded a delay for the lands in 1434.[72] In the towns, too, some soldiers were moving out of their garrisons and by means of intermarriage, property transactions and small business dealings were becoming absorbed into the urban community.[73] For such men, land and property meant a regular, modest income and the chance of social advancement. Land tenure also acted as a means of access to an Anglo-French society which it was in their best interests to support and defend.

There were changes in the way that land was held during the course of the occupation. The predominance of grants in fee tail during the lifetime of Henry V gave way to a more varied pattern after 1422. Many of those rewarded for their good services at Verneuil were given life-grants, and in addition to the awards in tail male which remained common came a handful of grants at the king's pleasure.[74] The limits of Bedford's personal competence to make grants remain uncertain, but some light may perhaps be thrown on this difficult subject. The royal patrimony in France had to be carefully preserved until the king attained his majority, which imposed a particular responsibility upon Bedford to ensure that the demesne lands were not given away.[75] Grants in tail male therefore contained a provision to exclude demesne lands from individual awards, and the same condition applied when the tenure of land was upgraded. Thus, Roger Amiger, esquire, was successful in his petition to improve the status of his landownership in May 1432 from life to hereditary tenure, in return for his past good services and notwithstanding another grant which had recognised his attendance at Verneuil.[76] The appointment of royal lieutenants in Ireland reveals a corresponding concern to preserve the king's inheritance, otherwise permitting several forms of tenure.[77] The responsibility for the direction of the land settlement was adjudged to be a personal one, and it was by the authority of the provisions contained within their letters of appointment that successive lieutenants in France proceeded to approve requests and make awards of their own.[78]

There was nothing random about the allocation of landed patronage, for it was a declared aim to issue grants according to the merits and status of their recipients.[79] When Matthew Jouen, esquire, and Hugh Jouen and John Osaystre, archers, were granted lands in the Caux to the total value of 100 *livres tournois*, it was specified that the esquire should receive sixty *livres* and the archers twenty *livres* each.[80] This sharp distinction between the man-at-arms and the common soldier may well have been blurred as archers began to accumulate land and local influence for themselves, however, and the precise values attached to such grants raise the suspicion that the figures quoted were at best nominal and give only an approximate guide to the revenues which might be anticipated. Where the men who fell into that very broad category known as esquires derived further benefit from the war was in their appointment to office. Richard Talbot, constable and lieutenant of the garrison at Touques, received lands in the *pays d'Auge* in January 1425 and was holding lands in fiefs near Pont-l'Évêque in 1429, not too far from his garrison.[81] Examples could readily be multiplied.

Within the compass of the rank of esquire came the men who formed the backbone of the Lancastrian occupation throughout the period under consideration, for their presence within the military and civilian administration was constant. Some, indeed, had abilities in both spheres. The Cheshireman Thomas Maisterson was *bailli* of the Caux from 1423 until his death in 1428 and captain of Pont-de-l'Arche and Neufchâtel-en-Bray;[82] one grant by Henry V and three more by Bedford gave Maisterson lands in those very areas where his duties were performed, as well as two houses in Rouen for his visits to the regent.[83] Griffith Don already held fiefs to the south of Lisieux at the time of his commission as captain there in 1441,[84] and the grant of a manor house and garden within the town two years later was probably the result of a request by him for suitable accommodation.[85]

What was involved in the tenure of land in Lancastrian Normandy? The situation of one English family in the Cotentin may illustrate several themes of relevance to this question. By a grant in 1419 of the fiefs of La Luthumière and Gonneville, Thomas Burgh, esquire, became a landowner in an area that was to

become his home.[86] He held captaincies at Valognes, Avranches and Tombe-
laine,[87] survived capture in 1421 and died in December 1432, an *information*
being carried out the following February at the request of his brother John.[88]
Thomas held some eleven fiefs scattered across the peninsula, including that of
Quinéville, situated to the east of Valognes close to the coast. Its revenues
included 176 bushels of wheat and 85 bushels of oats worth a total of 13 *livres*, 13
sous and 4 *deniers tournois*, as well as 54 *sous* and 2 *deniers tournois* in cash, all due
at Michaelmas; in addition there came bread and poultry at Christmas and eggs
at Easter. Further revenue was due from a dovecote, a water mill, from lands
farmed out for rent in cash and kind and from the presentation to Quinéville
church which was worth 27 *livres tournois*, a large sum. From this income were
paid the wages of a seneschal, a receiver, a proctor and an advocate. The total
revenue of Burgh's lands was estimated at 484 *livres tournois*, of which 100 *livres*
was needed for repairs to buildings. It should be stressed that this figure was only
an estimate of the landed income due and was not derived from an estate
account listing revenue and expenditure. Nevertheless, the *information* stands as
a detailed and valuable inventory of the sums which a landholder might expect,
their sources, and the obligations attached to seigneurial administration.
Reference was made to a manor at Quinéville which had been in ruin for the
previous forty years, and to the presentation to the chapel at Gonneville which
had greatly fallen in value during the same period, indicating the problems
which a settler could inherit. The value attached to Burgh's lands in 1419 was
800 *écus*, so an estimated income of 384 *livres tournois* in 1433 represents a fall in
seigneurial revenues of over fifty per cent, and this in an area that was relatively
prosperous and little-troubled by the war. On the other hand, there may have
been some under-estimation of revenue due, according to the efficiency or
otherwise of the *vicomte* charged with carrying out the survey, and it was not in
the family interest to put the *chambre des comptes* completely in the picture
regarding its landed wealth. In July 1433 Burgh's French widow, Elizabeth de
Pressy, was entrusted with the care of the estate and with the wardship of
Thomas junior, aged only eight months, and by this time Elizabeth was known
to be pregnant again.[89] Burgh had another daughter who had married the
Englishman Richard Hayton, esquire, a member of the Cherbourg garrison who
held a rent of 100 *livres tournois* granted to him by his father-in-law.

What emerges from this *information*, and others which have been examined, is
the importance of land as a means of livelihood to those men of middle rank who
spent long years in service to the Lancastrian cause.[90] Its diverse revenues
provided a means by which a family could settle and, by mutual support, secure a
reasonable living sufficient to encourage the appearance of a second generation
of settlers, Anglo-French in origin and upbringing. To a soldier and office-
holder like Thomas Burgh, the ownership of land was most unlikely to produce a
substantial profit after the necessary outgoings and expenses had been deducted.
Rather did it afford him a status within the *bailliage* which could not otherwise be

achieved, with a local income independent of his crown wages, albeit a reduced
one. The long-term commitment to the occupation was precisely that which
Henry V had promoted by the distribution of confiscated French fiefs in tail
male.

Consideration of appointments to office and their relationship to land tenure
within a particular region raises the question of the operation of patronage and
'connection' in Lancastrian France. It needed a firm hand to apportion the royal
prerogative in a manner that could be seen to be equitable and just, for military
success raised expectations of landed gain at every level of society. As late as
1437 William Bron, esquire, reminded the duke of York that he had been
present at Verneuil but since then had received no reward in lands.[91] The
examples of Bron and Thomas Maisterson illustrate an awareness that length of
service merited suitable recompense, since it was expected that service in a great
household would yield its own benefits. Henry V and Bedford had to balance the
demands of their households for lands, titles and offices against the broader and
perennial need of the occupation to attract and reward new men who bore no
connections or influence on foreign soil. Moreover, it was recognised that the
settlement formed an essential part of the stated policy of making the occupation
pay for itself, since landed income in cash and kind might at least reduce the
persistent demands made upon crown resources for immediate monetary reward
for services performed.[92]

The considerable expense attached to the running of a large household could,
therefore, be reduced by the application of the same principle: estates and
properties provided an alternative or supplementary form of income to regular
wages. This benefit to the patron was met by a corresponding improvement of
the social and professional status of the client. John Barton was promoted from
the rank of *serviteur* in 1422 to that of treasurer of Bedford's household by
November 1423, and by 1429 he was *maître d'hôtel*, having collected lands in at
least three *bailliages* along the way.[93] Bedford's second chamberlain, Sir Andrew
Ogard, was another who did very well for himself.[94] After receiving the lordship
of Blangy-le-Château in October 1422, he built up a considerble patrimony in
the area to the east and south of Caen by acquiring the lands of two men killed
during the siege of Orléans.[95] Salisbury's former lordship of Auvillars, conve-
niently close to Blangy, was augmented by that of Le Merlerault north-east of
Alençon, which was once held by William Glasdale.[96] Other lands later came
into the possession of Ogard, who rose from the position of an esquire in 1422 to
that of a senior counsellor of York with notable estates on both sides of the sea.[97]

There is no doubt that membership of the Bedford household was highly
advantageous. For all the fairness and moderation which is so often attributed to
his administration, Bedford was certainly generous in his disbursal of landed
patronage to retainers and household men. Such men were in a good position to
have their petitions read and to make their voices heard, enjoying the double
advantages of their lord's princely rank and his official status as the king's

representative in France. Attachment to the regent's household brought prestige and opportunity for social advancement which no one else could equal, but patronage was in essence a two-way relationship: good service prompted landed reward which prompted further good service. The series of temporary and short-lived appointments to the governorship of Lancastrian France after 1436, however, meant that the consistent application of the principles which had formerly underpinned the settlement became more difficult. Private gain began to outweigh public responsibility in the allocation of lands, as the balance of issuing grants for reward and for long service tilted toward a more pressing need to attract and favour followers.

The continuity of personnel between the households of Bedford and York was at first matched by a reasonable continuity in the apportioning of lands.[98] Robert Martin had been *valet de chambre* of Bedford and held the same position with York when given land in July 1436.[99] It should be emphasised, too, that the new men vital to the healthy maintenance and development of the occupation did arrive and take up lands during 1436 and 1437 as they had always been encouraged to do. At the same time, the number of household servants rewarded during York's first and second terms of office indicates that connection had become a more important consideration in the securing of land grants than had once been the case. They included the Welshman Griffith Don and his son Robert,[100] John Russell and John Leche.[101] It was not so much the range of advantages which had changed as the number of men enjoying them. Known household men and personal retainers were excused performance of their valuations and other obligations owed on lands held, and some gained an improvement in the terms by which existing estates were held, benefits which they had previously been able to obtain. Grants to officials of the royal household and, to a lesser extent, to those attached to the retinues of John and Edmund Beaufort point to the development of individual and factional interests in Lancastrian France which were not in the best interests of existing land and office-holders or of new men seeking land as- a base for careers abroad.[102]

The revocation of the crown's customary right to reversions and other specified revenues which would normally have been reserved to the royal demesne was, increasingly, the price which had to be paid for the loyal service of magnates in the war. To take one example recently brought to light: Edmund Beaufort was allowed to make small grants from lands returning to the royal demesne in his capacity as captain-general and governor of Anjou and Maine, and we know that he did so.[103] The fact that he was sparing in the reward of members of his household and affinity, as far as is known, does not detract from the view that a dangerous precedent had been set which rendered the land settlement open to abuse from a less responsible commander. The creation of a parallel system of grant-making hardly made the administration of the settlement any easier, and compromised the ability of successive lieutenants-general to direct a single and undivided policy. Although laudably intended to reinforce the military occupation of Maine and to settle new lands brought into the English obedience, aims which Bedford had also pursued, independent grants instead undermined the carefully-delimited powers of the governors of Lancastrian Normandy to distribute lands to a certain value.

The operation of patronage can be detected at different levels. John, Lord Talbot was swiftly able to acquire from Bedford lands appropriate to his status after his arrival in France, including a frontier grant at Amboise near Tours which was only briefly held and lands in the *bailliage* of Gisors once owned by Sir Reginald Grey.[104] Himself a York retainer and connected by marriage to the earl of Warwick, Talbot received a further grant in the *bailliages* of Rouen and the Caux in October 1438.[105] The members of his retinue who were recompensed included the Irishman Thomas Dalton, esquire, who was given lands in 1440,[106] and the long-serving lieutenant and then captain of Caudebec, Fulk Eyton.[107] Further research is necessary before the mechanics of patronage and connection at garrison level can be properly understood, but evidence for the integration of soldiers into urban communities suggests that such ties were of some importance in the securing of lands and urban properties closeby, in the collection of their rents and in their upkeep, and in the pursuit of what men-at-arms and archers regarded as legitimate livelihoods. Certain Englishmen were enterprising enough to set out their stalls as hostel-keepers and taverners, moving outside the town walls to avoid the levying of the *quatrième* and similar taxes on beverages.[108] These activities probably met with official disapproval, but at a local level much may have depended on the goodwill of the garrison captain or his lieutenant. It was not intended that the patronage of the minority should endanger the security of the majority.

It must be remembered, therefore, that patronage was, by its very nature, not available to all.[109] Whether such ties originated in England and subsequently underwent stress and change according to the fortunes and misfortunes of war, or whether connections were formed in France by men eager to advance themselves in the service of one or several lords, they constitute only one element, though an important one, of a society at war. The Lancastrian occupation of northern France, by virtue of its success and longevity, brought men into the landed settlement who had no patrons, masters or positions. Furthermore, it afforded an excellent opportunity for men of independence and resourcefulness to sweep away past associations and to develop new lives and careers. Mixed marriages introduced Englishmen to the urban centres by making them responsible for their wives' properties: ties of kinship had significant implications for social and economic integration in civic life.[110] The tenure of land and property generated associations between Normans and English at a commercial level, as holdings acquired by gift, marriage, purchase or exchange were themselves bought and sold regardless of ordinances to the contrary.[111]

By means of such transactions, by means of a readiness to be versatile and mobile and with a willingness to pick up some knowledge of the French language and local customs, it was possible to achieve a little and sometimes a lot. The scale of the land settlement, involving large numbers of settlers of all ranks, and its permanency, by which many chose to stay to the very end, reveals that livelihoods were available even in difficult conditions to men prepared to commit themselves to the cause which Henry V and Bedford had stood for. It was not through a lack of commitment by such men that Normandy and its lands were lost.

Notes

1. I am grateful to Dr C.T. Allmand for reading a draft of this paper.
2. *Paston Letters and Papers of the Fifteenth Century*, ed. N. Davis (2 vols., Oxford, 1971–6), II, pp. 40–2.
3. K.B. McFarlane, 'The Investment of Sir John Fastolf's Profits of War', *TRHS*, fifth series, VII (1957), 91–116; *English Suits before the Parlement of Paris, 1420–1436*, ed. C.T. Allmand and C.A.J. Armstrong (Camden Society, fourth series, XXVI, 1982), no. XX and pp. 292–3.
4. Davis, *Paston Letters*, I, pp. 7–12; II, pp. 505–7. This dispute is discussed by E. Powell, 'Arbitration and the Law in England in the Late Middle Ages', *TRHS*, fifth series, XXXIII (1983), 61–2.
5. C.T. Allmand, 'The Lancastrian land settlement in Normandy, 1417–50', *EconHR*, second series, XXI (1968), 461–79; *idem, Lancastrian Normandy: The History of a Medieval Occupation* (Oxford, 1983), ch. 3 *passim*.
6. 'The conquest of France has been called the Norman Conquest in reverse, with all its implications of a lavish endowment of the conquerors with estates as a new aristocracy. This confident assumption is based on a very slender stock of facts.' (J.R. Lander, *Conflict and Stability in Fifteenth-Century England* [3rd. ed., London, 1977], p. 62). See also M. Mollat in *Histoire de Rouen*, ed. Mollat (Toulouse, 1979), p. 132.
7. R. Jouet in *Histoire de Caen*, ed. G. Désert (Toulouse, 1981), pp. 97–8; Lander, *Conflict and Stability*, p. 62.
8. See *Patronage, Pedigree and Power in Later Medieval England*, ed. C.D. Ross (Gloucester, 1979) and *Patronage, the Crown and the Provinces in Later Medieval England*, ed. R.A. Griffiths (Gloucester, 1981), *passim*.
9. P. Contamine, *Guerre, état et société à la fin du moyen âge: études sur les armées des rois de France, 1337–1494* (Paris and The Hague, 1972), pp. vi, x.
10. G.R. Elton, *England, 1200–1640* (London, 1969), p. 40: 'nothing was so likely to get a man into the record as possession of land'.
11. M. Le Pesant, 'Les manuscrits de Dom Lenoir sur l'histoire de Normandie', *Bulletin de la Société des Antiquaires de Normandie*, I (1946–8), 125–51; C.T. Allmand, 'The Collection of Dom Lenoir and the English Occupation of Normandy in the Fifteenth Century', *Archives*, VI (1963–4), 202–10.
12. Allmand and Armstrong, *English Suits*, pp. 1–19.
13. A. Barabé, *Recherches historiques sur le tabellionage royal, principalement en Normandie* (Rouen, 1863); A. Dubuc, 'Le tabellionnage rouennais durant l'occupation anglaise (1418–1445)', *Bulletin Philologique et Historique*, II (1967), 797–808.
14. *Annual Reports of the Deputy Keeper of the Public Records* [hereafter DKR], XLI, XLII (London, 1880–1).
15. J.H. Wylie and W.T. Waugh, *The Reign of Henry the Fifth* (3 vols., Cambridge, 1914–29), III, pp. 74–5.
16. For example, the tenement granted to William Bell in the rue des Billettes in Harfleur owed 13 *sous* 4 *deniers* per year in rent and two nights' watch and guard duty; his vacant land on the rue Colyn Sery owed 12*d.* and half a night's watch (PRO, C64/12, m.3; DKR, XLII, p. 353). Multiple entries compound the problem, e.g. DKR, XLII, pp. 335, 350, 352.
17. 'Rôles normands et français et autres pièces tirées des archives de Londres par Bréquigny en 1764, 1765 et 1766', ed. L. Puiseux, *Mémoires de la Société des Antiquaires de Normandie*, XXIII (1858); hereafter cited as Bréquigny.
18. Cf. Bréquigny nos. 74, 189, and the omission of an important grant to Sir Gilbert Umfraville on 1 February 1419 (PRO, C64/10, m.28; DKR, XLI, p. 733).

The Land Settlement in Lancastrian Normandy

19. See especially *Gesta Henrici Quinti: The Deeds of Henry the Fifth*, ed. and trans. F. Taylor and J.S. Roskell (Oxford, 1975), pp. 16, 36; also P. Chaplais, *English Medieval Diplomatic Practice* (2 vols., London, 1983), II, pp. 456–7, 648–52, for Henry V's justification of renewed warfare.
20. *DKR*, XLI, XLII, *passim*.
21. PRO, C64/9, m.33; Bréquigny no. 88. In February 1420 Cheyne was granted La Roche-Tesson, to the west of Vire, to the value of 1,200 crowns (PRO, C64/12, m.13; Bréquigny no. 755).
22. PRO, C64/9, m.40; Bréquigny no. 99; R.A. Newhall, *The English Conquest of Normandy, 1416–1424: A Study in Fifteenth Century Warfare* (Yale and London, 1924), pp.55–6, 93–4.
23. A.L. Brown, 'The Authorization of Letters under the Great Seal', *BIHR*, XXXVII (1964), 127, 141, 145–7.
24. *Ibid.*, pp. 136–49; *Calendar of Signet Letters of Henry IV and Henry V (1399–1422)*, ed. J.L. Kirby (London, 1978), pp. 8–9. The non-survival of the petitions may be explained, in part, by the fire of 1619 (Brown, 'Authorization of Letters', pp. 126, 136).
25. PRO, C64/11, m.47; Bréquigny no. 425, dated 19 April 1419; PRO, C64/11, m.65; Bréquigny no. 482, dated 28 April 1419.
26. PRO, C64/10, mm.37d, 32d; Bréquigny no. 297.
27. PRO, C64/10, mm.35; 34; Bréquigny nos. 205, 277.
28. Newhall, *English Conquest*, pp. 131 n.233, 141.
29. PRO, C64/14, m.2; Bréquigny no. 911.
30. PRO, C64/11, m.29; Bréquigny no. 620. These lands were given to Sir Reginald Grey in December 1421, after Noon's death (PRO, C64/16, m.18; Bréquigny no. 1059).
31. PRO, C64/11, m.64; Bréquigny no. 465. Baskerville was a member of the Harfleur garrison in 1415 and was captain of Arques in 1421 (J.H. Wylie, 'Notes on the Agincourt Roll', *TRHS*, third series, V [1911], 112; BN, f.fr. 26043, no. 5583).
32. PRO, C64/11, m.53; Bréquigny no. 433.
33. The fief of La Bucaille (AN, Collection Lenoir 4/239) was worth up to 500 écus per year (PRO, C64/11, m.49; Bréquigny no. 370).
34. PRO, C64/11, m.76; Bréquigny no. 376.
35. PRO, C64/16, m.28; Bréquigny no. 1015. On 24 April 1419 these lands had been given to Hugh Whitlond (PRO, C64/11, m.51; Bréquigny no. 453).
36. PRO, C64/10, m.12; Bréquigny no. 281.
37. *DKR*, XLI, p. 806; XLII, p. 345.
38. One example was James Reede, granted lands south of Mantes on 22 April 1419 (PRO, C64 11, m.68; *DKR*, XLI, p. 770).
39. AN, JJ 172 no. 518; JJ 173 no. 315.
40. Compare B.J.H. Rowe, 'John, Duke of Bedford, as Regent of France (1422–1435): his policy and administration in the north' (Oxford B.Litt. thesis, 1927), p. 57. Miss Rowe's point that this grant rendered Bedford a vassal of the French crown is, however, a valuable one.
41. Many Frenchmen lost their estates: *comme de leurs terres et autres biens meubles quy furent prins et confisquies et mis realement en la main du roy dAngleterre pour aplicquier a son demaine, ou baillier en recompence a aulcuns qui lauroient mery par leur loyaulte et bon service* (J. de Waurin, *Recueil des croniques et anchiennes istoires de la Grant Bretaigne (1422–1431)*, ed. W. Hardy (RS, 5 vols., 1864–91), III, pp. 120–1.
42. AN, JJ 173 nos. 293, 299.
43. AN, JJ 174 nos. 162, 182. Chetwood was a member of Bedford's household, and Barneby of that of the duchess of Bedford.
44. AN, JJ 174 no. 23.
45. See Allmand, *Lancastrian Normandy*, ch. 6.
46. AN, Collection Lenoir 26/257.
47. BN, f. fr. 26063, no. 3283.

48. They included Richard Dyaron, granted lands in the *bailliage* of Alençon and *comté* of Maine to the value of 60 *l.t.* in 1437, and William Lenfant, given lands in both areas worth 40 *l.t.* in the same year (AN, Collection Lenoir 5/67; 5/17).

49. Although neither of the two royal commissioners appointed to surrender Maine held land there, Matthew Gough held extensive interests in Normandy and Fulk Eyton had recently received a small grant in the *bailliages* of Rouen and the Caux (AN, JJ 175 nos. 92, 107 for grants to Gough in 1432; AN, Collection Lenoir 28/11, a grant to Eyton in 1446). These were indeed good reasons for a lack of enthusiasm and for obstinacy in their task (R.A. Griffiths, *The Reign of King Henry VI: The Exercise of Royal Authority, 1422–1461* [London, 1981], pp. 500–4).

50. Over 300 Englishmen were granted town properties between 1417 and 1422 (a provisional estimate from the Norman Rolls).

51. See e.g. PRO, C64/14, m.20; Bréquigny no. 886. Thomas Hywey, *mercatori*, was given a house on the rue du Château and a garden nearby, *una cum quodam vacuo humo in humfreystrete*, named after the duke of Gloucester.

52. PRO, C64/16, mm.7, 14; Bréquigny nos. 1082, 1071. In 1437 Sir William Oldhall was granted an *hôtel* there, though his duties elsewhere must have precluded regular occupation (AN, Collection Lenoir 4/401).

53. PRO, C64/12, m.49; DKR, XLII, p. 334.

54. Walter, Lord Hungerford was given the *hôtel* de Novion, since *il est besoing que nostre dit conseillier reside souventesfoies en nostre bonne ville de Paris, en laquelle il n'a aucune demourance ne lieu ou il se peust logier si comme il dit* (AN, JJ 173 no. 340; A. Longnon, *Paris pendant la domination anglaise [1420–1436]: Documents extraits des registres de la Chancellerie de France* [Paris, 1878], pp. 196–7).

55. PRO, C64/12, m.23; DKR, XLII, p. 344.

56. ADSM, Tabellionnage de Rouen, 1419–20, fo. 148.

57. Ibid., fo. 327v.

58. ADSM, Tabellionnage de Rouen, 1421–2, fo. 290.

59. ADSM, Tabellionnage de Rouen, 1425–6, fos. 167–167v. Berkeroft was *seigneur* of Quenel in the Caux, probably the home of his wife Colette.

60. ADSM, Tabellionnage de Rouen, 1422–3, fo. 39; see also N. Périaux, *Dictionnaire indicateur des rues et places de Rouen: Revue de ses monuments et de ses établissements publics* (Rouen, 1870), p. 651.

61. ADSM, Tabellionnage de Rouen, 1433–4, fo. 161. Miles was promoted from clerk to *maître* in 1438 (AN, Collection Lenoir 4/341–2).

62. ADSM, Tabellionnage de Rouen, 1439–40, *sub* 28 July 1440; ibid., 1442–3, *sub* 21 June 1443.

63. *Gallia regia ou état des officiers royaux des bailliages et des sénéschausées de 1328 à 1515*, ed. G. Dupont-Ferrier (6 vols., Paris, 1942–61), III, p. 401.

64. ADSM, Tabellionnage de Rouen, 1434, fos. 371–71v.

65. AN, Collection Lenoir 27/281; 4/239.

66. BN, f. fr. 25767, no. 42; 25773, nos. 1089, 1199; 25774, no. 1244. I am grateful to Miss Anne Curry for these references.

67. An, Collection Lenoir 4/369.

68. AN, K63/10, no. 22.

69. A.E. Marshall, 'The Role of English War Captains in England and Normandy, 1436–1461' (Wales [Swansea] M.A. thesis, 1975), pp. 53–4; J.S. Roskell, 'John, Lord Wenlock of Someries', *The Publications of the Bedfordshire Historical Record Society*, XXXVIII (1958), 12–48.

70. A figure calculated from AN, JJ 173, 174, and Collection Lenoir.

71. AN, Collection Lenoir 21/281–2, 287–8; Allmand, 'Lancastrian land settlement', p. 472.

72. AN, Collection Lenoir 21/389, 22/349 for Regnault; 21/383, 26/183 for Preston.

73. Thomas Roley, a garrison soldier at Cherbourg, was granted a house there in 1420 (PRO, C64/12, m.13; Bréquigny no. 709). At Rouen in 1426 John Magnitourne sold to fellow-archer John Coutin and his French wife a house and garden in the parish of St.-Jean-sur-Renelle (ADSM, Tabellionnage de Rouen, 1425–6, fo. 223v; see also *ibid.*, 1430–1, fo. 60).
74. AN, Collection Lenoir 21/275.
75. B.P. Wolffe, *The Royal Demesne in English History* (London, 1971), pp. 87–8.
76. AN, JJ 175, no. 134.
77. See, for example, the appointment of Sir John Sutton in March 1428 (*CPR, 1422–9*, pp. 475–6).
78. See *Foedera, Conventiones, Literae, etc.*, ed. T. Rymer (10 vols., The Hague, 1739–45), V. p. 42, for Warwick's appointment in 1437 and V, i, p. 85, for that of York in 1440.
79. *Letters and Papers Illustrative of the Wars of the English in France during the Reign of Henry the Sixth, King of England*, ed. J. Stevenson (RS, 2 vols, in 3, London, 1861–4), II, ii, [550–1]. Grants were made *secundum statum, gradum, et merita gentis Anglorum strenue in praenominato bello de Vernelle in Perche gerentem*.
80. AN, Collection Lenoir 21/345.
81. *Ibid.*, 21/331; 17/294.
82. *Gallia regia*, II, p. 11; II, p. 78; DKR, XLII, p. 422.
83. PRO, C64/11, m.51; Bréquigny no. 458; AN, Collection Lenoir 21/245; AN, JJ 174, nos. 41, 305.
84. *Gallia regia*, V, p. 209; AN, Collection Lenoir 5/89; 26/421–2. The fiefs of Auquainville and Fervaques lie some eleven miles south of Lisieux.
85. *Ibid.*, 27/267.
86. PRO, C64/11, m.35; DKR, XLI, p. 789. See also PRO, C64/11 M.61; DKR, XLI, p. 773, for another grant to Burgh.
87. BN, f. fr. 26043, no. 5574; BL, Add. Ch. 7954, 7957; *Gallia regia*, II, pp. 262–3, 290–1.
88. The details given here come from AN, Collection Lenoir 9/154–60.
89. *Ibid.*, 8/385.
90. See Allmand, 'Lancastrian land settlement', p. 474, and Allmand, *Lancastrian Normandy*, pp. 64–6, for further evidence of family settlement.
91. AN, Collection Lenoir 26/291; 26/255.
92. Landed income was of particular advantage when hard currency and bullion were in short supply (J.L. Bolton, *The Medieval English Economy, 1150–1500* [London and Totowa, New Jersey, 1980], pp. 79–80, 297–300).
93. AN, Collection Lenoir 21/237; 17/413; AN, JJ 172, no. 359.
94. Stevenson, *Letters and Papers*, II, ii. 434.
95. AN, Collection Lenoir 3/220.
96. AN, JJ 174, no. 27; AN, Collection Lenoir 13/129.
97. *Itineraries of William Worcester*, ed. J.H. Harvey (Oxford, 1969), pp. 47–9; Griffiths, *Reign of Henry VI*, p. 670.
98. Marshall, 'The Role of English War Captains', pp. 42–6.
99. AN, Collection Lenoir 5/23.
100. *Ibid.*, 4/191; see above, nn. 84, 85.
101. AN, Collection Lenoir 5/71; 27/145. Russell was usher of York's chamber, Leche a *serviteur et familier domestique*.
102. Delays for valuations of lands held were granted to John Wykes and John Stanley of the royal household (BL, Add. Ch. 1470, 14388). John Beaufort rewarded his usher Thomas Vaughan with a life-grant in 1440 (AN, Collection Lenoir 26/485), and Edmund Beaufort gave John Maydston, a member of his household, lands in Maine in 1439 (*ibid.*, 27/455).
103. M.K. Jones, 'The Beaufort Family and the War in France, 1421–1450' (Bristol Ph.D. thesis, 1982), pp. 99–102, 296–7.

104. AN, JJ 174, nos. 112, 150. The fief of Heuqueville passed from Henry Noon to Reginald Grey to Talbot (see above, n.30).

105. AN, Collection Lenoir 26/413–4.

106. *Ibid.*, 75/21; A.J. Pollard, *John Talbot and the War in France, 1427–1453* (1983), pp. 90, 93.

107. *Ibid.*, p. 79 and ch. 5 for an examination of the nature and origins of the Talbot affinity.

108. AN, JJ 175 no. 310; P. Le Cacheux, *Actes de la Chancellerie d'Henri VI, concernant la Normandie sous la domination anglaise (1422–1435)* (2 vols., Rouen, Paris, 1907–8), II, pp. 282–4. John Wakefield and his French wife were engaged in this hazardous profession at Ellecourt near Aumale.

109. See the apposite remarks of C.F. Richmond, 'After McFarlane', *History*, LXVIII (1983), 46–60, esp. 58–9.

110. Richard Bic made a propitious marriage to Alison, daughter of Guillaume Paon, *bourgois de Rouen*, by which he came into property in the city (ADSM, Tabellionnage de Rouen, 1440–1, *sub* 14 October 1440).

111. Archives du Calvados, Tabellionnage de Caen, 7E 90, fos. 68v–69.

5

The Financing of the Lordship of Ireland under Henry V and Henry VI[1]

Elizabeth Matthew
Reading

Finance has been described as 'the great weakness in Lancastrian relations with Ireland'.[2] The inadequacy of English support for the Dublin government has been held in large measure to blame for an apparent deterioration in the state of the Irish lordship in the first half of the fifteenth century.[3] However, a study of the survival of scutage in later medieval Ireland has suggested that Lancastrian economies may also have had some more positive results. The incidence of scutage was found to have increased between 1415 and 1445, an indication that the Dublin government was making some attempt to exploit local financial resources more fully in this period than before.[4] It is the intention of this paper to examine, on the one hand, the decisions and omissions by which Lancastrian government reduced its financial commitment to Ireland, and, on the other, the effects of this reduction upon the finances of the Dublin government under the lieutenants, deputies and justiciars, and, in a wider sense, upon the outlook of the Anglo-Irish community under the crown.

The driving force behind the reduction in English financial support for the government and defence of the lordship of Ireland in the first half of the fifteenth century was Henry V. His ambitions in France, and the cost of their realization, provide obvious motives. The circumstances of Richard II's deposition had given Henry IV good reasons both for avoiding extensive personal involvement in Ireland and for not seeming to neglect the onus of lordship. Despite some initial inclination to spare the English exchequer as much of the cost of governing Ireland as possible,[5] the appointment of the king's second son,

Thomas, as lieutenant in 1401 with 12,000 marks from England a year, suggests that it was then considered important to attempt to maintain a level of financial support for the lordship consistent with late-fourteenth-century precedent.[6] Between 1361 and 1399, lieutenants had been granted at least £6,000–£8,000 from England a year, and sometimes more.[7] As the gravity of Henry IV's financial difficulties became apparent, English funds promised to Thomas were reduced to £6,000 a year in 1406, then to 7,000 marks a year in 1408.[8] Pressure for a further reduction was exerted by the English council and, in particular, the prince of Wales, in 1409.[9] Such a move was, however, resisted for the rest of the reign, notwithstanding the lieutenant's considerable and continual difficulties in securing the sums due.[10] When Henry IV died, Thomas of Clarence's appointment as lieutenant was not renewed. Instead, the new king at once set in train the first of two determined attempts to reduce the lordship's expectations of English financial aid.

The indentures sealed by Sir John Stanley as lieutenant of Ireland in June 1413 offered him English exchequer support of a mere 4,000 marks for his first year in office and 3,000 marks *per annum* thereafter, in addition to the (by this time) customary grant to lieutenants of the lordship's own revenues.[11] When Stanley died in office the following year, the same financial terms were agreed for his successor, John Talbot, Lord Furnival.[12] The decision of 1413 reduced the lordship to a level of English exchequer backing that was slightly less generous than that fixed two years earlier for the warden of the east march towards Scotland in time of peace.[13] This new rate set a standard to which all subsequent Lancastrian appointments to the lieutenancy adhered fairly closely, though with constant reviews and minor adjustments; it was not in fact until 1453 that these figures seemed securely established as the fixed rate for the job.[14]

The new terms put the lieutenants, particularly John Talbot, who held office for his full six-year term, in a difficult position in the lordship. The problem was not so much that the English exchequer failed to issue the sums promised: Stanley received all of, and even slightly more than, what was owing to him for a full first year in office;[15] payments to John Talbot, before the expiry of his term of office, covered eighty-six per cent of the sum due.[16] Delays in English payments did from time to time exacerbate Talbot's problems; when unable to pay his soldiers, he had to resort to the highly unpopular practice of coign or forced billeting without compensation, which a Dublin parliament of 1410 had attempted to prohibit.[17] However, in Ireland there seems to have been considerable resentment that Stanley and Talbot should have been promised so little support from the English exchequer when their limited personal resources within the lordship made it difficult – ultimately impossible – for their Anglo-Irish creditors to pursue their debts.[18] Early in 1417, complaints about the oppressions, extortions and inadequacies of the Dublin government were made in a petition from Ireland to the king. Specific accusations of improper conduct on Talbot's part were also drawn up, though it is not certain whether these reached Henry at this stage. At all events king and council took the complaints seriously. Henry announced that remedy would be provided by the appointment of good and sufficient officers when Talbot's lieutenancy expired.[19]

Although the arrangements of 1413 had proved unsatisfactory, determination to reduce the level of English exchequer support for the lordship did not slacken. In France Henry began to attempt to transfer some of the burden of the war to Normandy;[20] for Ireland a new initiative was launched, giving the lordship much more direct encouragement to pay for itself. The man appointed to succeed Talbot in February 1420 was James Butler, fourth earl of Ormond. In many ways it was a surprising choice; with the advantage of hindsight and some knowledge of the damage to be inflicted on the Dublin government by the Talbot-Ormond feud, it might seem politically unfortunate.[21] However, in terms of royal policy for Ireland, it made excellent sense. Although, when the indentures were sealed, Henry had recently departed for France leaving the duke of Gloucester as keeper of England,[22] it is unlikely, in the light of the king's announcement in 1417, that the choice of candidate was not his own. Well-cultivated as Ormond's English connections by blood, marriage and patronage were,[23] the earl, unlike Stanley, Talbot and Thomas of Clarence, was Anglo-Irish – a man whose main power-base and sphere of action lay not in England, but in Ireland itself. Here was 'sufficiency' in full measure. After inheriting from his father in 1405 one of the Anglo-Irish earldoms originally created in the second and third decades of the fourteenth century, Ormond's majority in 1411 had brought him full possession of the Butler lordship.[24] Centred on Kilkenny, these lands were as extensive as, and probably more valuable than any in the hands of an Anglo-Irish magnate.[25] At an earlier stage, Ormond had already gathered some brief, first-hand experience of the Dublin government: in 1407–8 he served as deputy to one of Thomas of Lancaster's deputies, Stephen Scrope.[26] The choice of such a man as lieutenant was also perhaps a natural extension of the well-established policy of appointing local magnates to the wardenships of the Scottish marches.[27] Certainly there was a similar calculation that such an appointment would provide the opportunity to harness local resources more effectively to the needs of defence at less cost to the English exchequer.

Talbot's confiscation of Ormond's Irish lands after an unsuccessful pursuit of mid-fourteenth-century Butler debts at the Irish exchequer in July 1417,[28] gave the earl a personal reason for seeking control of the lordship's administration at this time. He had every incentive to submit a low proffer, or to agree to whatever terms the king or Gloucester proposed. By the terms of his indentures, Ormond undertook the lieutenancy in return for a mere lump sum of 1,250 marks from England. His salary was set at 2,500 marks a year – less than Talbot's – and Ormond was to attempt to raise the bulk of it from the lordship's own revenues. Only upon Irish-seal certification of the Irish exchequer's inability to pay was Ormond to have warrants for further English issues to make up any shortfall.[29] Nor was Ormond to have the free disposal of Irish revenue enjoyed by

previous lieutenants. The treasurer of Ireland was from this time to account at
the English exchequer, as had been the practice before 1379.[30] It seems likely
that under the new arrangements there was to be a thorough assessment at
Westminster of the lordship's financial resources. Not only did various Irish
exchequer rolls and warrants of the period of this lieutenancy find their way to
the English exchequer, but details were also submitted of subsidies granted to
Ormond in Ireland, extra funds which were not collected through the Dublin
exchequer.[31]

A slight tightening of the lieutenant's powers and the unusually short term
which Ormond was given – two years, compared with Stanley's and Talbot's six,
and Thomas of Lancaster's twelve – further contribute to the air of experiment
which the 1420 appointment conveys. Financially it seems to have proved a
success, from the point of view both of the English exchequer and – unlike the
arrangements of 1413 and 1414 – within the lordship itself. Although Ormond
mounted a fairly ambitious set of military expeditions in defence of the outlying
areas of English obedience,[32] the total cost to the English exchequer was £1,270,
or little more than a third of the sum issued to Talbot during his first two years in
office up to April 1416. Contributions to Ormond's salary from the Irish
exchequer totalled nearly £1,344.[33] The remaining arrears of his salary – just
over twenty per cent of the total – were never paid, but there is no indication
that Ormond found shortage of funds a serious embarrassment. Unlike Talbot,
he had, of course, substantial private resources at his command on the spot: a
petition to the king from the Dublin parliament of 1421 confirms that they were
used.[34]

While the £1,344 that Ormond extracted from the Dublin exchequer seems
very little by English standards, in Irish terms it was no mean sum. No evidence
survives for the rate of Irish exchequer receipts in the period immediately
preceding Ormond's lieutenancy, but between 1420 and 1422 they were of the
order of £1,500 a year,[35] significantly above the £1,000 average for the period
1420–45 as a whole.[36] How was this achieved? It seems likely that Ormond's
vigorous general resumption of Irish-seal grants since Henry V's coronation
owed as much to financial considerations as it did to personal political ones.[37]
The receipt rolls for 1420–22 suggest that his lieutenancy may well have seen a
lengthening of the exchequer arm. While the bulk of receipts came from the
cities of Dublin and Drogheda and the surrounding counties of Dublin, Meath
and Kildare, there were some contributions from Kilkenny, Louth, Wexford,
and the ports of Waterford, Cork and Galway. Hanaper profits were a significant
item, and, after a proclamation of royal service at Louth on 8 July 1421, so were
scutage returns.[38] While payments to Ormond absorbed a substantial proportion
of available revenue, some fifty-five per cent was left for the wages of other
officials and other expenses.[39] In addition, the lordship granted Ormond over
1,400 marks in subsidies for defence, twice the sum John Talbot had been
promised during his last three years in office. A further, local, subsidy was

granted by the commons of Meath in July 1421 and there may have been others.[40] The earl's success in this respect seems to have been due at least in part to a pledge to avoid the detested coign to which Talbot had succumbed. Ormond was sufficiently persuaded of the evils of coign to legislate against its abuse within his own lands.[41] His concession on the matter as lieutenant was likely to be popular amongst the Anglo-Irish, and the attempt to ensure more equitable distribution of the burden of defence costs *via* the subsidies seems, literally, to have paid off, though the total actually raised probably fell a little short of the total granted.

Henry V's death in France, within months of the conclusion of Ormond's term of office in April 1422, left the king's initiative in relation to the financing of the lordship in disarray. No provision had been made for a successor to Ormond; possibly the intention had been to make a decision in the light of the investigation of the practical workings of the 1420 arrangements in Ireland. The minority council's first appointment to the lieutenancy, that of the earl of March in May 1423, owed more to politics and former precedents than it did to Henry V's new policy,[42] beyond its confirmation of the recent revival of English audit of the Irish treasurers' accounts. Although there was initial talk of lower rates of payment, March, perhaps in recognition of his high rank, was finally offered 5,000 marks a year, all from the English exchequer.[43] However, when, some months later, the finances of Ormond's lieutenancy were investigated at the English exchequer,[44] the council apparently found the evidence encouraging. When March's lieutenancy came to an abrupt end with his unexpected death in Ireland in January 1425, it was decided that the arrangements of 1420 should be given a further trial. Ormond, whom March had made deputy in 1424, was reappointed lieutenant from April for one year with 3,000 marks, only half of which was intended to come from England.[45] From this date until 1445, the essential elements of the financial provision of 1420 were upheld in every appointment to the lieutenancy. Rates of payment varied somewhat (from 5,000 to 3,000 marks a year) but the English exchequer was, for each lieutenant, initially only responsible for issuing a lump sum of between £1,000 and 4,000 marks. Thereafter, further salary instalments were only payable from the English exchequer upon receipt of Irish-seal certification of the Irish exchequer's inability to find all or part of the quarterly sums due. However, the success with which this system of payment and audit reduced the burden on the English exchequer very rapidly diminished. The initial determination, on the part of English government to use these arrangements to encourage the lordship to meet more of the costs of its government and defence, and, on the part of the lieutenants, to achieve this end, seemed to evaporate.

Lack of evidence makes it difficult to compare the finances of Ormond's lieutenancy of 1425–26 with those of his first. Little can be discovered beyond the bare figures for English and Irish exchequer contributions to his salary. As before, he raised slightly more from Ireland than from England, but both figures represent rather lower rates of issues than those made in respect of a smaller salary between 1420 and 1422.[46] The lack of further details may be explained by a clause peculiar to his 1425 indentures, namely, exempting him from presenting any personal account at the English exchequer. This in itself is probably of significance. During his previous lieutenancy of 1420–22, he had entertained hopes of sufficiently interesting Henry V in the state of Ireland, and in the origin and responsibilities of the crown's lordship, to persuade him to organise a major expedition to Ireland in the Ricardian style.[47] Such a prospect was likely to be popular in the lordship, and may actually have stimulated co-operation in raising funds there for the lieutenancy. But these extravagant hopes were probably dampened by the king's death. Under changed circumstances, the flourishing of the lordship's potential under the noses of the English council may have seemed less worthwhile – if not positively damaging – for prospects of securing even a modest flow of English financial aid. There was still considerable willingness to grant Ormond substantial defence subsidies, for which Irish treasurers did not account. An anonymous refutation (probably the work of supporters of Ormond's chief political opponent in Ireland, John Talbot's brother, Richard, archbishop of Dublin) of a petition sent to England by an Irish parliament of 1428 was to include the jibe that, as Ormond had been so successful in raising funds within the lordship as lieutenant, there was no need for the English exchequer to pay his arrears at all.[48]

As the 1420s progressed, the Talbot-Ormond feud, despite an official attempt to reconcile the protagonists in England in 1423,[49] became an increasingly serious problem in Ireland.[50] Its persistence and ill-effects upon the Dublin government no doubt influenced decisions to appoint a succession of English lieutenants from 1427 to 1438: John, Lord Grey, Sir John Sutton, Sir Thomas Stanley and Lionel, Lord Welles. Although the English council was at this time still concerned to be as economical as possible in its funding of the lordship,[51] the English lieutenants from 1427 to 1442 were very much less successful in extracting salary contributions from the Irish exchequer. At best they obtained £100–£300 in a year, sometimes considerably less.[52] Lacking Ormond's ability to breathe new life into the ailing Dublin exchequer, the English lieutenants took what little they could easily extract and prosecuted their claims in England more vigorously. The requirement to send quarterly Irish-seal certifications of the Irish exchequer's inadequacy, in order to secure further English issues towards salary payments, was cumbersome and invited delay. However, it had the advantage of securing fresh English-seal warrants for each salary instalment, thus providing some additional help in obtaining exchequer issues.

The English government seems to have been more attentive to the lieutenants' pleas for English funds (particularly in the late 1420s and early 1430s) than concerned that they should raise more money in Ireland. John Sutton, lieutenant from April 1428 to April 1430, was treated particularly well. Over ninety-six per cent of the money due to him was paid within his term of office, almost entirely from the English exchequer.[53] This was perhaps a reflection of the English council's special, though short-lived, interest in Ireland at this time, in consequence of the presence there of James Stewart, cousin and political opponent of King James I of Scotland. (Stewart had fled to Ireland in 1425; by 1429 the English council woke up to his possible use as a diplomatic lever against King James, and hoped to lure the fugitive to England.[54]) John Sutton's successor as lieutenant, Thomas Stanley, was not quite so fortunate. At least twice an increasingly hard-pressed English exchequer attempted to shelve his claims, both at the time of his first appointment in 1431 (when, after five months, his indentures had to be rewritten specifying different starting dates because of the non-payment of his initial lump sum) and again in 1434.[55] Each time Thomas Stanley sought, and obtained, from the council new warrants giving him special, and effective, preference over other creditors. However, although Stanley had to work harder to obtain his money than Sutton (assignments were frequently exchanged),[56] he secured nearly two thirds of his salary in office and a further twenty-two per cent in arrears thereafter.[57]

It was not until the late 1430s and the early 1440s that the system began to break down. Competing for funds, not only against increasingly urgent demands for the defence of English positions in France, but also with the young king's many generosities at home,[58] the first two lieutenants appointed by Henry VI himself fared less well. Lord Welles (lieutenant from 1438 to 1442) seems actually to have resigned his office prematurely over the English exchequer's failure to pay his arrears with the promptness promised in his indentures;[59] this threat was employed successfully by John Talbot in 1415 and unsuccessfully by Richard of York in 1450, but was not otherwise carried out under the Lancastrians.[60] Welles only secured fifty-five per cent of his salary in office and just over sixty-four per cent overall. Ormond, lieutenant a third time from 1442 to 1444, was paid a mere twenty per cent in office and only thirty-five per cent overall.[61] Increasing difficulty in extracting funds from the English exchequer was not offset by an increase in salary contributions from Ireland. On the contrary, a mere £107 was issued from the Dublin exchequer towards Welles's salary, and all the certifications sent from Ireland during Ormond's third lieutenancy (from 1442 to 1444) protested that Irish revenue could not contribute anything at all to the lieutenant's salary.[62]

By this time, the earl himself was very much less keen to spare the English exchequer than he had been as lieutenant in the 1420s. Before his appointment in 1442, he asked for a salary of 4,000 marks a year, to be drawn entirely from the English exchequer (though the refusal of this request was not sufficient to deter him from taking office).[63] The Irish treasurer at the time, Giles Thorndon, appalled by the poor state of the Dublin exchequer, was determined that none of Ormond's salary payments should be drawn from Irish revenue and received English-seal authorisation to give preference to other charges.[64] But while it may have been unwillingness, rather than sheer inability, which precluded any formal Irish contribution to Ormond's salary in the early 1440s, it is clear that at this point the 1420 arrangements for financing the lieutenancy gave every appearance of total breakdown.

No attempt seems to have been made to investigate properly what had gone wrong. Giles Thorndon's eagerness for a thorough reform of the Irish exchequer met with little encouragement in England.[65] Instead, when John Talbot was reappointed as lieutenant in 1445, the policy of 1420, initially so promising, was simply abandoned. Talbot himself was no doubt unwilling to return to Ireland as earl of Shrewsbury on financial terms seemingly less generous than those he had found so unsatisfactory in 1414. It was, however, agreed that the financial terms of his 1445 appointment should mirror those of 1414 exactly, as did those of Richard of York and the earl of Wiltshire up to the end of the reign.[66] This time, however, Shrewsbury had distinctly greater difficulty in obtaining the payments due to him from the English exchequer,[67] and in the 1450s English financial aid to Ireland more or less dried up.[68] The lordship was thus deprived of most of the benefit that it might otherwise have received from this belated acknowledgement that, as before 1420, the lieutenants' salaries were to be paid exclusively by the English exchequer.

The failure of the 1420 policy to achieve its purpose from 1427 onwards provides yet another contrast between the success and coherence of Lancastrian government under Henry V and the frequent absence of powerful central direction under Henry VI. But while Henry V's originally promising initiative suffered a slow death at the hands of the minority council and Henry VI, other aspects, or defects, of the Lancastrian provision for Ireland indirectly encouraged the lordship to provide for itself to a considerable extent.

In 1420, and again in 1425, Ormond's lieutenancy had been conditional upon his holding office in person. But all the other appointments of Henry VI's reign permitted lieutenants to appoint deputies should they wish to return to England during their term of office. The earl of March in 1423, and Shrewsbury, York and Wiltshire after 1445 (following the pattern of Henry V's earlier appointments in 1413 and 1414) were additionally empowered to hold office by deputy before their own arrival in Ireland.[69] There were also gaps in the succession of lieutenants created in two cases by sudden death and more commonly by delays in the process of appointment and departure. Such gaps were filled by the appointment of temporary justiciars, in one case appointed from England,[70] but usually chosen by the Irish council. Between 1413 and 1461, deputies held office for a total of between twenty and twenty-four years, justiciars for about eight years.[71] Unlike the lieutenants, the deputies and justiciars were very largely – often entirely – dependent on whatever financial resources they could raise within Ireland itself.

No deputy under Henry V or Henry VI was given direct access to English exchequer funds,[72] though in 1406 Stephen Scrope, as deputy for Thomas of

Lancaster, had sealed special indentures by which the English exchequer was to bear direct responsibility for the payment of his troops.[73] By contrast, under Henry V and Henry VI deputies made private financial arrangements with the lieutenants. Frequently the deputies chosen were prominent lay or ecclesiastical figures within the Anglo-Irish community;[74] this in itself may be an indication that they were generally expected to conduct government and defence using local resources. While deputies were from time to time responsible for sending the appropriate certifications of the Irish revenue's inability to pay all or part of the lieutenants' salary instalments,[75] the resulting English issues were always made to the lieutenants. Sometimes the lieutenants may have sent extra funds to deputies in Ireland, but no evidence confirms this. A letter written by Archbishop Mey of Armagh as the earl of Wiltshire's deputy in the mid-1450s shows that, while he had requested Wiltshire to send him money from England, Mey doubted very much whether it would ever arrive.[76]

The salary long-associated with the justiciarship was £500 a year from the Irish exchequer.[77] In this period the justiciars were, at least in some cases, granted additional sums from Irish revenue to support a small standing defence force of twelve men-at-arms and sixty archers.[78] The office had no established claim on English funds. The only justiciar of this period known to have petitioned for English financial aid was Archbishop Richard Talbot, who in the late 1430s and the late 1440s claimed arrears for two of his five justiciarships at the English exchequer, with some limited success.[79] No other justiciar received any financial assistance from England under Henry V or Henry VI, either in or out of office.

Thus, for well over half the period of the second and third Lancastrian reigns, the Dublin government lacked direct access even to the limited English funds that were found for the lieutenants. The real extent of the Irish government's influence and competence within Ireland is difficult to ascertain; nevertheless, it certainly continued to function. The ways and means by which it did so are frequently obscure, so severely limited is the surviving evidence for the lordship's internal financial resources and their management.[80] The extent of the available sources for 1420–22 is exceptional; thereafter, the records appear to offer only one detailed insight and a few slender indications of the Dublin government's ability to exploit local resources to meet its needs when little or no English aid was available.

A group of Irish exchequer documents bridging a brief chronological gap in the sequence of Irish treasurers' accounts at the English exchequer suggests that the finances of Ormond's only justiciarship of 1426–27 were, by Irish standards, remarkably healthy.[81] The documents concern part of the year 1427, coinciding with the last seven months of the justiciarship before the arrival of Lord Grey as lieutenant on 1 August 1427. During Ormond's second lieutenancy, Irish revenue had contributed only just over £541 towards his salary.[82] But between January and July 1427 the Irish exchequer was able to provide the earl with nearly half a year's salary as justiciar, and to meet the full cost of retaining his standing force of twelve men-at-arms and sixty archers over the whole period of this fifteen-month justiciarship. Together these payments totalled £988. In addition, a further £149 was issued in rewards to men to whom the justiciar had deputed some of the work of defence. (Despite the lack of English resources, military expeditions, with the help of at least one Irish parliamentary subsidy, were ambitious and wide-ranging.[83]) Nor did this preclude the spending of a further £511 on the wages of other officials of the Dublin administration, and £163 on additional administrative expenses and extra rewards, mainly to officials. The rate of spending in these two areas was at least equivalent to, if not slightly higher than, it had been over the period of the preceding Irish treasurer's account, August 1424–September 1426.[84] The seven months from January to July 1427 in fact represented three quarters of an Irish exchequer year;[85] but even allowing for this, expenditure during these months of between £1,562 (the sum for which satisfied creditors presented acquittances) and £1,638 (gross issues, less 'bad' assignments) was at a rate significantly higher than the average of £1,000 a year suggested by the totals on the Irish treasurers' accounts for 1420–42.

Clearly the absence of English subsidies led to a determined effort to increase Irish exchequer revenue. The rate of assignment during these months was very high: only £5 of issues were made in cash.[86] While assignment necessarily involved an anticipation of receipts, there is little indication that, within the limits of this brief period, available revenue was being seriously overstrained. According to the acquittances, eighty-six per cent of issues by assignment did satisfy their recipients.[87] Indeed, it seems that assignment may have been regarded as the most effective means of revenue collection in the areas furthest from Dublin.[88]

Reports on the state of the Irish exchequer in the early 1440s, which were submitted to the king and English council by the treasurer, Giles Thorndon, suggest that by this time the point of overstrain had been reached.[89] This in itself was not enough to daunt an official of Thorndon's energy and experience.[90] However, his detailed plans and considerable efforts to put matters right made him clash head-on with the determination of the earl of Ormond to raise extra funds during his lieutenancy of 1442–44, which was particularly poorly supported by the English exchequer.[91] The quarrel between treasurer and lieutenant reached such a pitch that in March 1444 Thorndon was driven to flee secretly from Dublin to England.[92] Baulked of official exchequer payments by Thorndon's determination to reserve available revenue for the wages of the rest of the Dublin administration, it seems that Ormond nevertheless managed to intercept certain revenues before they reached Thorndon's hands.[93] Thus, the official certifications to England suggesting that Ormond was paid nothing at all at this time from Irish revenue perhaps concealed rather more than they revealed about the extent to which his lieutenancy was supported by Irish resources.

Details of the terms of appointment of deputy lieutenants are scarce. For the period from 1413 to 1461, full indentures have survived apparently in only two cases. By coincidence the first of these were drawn up within months of Thorndon's flight. The financial provision which Ormond as lieutenant made for Richard Nugent, Lord Delvin, as deputy in August 1444 depended entirely upon resources within Ireland. The indentures specified not only the sum Delvin was offered (210 marks a quarter) and the use to which it was to be put (90 marks for household expenses, 120 for the wages of his retinue), but also precise details of the debts, rents and subsidies which were to make up the payments. Delvin's salary, however, apparently represented only a part of the funds that he was likely to find at his disposal. All profits from offices and benefices falling vacant, from prisoners' ransoms and the making of war and peace with the Gaelic Irish were to be divided equally between the deputy and the lieutenant.[94] Apparently both parties expected such sums to be of significant value.

The second case is that of the duke of York's appointment of the earl of Ormond as deputy on 23 August 1450. Some of the details of Ormond's proposed finances are unfortunately obscure: references are made to the terms of an earlier draft, now missing, agreed upon the previous day. However, according to the surviving indentures, Ormond was to have £1,000 for his first year in office. At least the first quarterly instalment of this sum was to be drawn entirely from taxation and fines raised within Ireland. No specific mention is made of any payments to be received from York in England, but in addition to his £1,000 Ormond was to draw upon the issues and profits of York's earldom of Ulster, with the proviso that the earl should first make payment to the seneschal of Ulster, the constable of Carrickfergus and towards the keeping of the castle of Ardglass.[95] Clearly there were hopes of a lasting recovery of government influence in this area, in the wake of York's successful personal intervention.[96]

Although the sums that could be raised within the lordship to finance government and defence as English aid diminished seem small – by English standards, very small indeed – it must be remembered that the responsibilities of the Dublin government, especially in the fragmented lordship of the later medieval period, were limited. Outlying Anglo-Irish communities depended to a considerable extent on self-help in defence, spending much local revenue at source.[97] Under such conditions, these small sums were considered well worth having.

The reigns of Henry V and Henry VI saw a major shift in the burden of financial provision for the lordship from England to Ireland. What is perhaps remarkable, in view of the fate under Henry VI of his father's initially promising policy for engineering just such a change, is that it took place gradually and relatively smoothly.

Under Richard II and Henry IV there had been evidence of considerable reluctance on the part of Anglo-Irish magnates to fill gaps in English lieutenancies on the grounds that a justiciarship unsupported by English funds entailed too great a financial burden.[98] Whether genuine or consciously exaggerated, this reluctance is evidence of the extent of the sense of dependence upon English financial resources at this time. Similarly, Henry V's initial reduction of the lieutenant's English salary aroused serious resentment. Yet under Henry VI the leading figures of the lordship were generally eager to take on the chief governorship, either with, or more usually without, English financial backing.[99] Their willingness and degree of success in so doing decreased the actual and conscious dependence of the Anglo-Irish community upon English aid with striking consequences. Recent analyses of the proceedings of Richard of York's famous Drogheda parliament of 1460 have argued convincingly that they were not simply the result of York's manipulation of the Anglo-Irish to serve his own ambitions, but of a bargaining process in which the duke found it politic to make certain concessions to the assembly.[100] Demands of the Anglo-Irish for acknowledgement of their separate identity under the crown and for the opening of an Irish mint to ease their internal monetary problems[101] at once emphasised and increased their sense of detachment from English government.

The first crucial turning-point in Anglo-Irish attitudes was the success of the experimental lieutenancy of the earl of Ormond from 1420 to 1422. From the experience of his first lieutenancy, Ormond himself no doubt derived much of his own confidence in the feasibility of financing government and defence from the lordship's own resources. The escalation of the Talbot-Ormond feud provided a more general and pressing incentive. For the three decades during which the feud held Anglo-Irish politics in its tenacious grasp, the possession of the patronage and powers that the chief governorship conferred was of vital importance to the protagonists and their supporters. While the feud lasted there was more to be gained than to be lost from seeking the office of chief governor; without control of its powers, neither faction could ensure the protection of its personal interests.[102]. When the much reduced level of English exchequer support finally dwindled away to virtually nothing in the 1450s, men of the lordship had already become accustomed to finding ways of surmounting financial problems which had previously been declared insuperable and still remained considerable.

Notes

1. I am grateful to Dr R.F. Frame of the University of Durham for reading an earlier draft of this paper and for contributing valuable suggestions and comments at various stages of its preparation.
2. J. Lydon, *Ireland in the Later Middle Ages* (Dublin, 1973), p. 125.
3. A.J. Otway-Ruthven, *A History of Medieval Ireland* (London, 1968), p. 375.
4. S.G Ellis, 'Taxation and Defence in Late Medieval Ireland: the Survival of Scutage', *Journal of the Royal Society of Antiquaries of Ireland*, CVII (1977), 5–28, esp. 17.
5. Henry IV's first lieutenant, John Stanley, was appointed with a salary of only 8,000 marks. It was hoped that all but the first 3,000 marks could be drawn from Irish revenue (PRO, E404/15/133). An earlier draft of his indentures suggests that there had been hope that all his salary might be drawn from Ireland (PRO, E101/69/2, no.307).
6. PRO, E404/16/728.
7. For the initiation of English subsidizing of government and defence in the lordship, see P. Connolly, 'The Financing of English Expeditions to Ireland, 1361–1376', *England and Ireland in the Later Middle Ages*, ed. J. Lydon (Dublin, 1981), pp. 104–21; for further details up to 1399, see H.G. Richardson and G.O. Sayles, *The Irish Parliament in the Middle Ages* (2nd ed., Philadelphia, 1964), pp. 151–2; Otway-Ruthven, *Medieval Ireland*, p. 313.
8. *Foedera*, VIII, 431.
9. *PPC*, I, 320.
10. See Otway-Ruthven, *Medieval Ireland*, p. 346, and further details in G.L. Harriss, 'Preference at the medieval exchequer', *BIHR*, XXX (1957), 17–40, and 'Fictitious loans' in *EconHR*, VIII, no.2 (1955), 187–99, esp. 190.
11. *PPC*, II, 130–1.
12. PRO, E404/29/190
13. £2,500 a year: see R.L. Storey, 'The Wardens of the Marches of England towards Scotland 1377–1489', *EHR*, LXXII (1957), 593–615, esp. 604. For comparisons with the far greater amounts spent on Calais and Normandy under the Lancastrians, see J.F. Lydon, *The Lordship of Ireland in the Middle Ages* (Dublin, 1972), p. 249.
14. The earl of Wiltshire's indentures of 1453, quoting these rates of payment, added that this was what other lieutenants of Ireland had received before him (PRO, E404/69/168). The same phrase occurs in Richard, duke of York's indentures of 1457, printed by Sir J.T. Gilbert in *History of the Viceroys of Ireland* (Dublin, 1865), pp. 585–6.
15. Before his death in office in January 1414, he had been issued his first year's 4,000 marks in full, £37,10 *s. 0d.* for supplies of arrows and £120 for his shipping expenses. All payments were in cash (PRO, E403/612, mm.3, 9; 614, m.5).
16. Of the £12,666 13 *s.* 4*d.* owing to him for his six-year term, just over £11,130 was issued to him within this period. Only one assignment of just over £185 was subsequently cancelled (PRO, E403/617, mm.2, 14–15; 624, mm.2, 22; 627, m.29; 633, mm.9, 16; 636, mm.1, 2; 638, mm.5, 6, 7; 640, mm.2, 5, 7, 15; 643,m.10; E401/667, 25 June; 646, m.12).
17. *Statutes and Ordinances and Acts of the Parliament of Ireland, King John to Henry V*, ed. H.F. Berry (Dublin, 1907), pp. 520–1; for John Talbot's difficulties, see Otway-Ruthven, *Medieval Ireland*, pp. 349–52.
18. *Statutes, John to Henry V*, pp. 568–71; 'Chronicle of Ireland' by Henry Marlborough in *The Historie of Ireland*, (Hanmer, Campion and Spenser, Dublin, 1633), pt. ii, p. 221. Talbot inherited his family's disputed claim to the lordship of Wexford, but not until 1421, after his first lieutenancy in Ireland had terminated: see A.J. Pollard, 'The family of Talbot, lords Talbot and earls of Shrewsbury in the fifteenth century' (Bristol Ph.D.thesis, 1968), pp. 104–6.

19. *PPC*, II, 43–50, 219–20.
20. R.A. Newhall, *The English Conquest of Normandy, 1416–24* (New Haven and London, 1924), pp. 150–76.
21. For the subsequent effects of the feud, see M.C. Griffith, 'The Talbot-Ormond Struggle for Control of the Anglo-Irish Government, 1414–47', *Irish Historical Studies*, II (1940–41), 376–97.
22. From 3 January 1420: *CPR, 1416–22*, p. 214.
23. His first wife, Joan Beauchamp, then living, was English, as was his mother, Anne de Welles, wife of the third earl (*CP*, X, pp. 122–3, 125). The first and second earls of Ormond had also seen distinct advantages in choosing brides from English, rather than Anglo-Irish, families (R. Frame, *English Lordship in Ireland, 1318–1361* [Oxford, 1982], pp. 50–1). On the death of the third earl in 1405, Thomas of Lancaster gained custody of the lands and the marriage of the heir; the fourth earl served with him in France in 1412 and 1418: *COD*, II, pp. 277–8, no. 386; Marlborough, 'Chronicle', p. 218; *The Brut, or the Chronicles of England*, ed. F.W.D. Brie, II (EETS, CXXXVI, 1908), pp. 387,395; *Collections of a London Citizen*, ed. J. Gairdner (Camden Society, new series, XVII, 1876), p. 7.
24. *COD*, II, p. 297, no.413.
25. See C.A. Empey, 'The Butler lordship', *Journal of the Butler Society*, I, no.3 (1970–1), 181–7.
26. *COD*, II, pp. 282–3, no.391. The correct date of this document is 18 (not 8) December (*NLI*, D.1457).
27. From 1386: see R.L. Storey, 'Wardens', esp. p. 599.
28. See C.A. Empey, 'The Butler lordship in Ireland, 1185–1515' (Dublin Ph.D. thesis, 1970), pp. 261–7 and Appendix V, p. xxxii.
29. PRO, E101/247/13, no.5.
30. This later caused some initial confusion at the English exchequer. The treasurer, Hugh Burgh, had to be officially exempted from responsibility to account for the previous period of John Talbot's lieutenancy when he presented his records for 1420 (*Analecta Hibernica*, II [1931], 223–4).
31. PRO, E101/247/8–10,14–16. E101/247/16 is printed in *Parliaments and Councils of Mediaeval Ireland*, ed. H.G. Richardson and G.O. Sayles (Dublin, 1947), pp. 131–85.
32. There were two campaigns to the north to defend Louth and southern Ulster, short campaigns in western Meath and western Kildare, one, possibly two, tours of the south and south-east and a foray as far west as Thomond: PRO, E101/247/17 no.1; Marlborough, 'Chronicle', pp. 221,223; *Three Prose Versions of the Secreta Secretorum*, ed. R. Steele, I (EETS, 1898), pp. 164,203–4; *RPC*, p. 217, 8 Hen. V, no.4 & p. 219, 8 Hen. V, no.2; M.C. Griffith, 'Talbot-Ormond Struggle', Appendix I, p. 392; K. Simms, '"The King's Friend": O'Neill', in Lydon, *England and Ireland*, pp. 214–35, esp. p. 219.
33. See Ormond's account as lieutenant: PRO, E101/247/11, enrolled E364/57,m.C.
34. *Statutes John to Henry V*, pp. 572–3.
35. Calculated from Hugh Burgh's receipt rolls for February–July 1420 and Hugh Bavent's receipt roll and account as treasurer from July 1420 to December 1421 (PRO, E101/247/8,9,15; E364/57, m.G).
36. Calculated from the series of Irish treasurer's accounts (PRO, E101/247–8; /540; E364/57–80) by Lydon, *Lordship of Ireland*, p. 259. For indications of the poor state of the Irish exchequer earlier in the fifteenth century, see Otway-Ruthven, *Medieval Ireland*, p. 343.
37. PROI, R.C. 8/38 (transcript of Irish memoranda roll for 8 Hen.V), pp. 9,13–16.
38. These totalled nearly £183 between July and November 1421 (PRO, E101/247/15, mm.13–17), but in the absence of a receipt roll for 1422, the total yield remains uncertain. For the Tudor period, Dr. Ellis estimates an average yield from scutage of about £200, but he believes this figure may have been higher under the Yorkists (S.G. Ellis, 'Taxation and Defence', p. 16). The 1420–1 rolls also note small receipts from Kerry, Ulster and Limerick.
39. Calculated from the Irish issue roll for February–July 1420 and from Hugh Bavent's account as treasurer, July 1420–December 1421: PRO, E101/247/10; E364/57, m.G.

40. See Richardson and Sayles, *Parliaments and Councils*, I. pp. xxv–vi, 131–85, and *Irish Parliament*, pp. 234–40. For Talbot's subsidies, see also Marlborough, 'Chronicle', pp. 219,221.

41. Four of the subsidy indentures of June 1420 specified that the grant was to avoid resort to coign (Richardson and Sayles, *Parliaments and Councils*, I, pp. 140, 144–5, 148). Under Edward IV this clause was common in subsidy grants: see D.B. Quinn, 'The Irish Parliamentary Subsidy in the Fifteenth and Sixteenth Centuries', *Proceedings of the Royal Irish Academy*, XLII (1934–5) C, 225; but the special mention of Ormond's abolition of coign in the Irish parliamentary petition of 1421 suggests that it seemed unusual at the time (*Statutes, John to Henry V*, pp. 572–3). For Ormond's regulation of coign within his own lordship, see C.A. Empey and K. Simms, 'The Ordinances of the White Earl and the Problem of Coign in the Later Middle Ages', *Proceedings of the Royal Irish Academy*, LXXV (1975) C, 167–87.

42. See Otway-Ruthven, *Medieval Ireland*, pp. 362–3; R.A. Griffiths, *The Reign of King Henry VI* (London, 1981), pp. 164–5.

43. PRO, E28/41/45; E404/39/285; PPC, II, 49. There was an earlier suggestion that, like Ormond, March should draw as much of his salary as possible from Irish revenue (PPC, III, 68), but it was abandoned. The terms of neither his indentures nor his patent (*Foedera*, X, 282–5) gave him the free disposal of Irish revenue enjoyed by lieutenants before 1420.

44. His own account was completed in December 1423 when the council was notified of the result (PRO, E101/247/11).

45. *Analecta Hibernica*, I. 217–8.

46. In August 1425 he obtained assignment of the £1,000 due from the English exchequer, but from various cancellations it is clear that he cannot have realised more than £500 within his term of office; from the Irish exchequer he raised a total of £541 8s. 8d. (PRO, E364/60, m.C; E403/672, m.16; 675, m.7; 683, m.9; 691, m.10; E401/711, m.14; 713, 15 July; 717, 5 December; 721, 17 November; 723, 13 December).

47. See the first and fourth clauses of the petition to the king from the Dublin parliament of 1421 (*Statutes, John to Henry V*, pp. 562–7) and memoranda referring to letters concerning a royal visit to Ireland written by Ormond to the king's brothers and the earl of March, which also listed a number of points substantiating the crown's right to lordship over Ireland, similar in many respects to a fuller version in the translation of *Secreta Secretorum* made for Ormond in 1422 (PPC, II, 50–2; *Secreta*, I, 184–6).

48. Sir William Betham, *The Origin and History of the Constitution of England, and of the Early Parliaments of Ireland* (Dublin, 1834), p. 356; RPC., p. 248, no.13.

49. See Otway-Ruthven, *Medieval Ireland*, p. 361.

50. For a contemporary report on the seriousness of the feud c. 1428, see *The Register of John Swayne*, ed. D.A. Chart (Belfast, 1935), pp. 109–11, quoted by Griffiths, *Reign of Henry VI*, p. 164. The form of address, 'ryght hey and mighty Prince', suggests that the duke of Gloucester was the most likely intended recipient.

51. Grey's appointment in 1427 was made on the understanding that his term would be cut short if the council managed to find another candidate to serve at a lower rate of payment. Of his 4,000 marks p. a., only the first £1,000 was to be drawn from the English exchequer, unless Irish revenue proved insufficient to meet subsequent payments (PRO, E101/71/2, no.824).

52. Grey was paid nothing within the first two months of his arrival in Ireland, and only a small sum (unspecified) thereafter (PRO, E101/248/2; E364/66, m.E; E404/44/152). Sutton obtained just over £190 from Ireland between Christmas 1428 (when his first Irish payment fell due) and Christmas 1429, and probably no new issues before he left office in April 1430, although he succeeded in exchanging an earlier tally for the sum of £6 (E101/248/4, 6; E364/73, m.B; E404/46/154, 161, 177, 183). Thomas Stanley received just over £518 from Irish revenue between Michaelmas 1432, when his first Irish payment fell due, and Easter 1437, just before his lieutenancy expired (E404/49/172; 50/154, 280; 51/114, 139, 370, 383–4; 53/149–51, 165–6, 321–2). Welles seems to have obtained no more than £109 6s. 8d. from Ireland between 1438 and 1442 (E101/248/13; E364/73, m.B; 79, m.A; E404/57/318).

53. See Griffiths, *Reign of Henry VI*, pp. 165, 175, n.64. In contrast, Grey obtained just over sixty per cent of his payments during his short term of office, 1427–28 (*ibid.*, p. 175, n.62). This sum did, however, represent more than the lump sum of £1,000 which was all his indentures initially promised him from the English exchequer towards his salary (PRO, E101 71/2, no.824), Sutton and Stanley (both with salaries of 5,000 marks for the first year and 4,000 marks *p. a.* thereafter) were offered a slightly higher initial lump sum of 4,000 marks each (E404/44/183; 46/154; 47/161; 50/154).

54. PRO, E28/68, no.15; *PPC*, III, 327. For the background to the Stewart affair, see R. Nicholson, *Scotland in the Later Middle Ages* (Edinburgh, 1974), pp. 281–7; Griffiths, *Reign of Henry VI*, pp. 158–9; A. Cosgrove, *Late Medieval Ireland, 1370–1541* (Dublin, 1981), p. 84.

55. PRO, E404/48/283; Otway-Ruthven, *Medieval Ireland*, p. 368.

56. PRO, E403/698, m.7; 712, m.10; E404/47/328; 50/170; see also Griffiths, *Reign of Henry VI*, pp. 121, 167.

57. Calculated from the English receipt and issue rolls (PRO, E401; E403) for 1431–54.

58. See Griffiths, *Reign of Henry VI*, pp. 329–33, 376–77.

59. Welles's seven-year term from 1438 was abruptly curtailed early in 1442, by which time his payments from the English exchequer were more than three months overdue, a state of affairs which, according to his indentures, permitted his resignation (PRO, E101/71/4, no.901; E403/744, m.14; E404/57/88–9, 165, 318; and see Griffiths, *Reign of Henry VI*, pp. 415, 437, n.75). Welles then made his account (E101/540/17).

60. PRO, E404/31/258; for York, see Otway-Ruthven, *Medieval Ireland*, p. 382.

61. Calculated from English issue and receipt rolls for 1438–54. Welles's salary was fixed at 4,000 marks for his first year (of which the first £1,666 13s. 4d. was to be paid directly from the English exchequer) and 3,000 marks a year thereafter, supposedly from Ireland. Issues from the English exchequer during his four years in office totalled, in cash and uncancelled assignments, about £4,526; he obtained a further £753 after leaving office, mainly during the 1440s. Ormond's salary was lower – 3,000 marks a year, as in 1425, of which only the first £1,000 was to be paid directly from England (*Analecta Hibernica*, I, 215–16). During his two years and nine months in office, cash issues totalled £110 from the English exchequer, uncancelled assignments nearly £1,122. After leaving office, he obtained a further £806 by reassignment; there were no new issues.

62. PRO, E404/59/135,275; 60/170,210. For Welles, see n. 52 above.

63. PRO, C47/10/27, no.6: the document is undated, but from its contents appears to refer to Ormond's third lieutenancy rather than to either his first or second.

64. *PPC*, V, 203–6, 321–4; and see Otway-Ruthven, *Medieval Ireland*, p. 373.

65. Once in England, Thorndon was asked to shelve his accusations against Ormond in 1444 so that a 'higher matier', the charges of treason brought against Ormond by Thomas fitzGerald at this time, could be settled first (*COD*, III, p. 152). This was not accomplished until the second half of 1446 at the earliest ('John Benet's Chronicle for the years 1400 to 1462', eds. G.L. and M.A Harriss, in *Camden Miscellany*, XXIV [Camden Society, 1972] pp. 191–2) and possibly not until 1448 (*Six Town Chronicles*, ed. R. Flenley [Oxford, 1911], p. 122), by which time king and council had already delegated the supervision of the Irish exchequer to John Talbot by the terms of his appointment as lieutenant in 1445 (see n.66 below).

66. All three were offered 4,000 marks for the first year in office and £2,000 for subsequent years, with the free disposal of Irish revenue enjoyed by lieutenants before 1420: PRO, E101 71/4, nos.920–1; E404/61/138, 280; 69/168; Gilbert *History of the Viceroys*, pp. 585–6.

67. During his term of office, Shrewsbury seems only to have extracted just over half the sums due; his responsibility for Ireland lasted only a little less than four years, but on 10 March 1448 the crown still owed him as much as £3,527 6s. 8d. in respect of his service in Ireland (*CPR, 1446–52*, p. 146). For his further difficulties in extracting this debt, see A.J. Pollard, *John Talbot and the War in France* (Royal Historical Society, Studies in History no.35, London, 1983), p. 111.

68. While York extracted slightly over half the payments due for his first two years in office Griffiths, *Reign of Henry VI*, pp. 421–2), the exchequer made only two further assignments to him for Ireland thereafter (in 1451 and 1457), totalling a mere £1,104 7s. 7 d. (PRO, E401 822, 6 August; E403/810, m.10). The earl of Wiltshire had little difficulty in obtaining all the money due for his one year in office, 1453–4, but although he had then just succeeded his father as earl of Ormond, he did not go to Ireland as lieutenant, and it is unlikely that the money was spent there (either Griffiths, *Reign of Henry VI*, p. 423; Otway-Ruthven, *Medieval Ireland*, pp. 385–6).

69. Precise details of the lieutenants' powers to appoint deputies were normally included in the texts of the letters patent of appointment (PRO, C66/390, m.15; 393, m.13; 402, m.9; 416, m.2; 420, m.4; 423, m.20; 429, m.18; 441, m.3; 451, m.2; 460, mm.10, 22; 466, m.3; 477, m.14; 482, m.3; *Foedera*, X, 282–5). In the cases of Shrewsbury (1445) and York (1447, 1457), the power to appoint deputies was also included in their indentures (PRO, E101/71/4, nos.920–1; E404/61/138; Gilbert, *History of the Viceroys*, pp. 585–6).

70. Archbishop Richard Talbot of Dublin was appointed justiciar, during pleasure, under the English seal in October 1422 (CPR, *1422–29*, p. 3).

71. These figures are based on the new lists of chief governors to be published in *A New History of Ireland*, IX, *Companion to Irish History*, ii. ed. T.W. Moody, F.X. Martin, F.J. Byrne (Oxford, forthcoming).

72. No payments to lieutenants' deputies are recorded on any of the English issue rolls for 1413–61.

73. PRO, E404/21/305; and see J.H. Wylie, *History of England under Henry IV*, III (London, 1896), p. 162. This payment of troops in Ireland directly from the English exchequer was unusual: Lancastrian lieutenants were normally required to pay their retinues themselves out of their salaries, even between 1427 and 1444, when indentures specified the exact number of troops the lieutenants were required to maintain (see Griffiths, *Reign of Henry VI*, pp. 165–7, 413–5).

74. Among exceptions to this general rule were Thomas Talbot (deputy in 1418: BL, Add. MS 4797, f.52; Marlborough, 'Chronicle', p. 219) and William Welles (deputy in 1439: PRO, E28/62, 27 August; E368/211, m.109). Although both, before their appointment, were seneschals of the liberty of Meath and were subsequently escheators of Ireland (PROI, RC8 36, pp. 201, 615–6; 38, p. 197; Irish memoranda roll extracts, 1A/49/135, f.50; 148, p. 165), the main strength of their position in Ireland lay in their relationship with the lieutenants concerned – in both cases their elder brothers.

75. This happened at least twice during Thomas Stanley's lieutenancy (PRO, E404/50/154, 280).

76. *The Register of John Mey, Archbishop of Armagh, 1443–56*, ed. W.G.H. Quigley and E.F.D. Roberts (Belfast, 1972), pp. 372–3, no.356.

77. H.G. Richardson and G.O. Sayles, *The Administration of Ireland, 1172–1377* (Irish MSS. Commission, Dublin, 1963), pp. 8–15.

78. As were Ormond in 1426–27, and Archbishop Talbot in 1430–31, 1437–38 and 1445–46 (PRO, E101/248/2, 10; BL, Harleian Ch. 43.A. 72, 75, 77; and see n.79 below).

79. PRO, E28/62, 14 July; E404/55/310; 63/159. He was given assignments of £765 (and £10 in cash) in 1439 and £2,206 in 1447; tallies of over £1,000 were afterwards exchanged and reassigned up to 1458, nine years after his death in 1449 (E401/776, 22–3 December; 804, 6 December; E403/736, m.12).

80. Generally the Irish treasurers' accounts subdivide issues into various groups, that is, to all officials including the chief governors, for works, for returned tallies and for exchequer expenses, giving totals for each; details are rarely given for individual items. The accounts become more perfunctory towards the end of the sequence (for references, see n. 36 above).

81. An Irish receipt roll, an issue roll and over a hundred warrants and acquittances relating to 12 January–2 October 1427 (PRO, E101/247/20; 248/1, 2).

82. See above, n. 46.

83. *Reg. Swayne*, p. 56. In the summer of 1426 Ormond led a force against Gerald Kavanagh, and in 1427 he made a tour of Munster and Leinster (NLI, MS4, Harris Collectanea, f.302; *RPC.*, p. 244, no.39; p. 245, no.13). The earls of Kildare and Desmond, Archbishop Talbot, William Burke of Loughrea and Miles Bermingham were variously rewarded for military activities in the marches of cos. Kildare and Dublin, in Munster and in Connacht (PRO, E101/248/2; NLI, MS4, ff. 304, 306; *RPC.*, p. 244, nos.32, 34, 37, 41, 45; p. 245, nos. 15, 16).

84. From August 1424 to September 1426, a total of some £1,737 was spent on administrative expenses and officials' wages, excluding payments to Ormond as lieutenant (PRO, E101/247/19; E363/60, m.C).

85. They covered three terms – Hilary, Easter and Trinity – out of the four terms of the Irish exchequer year.

86. The assignment notation used at the Dublin exchequer at this time seems to have been different, and less complex, than that at its English counterpart. On the Irish receipt roll of 1427 (PRO, E101/248/1) assignments are distinguished by the note '*per* N.' (N. being the name of the assignee) at the conclusion of the entry of the item of revenue concerned. With a few minor discrepancies – probably clerical errors – the totals of the entries of revenue thus marked generally correspond, for each different name, with sums entered to the credit of the same people on the issue roll (E101/248/2). The entries with no *per* marking were probably genuine cash receipts; the acquittances (E101/247(20) confirm that a small proportion of issues were made in cash, but there are no notes of *in denarii* or *per assignationem* to distinguish cash from assignment on the issue roll (E101/248/2). With so many of the late-fourteenth- and early-fifteenth-century Irish receipt rolls now missing, there is no means of knowing when this notation for assignment was first developed, but it was not in use in this form in 1360–62. On the receipt roll for 34–5 Edward III, the *per* notation appears infrequently, with no apparent correlation with issue roll entries (PRO, E101/244/556).

87. PRO, E101/247/20. The high rate of assignment in 1427 may have been exceptional; a comparison of the only other pair of Irish receipt and issue rolls of this period to have survived, those for April–July 1420 (E101/247/8–10), suggests that twenty-five per cent of issues were in cash.

88. For instance, the earl of Desmond and William Burke of Loughrea declared themselves satisfied with assignments on the fee farm of Limerick and the customs of Galway and Sligo, revenues which would probably not have reached the exchequer at all as cash returns (PRO, E101/247/20, nos.33, 40; 248/1, Easter term).

89. *PPC*, V, 321–4, 327–34.

90. For Thorndon's career, see R.A. Griffiths, *The Principality of Wales in the Later Middle Ages*, I (Cardiff, 1972), pp. 216–18.

91. See n. 61 above.

92. For details, see Otway-Ruthven, *Medieval Ireland*, pp. 373–7; Griffiths, *Reign of Henry VI*, pp. 415–7.

93. *PPC*, V, 329–33; n. 64 above.

94. The text of the Delvin indentures is printed in *COD*, III, pp. 157–9, no.161, from NLI, D1718.

95. The seneschal of Ulster was to have 100 marks *p. a.*, and the constable of Carrickfergus £40 *p. a.* (Bodleian Library, Western MS. 31647, pt. i. 1–2).

96. The Ulster clause of the indentures may reflect some of York's over-optimism about the significance of the Gaelic submissions to him in 1449, but Ormond's close acquaintance with Ulster politics gave him a good chance of extracting whatever funds there might be, in York's name. For York, Ormond and Ulster, see K. Simms, '"The king's friend": O Neill', pp. 219–24; also E. Curtis, 'Richard duke of York as Viceroy of Ireland, 1447–60', *Journal of the Royal Society of Antiquaries of Ireland*, LXII, part 2 (1932), 165–74.

97. See J. Lydon, 'The City of Waterford in the Later Middle Ages', *Decies*,XII (1979), 5–15.

98. See Lydon, *Lordship of Ireland*, p. 253; Cosgrove, *Late Medieval Ireland*, pp. 8–12; Otway-Ruthven, *Medieval Ireland*, pp. 315–6. See also a letter in 1405 from the third earl of Ormond to Henry IV asking to be relieved of his temporary appointment as chief governor by the Irish council because of his inability to find sufficient funds: *Royal and Historical Letters during the Reign of King Henry IV*, ed. F.C. Hingeston, II (RS, 18, 1965), pp. 29–32.

99. See Lydon, *Lordship of Ireland*, p. 254.

100. See S.G. Ellis, 'The Struggle for Control of the Irish Mint, 1460–c. 1506', *Proceedings of the Royal Irish Academy*, LXXVIII, C, no.2 (1978), 17–36, esp. 18–20; A. Cosgrove, 'Parliament and the Anglo-Irish Community: the Declaration of 1460', in *Parliament and Community: Historical Studies*, XIV, ed. A. Cosgrove and J.I. McGuire (Belfast, 1983), pp. 25–41.

101. Numismatic evidence suggests that there was an acute shortage of coin within the lordship in the 1450s: see M. Dolley, *Medieval Anglo-Irish Coins* (London, 1972), pp. 17–19.

102. This is well illustrated by the terms of a tripartite indenture between Lord Welles, Archbishop Talbot and Ormond in 1441 specifically designed to protect the interests of Talbot and his supporters during Ormond's subsequent deputyship (PRO, C47/10/26, no. 7). Ormond and Talbot each secured appointment as chief governor seven times between 1419 and 1452.

6

The Commission of the Peace for the West Riding of Yorkshire, 1437–1509

Carol Arnold
University of Manchester

The commission of the peace had become an established part of the administration of local government in the shires during the fourteenth century and had taken over from the sheriff the primary responsibility for preserving the king's peace. Justices of the peace were required to enforce certain legislation concerned with the maintenance of law and order, to hold quarter sessions where indictments for felony and trespass were determined, and to take surety for the future good behaviour of those who threatened to break the peace.[1] The terms of reference of the commission empowered the J.Ps. to enter any liberty within the area of their responsibility, a right which the sheriff (unless he was given specific authority to do so in a particular matter) could no longer exercise where landowners had been granted the franchise of return to writs.[2] The work of the commission also involved the enforcement of legislation on a variety of social and economic matters and could include assisting in the collection of taxes and loans to the king.[3] The scope of the work performed by the J.Ps. increased during the fifteenth century, but the authority to grant bail to those indicted for felony was the only significant addition to the powers which they had acquired in the previous century.[4] Professor Putnam's study of the commission and its work led her to consider that by the fifteenth century the commission of the peace had become 'the dominant factor in local government in normal times'.[5] Excluding the towns which held county status, forty commissions had been established for the English counties. Although in most aspects of local government Yorkshire was considered as one county, the three Ridings were in this respect treated separately. In terms of the personnel appointed and the dates of renewal of each commission, there was as little similarity between the three Yorkshire commissions as between those of any other group of adjacent but separate counties. This, however, was to change in the reign of Richard III.

After the general review of July 1424, the form and content of the commission remained substantially unaltered until the reign of Henry VIII, despite the political upheavals of the period.[6] When a renewal was made, the government's prime concern was with the identity of those who were appointed J.Ps. The commission was composed of a number of lords, local gentry and lawyers. From 1424, members of the clergy (in practice the prelates) might also be included.[7] A brief attempt to establish commissions of the peace which excluded the lay lords had ended in November 1390 when it was accepted that the work of the J.Ps. was impossible to discharge without the prestige and authority given to the commission by the inclusion of lords, especially those with a substantial landed interest in the county concerned.[8] Legislation passed during the parliament of 1439–40 required the J.Ps. drawn from the local gentry should be resident in the county for which they were appointed and should possess a clear annual income from land of £20.[9] From what can be learnt of the wealth of the J.Ps. for the West Riding it seems that, except for a few appointed during the 1460s, probably all those nominated possessed incomes of at least this amount. Those who had had a formal training in the law, however, were exempt from these conditions.

Subject to the king's approval, the J.Ps. were selected by the chancellor and treasures of the realm and other of the king's councillors. There is little evidence regarding the actual mechanics of selection, but a letter from Godfrey Green to Sir William Plumpton suggests that the initiative, as with most royal grants, could come from the prospective recipient.[10] Plumpton had submitted a petition to the king's council in an effort to secure re-appointment after his removal from the West Riding commission on 10 November 1475. A J.P. was, in theory, disqualified from office if he were outlawed or, more honourably, if he were selected sheriff for the same county. It is not clear whether any heed was paid to the former disqualification with regard to the commissions in Yorkshire in the fifteenth century. There is some evidence, however, that J.Ps. in Yorkshire who were appointed sheriff for the county were removed from the commission during their year of office, though only after the accession of Edward IV in 1461.[11] By the early sixteenth century, such removal was apparently automatic.[12]

The justices of assize were always appointed to the commission. Two justices were named for each of the six circuits into which the English counties were divided, Yorkshire forming part of the northern circuit. Both justices were included in all commissions of the peace within their area of responsibility and were named in the *quorum*. This had become a permanent part of the commission from 1389, when the power to determine felonies had been finally restored to the J.Ps.[13] Those appointed were usually lawyers, but others could be included who had no formal training in the law.[14] The attendance of members of the *quorum* at quarter sessions was essential.

Such was the general form and composition of the commission of the peace. The commission was a powerful and potentially very flexible instrument of local government for the king was in theory able to exercise much freedom in deciding when to renew each commission and, within the framework of lords, gentry and lawyers, in the choice and number of J.Ps. appointed. There was no fixed interval between the issue of two commissions. In the West Riding one lasted less than a fortnight, another for more than four years.[15] Although a limit had been imposed during the Cambridge parliament of 1388 on the number of J.Ps. who could be appointed to any one commission, fifteenth-century governments proved adept at ignoring such legislation when it suited them.[16] In the West Riding, the limitation was adhered to only once during the adult reign of Henry IV and not at all after the accession of Edward IV.

It is not possible to give an explanation for every renewal of the West Riding commission. Most likely the date and composition of each were determined by a number of different considerations. A commission could be issued in response to local conditions or as part of the occasional general reviews of the commission of the peace affecting a large number of counties, the motives for which were not always overtly political.[17] The commission was flexible enough to be altered quickly in response to local or national politics but, by the same token, when the government was itself threatened, the commission became susceptible to the politics of faction and dynastic rivalry.

In the absence of surviving records, it is difficult to reconstruct much of the work of the commission.[18] The following account of the West Riding commission between the majority of Henry VI and the death of Henry VII is an attempt to examine those factors that determined appointment to the commission and how these might reflect the attitude of the several governments of the period to the role of the commission in local government, especially in the north of England. With large estates belonging to the duchies of Lancaster and York and the baronial families of Percy, Clifford and Talbot, the West Riding was an area which found it difficult to remain aloof from the severe political and dynastic conflicts of the period. The medieval king was the pivot of government. When the king was absent abroad, or a minor, steps had to be taken to ensure the continued effectiveness of local government, especially of those officers most concerned with the preservation of law and order. During the minority of Henry VI, which lasted fifteen years, a larger number of lords was appointed to the West Riding commission than had been customary in the past, and the major estate officials of the duchy of Lancaster were regularly included. There was no comparable increase in the number of J.Ps. drawn from the local gentry. In November 1439, after the king's majority had been announced, lords composed half the West Riding commission. Four of the nine lords appointed owned large estates in the Riding and two more held major offices within the administration of the duchy of Lancaster.[19]

The duchy of Lancaster was of vital importance in the affairs of the Riding. A third of the Riding was duchy property. In addition to the honours of Pontefract, Knaresborough and Tickhill, there were a number of lesser lordships mostly situated in the central area of the Riding alongthe Aire valley.[20] Since 1399, following the usurpation of the throne by Henry of Bolingbroke, duke of Lancaster, the estates had formed an important, but always separate, part of the property of the king. In 1417, Henry V had invaded France and his absence abroad was expected to be prolonged. This, it seems, had prompted the appointment of the two chief stewards of the duchy to the commissions of the peace for those counties where the larger duchy estates were situated.[21] Roger Flore, chief steward of the duchy north of the Trent, was appointed to the West Riding commission on 8 July 1420, taking the place of John, duke of Bedford, the king's brother, who had joined Henry V in France earlier that year. Flore and his successor, James Tyrell, continued to be appointed to the commission during the minority of Henry V's son. On 23 April 1437 William de la Pole, earl of Suffolk was appointed chief steward north of the Trent and joined the West Riding commission on 18 July that year.[22] Although the holder of this duchy appointment continued to be included in the commission until 1483, Suffolk was the last to join the commission by virtue of securing tenure of this office.

Pontefract was the largest and most valuable of the Yorkshire properties of the duchy. The steward had been a member of the West Riding commission since the renewal of 28 November 1399, the first to be issued after the seizure of the throne by Henry IV. For most of the reign of Henry VI, the stewardship was held by Richard Neville, earl of Salisbury. When granted the office on 30 January 1425, he was already a J.P. for the Riding, having joined the commission on 20 July 1424.[23] The inclusion of the steward of Knaresborough was a direct result of Henry VI's minority. It seems probable that this was part of the effort to maintain the authority of the commission and the duchy while the king was a minor. The two knights who held this office during the minority, Sir Richard Hastings and Sir William Ingleby, both joined the commission. Their appointment set a precedent. Ingleby's successor was Sir William Plumpton, who was granted the office on 9 January 1439.[24] Although the king was no longer a minor, Plumpton joined the commission when this was next renewed on 28 November of that year.

The commission to which Plumpton was appointed in November 1439 was the first to be issued for the Riding after the king took personal control of the government. During his adult reign the total number of lords appointed did not increase but neither did it return to the level of previous reigns. None of the lords appointed during the minority left the commission. There was a steady rise, however, in the number of J.Ps drawn from the local gentry. Their number rose from seven in November 1439 to fourteen in the renewal of 25 June 1456. From 1439 to November 1443 the membership of the *quorum* remained unaltered, but the number of knights and esquires rose from five to nine. After the renewal of 23 November 1443, however, the increase was confined almost entirely to the *quorum*. With the exception of Sir William Plumpton, all those appointed from local gentry families came from the central and south-eastern part of the Riding. This was indeed the area where quarter sessions where usually held, but as a result Plumpton was the only J.P. resident in the north-east of the Riding, the Lords Clifford the only J.Ps. in the north-west, and the Talbots the only J.Ps. in the south-west.[25] This can only have enhanced their influence in these areas. Both Thomas, Lord Clifford (d.1455) and Sir John Talbot (d.1460), later second earl of Shrewsbury, are known to have attended quarter sessions, the former, however, only on the one occasion when the sessions are known to have been held at Skipton, his own property.[26] Sir John Talbot and his younger brother, Sir Christopher, joined the West Riding commission on 4 May 1442. Their appointment at this time was doubtless complementary to the creation of their father as earl of Shrewsbury on 20 May. Although the Talbots were still primarily a Shropshire family, it does seem that both knights were expected to live on the family's properties around Sheffield.[27]

Only in the case of two J.Ps., both members of the *quorum*, can any appointment to the commission between 1437 and the general review of November 1458 be attributed to the influence of a particular magnate or his family. The first instance occurred in 1443. Sir Christopher Talbot died in August of that year. When the commission was next renewed, on 23 November, John Stafford was appointed to the *quorum*. Although the exact relationship is unclear, it seems that he was from the same family as Robert Stafford of Treeton, who by 1435 was a retainer of Sir John Talbot (d.1453), and Henry Stafford who was rector of Treeton and receiver of the Talbot property at Sheffield during the 1440s.[28] Talbot influence on Stafford's appointment seems probable. The second instance concerns Henry Sotehill who, when appointed to the *quorum* of the West Riding commission on 1 June 1454, was already established in the service of the earl of Salisbury and his eldest son, Richard, earl of Warwick.[29] Two of Salisbury's sons, Warwick and Sir John Neville, also joined the commission on 1 June. At this time the Nevilles were in a strong, if delicate, position. As a result of the king's illness, the duke of York had been appointed protector of the realm and Salisbury had accepted the office of chancellor. The following day, on 2 June, a commission of *oyer* and *terminer* was issued to examine the disturbances in Yorkshire during the previous few years. The commission was heavily weighted against the Percies, whose quarrel with Salisbury and his sons had been a root cause of the violence in the county.[30]

Such blatant factional considerations in appointments to the commission of the peace were not typical of the period between 1437 and November 1458. Except in the two instances given, no appointment suggests any interest in the composition of the commission on the part of any magnate. The government's response to the growing violence in Yorkshire, especially in the 1450s, was to increase the number of lawyers appointed to the *quorum*. In the renewal of 4 May 1448, there were six members of the *quorum* of the West Riding commission. By the time of the renewal of 25 June 1456, this figure had risen to eleven. Apparently it was not thought necessary to bolster the authority of the commission by the addition of more of the Riding's leading knights and esquires. A general lack of interest on the part of many of the more important gentry families seems more likely than a policy of exclusion by the government. Ten West Riding knights, for instance, held the office of sheriff or knight of the shire for Yorkshire between 1437 and 1458, but only three joined the commission of the peace: Sir William Plumpton who was steward of Knaresborough, Sir Robert Waterton and Sir Thomas Harington.[31] All three had joined the commission by the renewal of 12 October 1440. Of the eight West Riding esquires who held the office of escheator for the county during the same period, only Nicholas Fitzwilliam joined the commission, being appointed on 16 March 1442. During the next sixteen years, there was only one addition to the commission from amongst the Riding's leading families. John Hastings was an esquire in the royal household when he was appointed to the commission on 4 May 1448.[32] Hastings's appointment at this time was probably prompted by the outbreak of war with Scotland. His rank as an esquire belies his local importance, for he was the eldest son of Edward, Lord Hastings (d. 1438) of Fenwick (West Riding). It seems that during the adult reign of Henry VI, appointment to the commission conferred little additional prestige or authority on those who, by their rank and wealth, were the leaders of their community, and as a result few of these men sought the office. From what can be learnt of the work of the commission in the period up to 1458, it is clear that the bulk was performed, apparently quite adequately, by the members of the *quorum*.[33] This was composed almost exclusively of lawyers, and though most were native to the Riding, they were generally drawn from the families of the lesser gentry.

The government's concern with the exact composition of the commission increased dramatically in November 1458. By this time, the tension between the Lancastrian government and the 'Yorkist' lords was undisguised and near to breaking-point. In November, the commissions of the peace for fifteen counties in all parts of England were reviewed. Although there is no obvious common denominator between the counties concerned, each underwent a reduction in the number of J.Ps. appointed.[34] In the West Riding, the number of J.Ps. drawn from the local gentry was reduced from fourteen to six. This was the first renewal to be made during Henry VI's adult reign in which J.Ps. were dismissed from office. Since 1437 mortality had accounted for every departure from the West Riding commission. Sir John Neville was amongst those dismissed, but this was not simply a purge of potential supporters of the duke of York and the Neville earls. The six who remained in office included Sir Thomas Harington and Henry Sotehill, both closely and openly connected with the duke and the earls by this date. Perhaps their retention was a calculated attempt to prove that the Lancastrian government was not trying to undermine the position of those associated with its opponents. The bench was not yet an instrument in the politics of faction. The government's main intention was to retain the most notable of the knights and esquires and the most experienced of the members of the *quorum*.[35] There were no new appointments. On 29 August 1459 all six local J.Ps. were commissioned to inquire into the 'opprobious words' spoken against the king's person by Henry Walron, who was bailiff of the earl of Warwick's lordship of Bawtry in the West Riding.[36]

The attitude of the Lancastrian government towards the commission of the peace altered after the armed hostilities at Blore Heath and Ludford and the attainders, in November 1459, of the 'Yorkist' lords and a number of their supporters. The West Riding commission was renewed on 8 December, to take account of the attainders of the duke of York, the earls of Salisbury and Warwick, and Sir Thomas Harington. Sotehill, though not attainted, was also dismissed, his place in the *quorum* being taken by William Bradford, who was then clerk of the pleas in the county palatine of Lancashire. No additions were made to the lords to compensate for the removal of the 'Yorkists', but two members of the West Riding gentry, Sir John Tempest and William Gascoigne, joined the commission. Sir John and his eldest son, Richard, had been annuitants of the second earl of Northumberland (d. 1455).[37] Although there is no definite evidence that the annuities were continued by the third earl, this seems likely. Richard Tempest and William Gascoigne were both knighted after the battle of Wakefield on 30 December 1460 when York and Salisbury were killed.[38] All those appointed to the West Riding commission on 8 December 1459 were included in the commission of array issued for the Riding on 21 December against the 'Yorkists'.[39]

When the commission of the peace was next renewed, on 23 August 1460, Henry VI was still king but the central offices of government were under the control of Salisbury and Warwick. The duke of York had not yet returned from Ireland. A younger son of the earl of Salisbury, George Neville, bishop of Exeter, was chancellor. The aims of the earls in renewing the commission were principally to secure the restoration of those attainted in the previous year and to remove those too closely connected with the Lancastrian cause; Tempest, Gascoigne and Sir William Plumpton. Little else could be attempted realistically, for the Lancastrians were mustering in the East Riding and the castle of Pontefract, of which Salisbury was constable, was in the hands of the earl of Northumberland.[40] This was the last commission of the peace to be issued for the West Riding before the deposition of Henry VI in March 1461. There is no clear evidence to show whether the commission as such was employed to further the interests of the Nevilles or of the duke of York in the period before the accession of the duke's son as Edward IV, although at such a time and in such an area it is hard to believe that its activities were not dictated by political considerations.

The commission of 23 August formed the basis of the first commissions of Edward IV's reign. With the exception of Sir Thomas Harington, who had been killed at the battle of Wakefield, all the J.P.s drawn from local families were re-appointed during 1461. In addition, on 28 May three of the esquires who had been dismissed in November 1458 were restored.[41] None is known to have been prominent in the service of either the Nevilles or the duke of York during the civil war of 1459–61, but their past experience in office must have counted in their favour at a time when the Riding was unsettled. Edward IV probably also wished to avoid the appearance of relying on the support only of his father's or Warwick's men. The influence of the earl of Warwick, however, could not be ignored. Two new appointments were made on 28 May. Although both can be associated with the Neville family, their appointment shows how weak the position of the earl was in the West Riding itself. Sir James Strangeways was a prominent North Riding retainer of the earl of Warwick and was to be elected speaker during the first parliament of the reign.[42] William Scargill was the son of an esquire, with property in the North and West Ridings, who had served the earl of Salisbury. William Scargill the elder had died in May 1459. The son had been included in a commission of 14 October 1460 which was intended to prevent the Lancastrians mustering in Pontefract.[43] Despite his appointment to the commission of the peace, the younger William Scargill is not known to have served the earl of Warwick during Edward IV's first reign.

The forfeited property of John, Lord Clifford, who was attainted during the first parliament of the reign, was granted on 1 February 1462 to Sir William Stanley.[44] On 12 October of that year, Stanley joined the West Riding commission of the peace. There is no evidence to suggest how effective Stanley proved in office. That he owed his appointment solely to his position as lord of Skipton is shown by his departure from the commission when he surrendered the lordship to the king's brother, Richard, duke of Gloucester, in 1475.[45] Stanley was the only J.P. appointed for the Riding as a direct result of the attainders of prominent Lancastrians in 1461.

During the first eight years of Edward IV's reign, the numbers of J.P.s rose from seventeen to thirty. There were several reasons for this increase. From the renewal of 12 October 1462, the king began to appoint members of the royal household and servants of the duchy of York. On 12 October Richard Fitzwilliam joined the commission. He had been granted an annuity of twenty marks by the duke of York in November 1460 and this had been confirmed by Edward IV on 10 July 1461.[46] In March 1465, he joined his father as constable of Conisborough.[47] It is not known when he joined the household, but he was a king's knight by 25 January 1470.[48] John Pilkington was an esquire from the duchy of York lordship of Wakefield. He had been an esquire of the body since 7 July 1461 and joined the West Riding commission of the peace on 8 July 1464.[49] On 8 May 1467 Sir John Saville was appointed to the commission with his younger son William, who was a lawyer and joined the *quorum*. Sir John was steward of Wakefield, an office which he had held since 1442.[50] The following month, on 27 June 1467, John Fitzwilliam was added to the commission. He had been an esquire of the king's household since Michaelmas 1466 at least.[51] The appointments of 1467 may have been a result of the widening breach between the king and the earl of Warwick, but more probably they were caused by circumstances within the Riding. By 1467 there had been a great increase in disturbances throughout the country.[52] A notable example in the West Riding was the outbreak of violence in the long-running dispute regarding the payment of thraves of corn to the hospital of St. Leonard's York. This had been brought to the attention of the king's council by June 1467.[53] Such violence would explain why there were three renewals of the commission that year. As in the 1450s, the government's response to violence was to increase the number of men with a formal legal training appointed to the *quorum*. In the commissions of 5 January 1466 and 8 May 1467, the *quorum* was increased from seven members to twelve (including the justices of assize). Three of the five new members had definitely had a formal training in the law.[54]

The growing hostility of the earl of Warwick, combined with the duplicity of the king's brother, George, duke of Clarence, resulted in rebellion and, in September 1470, in the flight of the king from England. For the next six months the earl of Warwick was in uneasy charge of a government ruling in the name of Henry VI. The commissions of the peace were reviewed in November and, as in November 1458, there was a general decrease in the number of J.Ps. appointed. In the West Riding commission, which was renewed on 19 November, the number was reduced from twenty-nine to fourteen. Predictably, all those who were too closely associated with Edward IV, were dismissed, that is, the members of the royal household and the servants of the duchy of York. Sir William Stanley, who lost the lordship of Skipton at this time, was also removed from office.[55] Similarly dismissed were Sir James Strangeways and William Scargill. The commission was in effect stripped of all political nominees. Four were removed from the *quorum* but one, Brian Roucliff, was replaced by his own son and there is no reason to believe that any of the other three, with the possible exception of William Saville, was mistrusted by Warwick. The members who retained their appointment were those with most experience in the law. Of the fourteen J.Ps., therefore, no fewer than eight were lawyers appointed to the *quorum*. The composition of the commission reflected the failure of the earl of Warwick to create a coherent affinity in the West Riding during the previous ten years. This was despite the monopoly of the major offices in the administration of the duchy of Lancaster enjoyed by the earl and by his brother, John, Marquis Montagu.[56]

Edward IV returned from exile in March 1471 and regained the throne through his victories at the battles of Barnet and Tewkesbury on 14 April and 4 May respectively. The first few months after the king's return were spent in removing from office those too closely identified with Warwick and in distributing the considerable patronage freed by his death and by that of Marquis Montagu. The West Riding commission of the peace appointed during the Readeption proved sufficiently acceptable to be allowed to remain in force until

February 1472. From this time, appointments to the commission suggest a far greater concern with its exact composition.

The vacuum created by the deaths of the earl of Warwick and Marquis Montagu in the government of the north of England was filled by the king's brother, the duke of Gloucester, and by Henry Percy, fourth earl of Northumberland, who had been restored to his father's lands and title in March 1470. Both lords joined the commission for the West Riding on 24 February 1472. This was also the first commission to which the young earl of Shrewsbury was appointed. He died, however, only eight months later.[57] Sir William Stanley, who was again in possession of Skipton lordship, was restored to the commission in February, as were the more prominent of the king's supporters from amongst the local gentry: Sir John Saville, Sir Richard Fitzwilliam and Sir John Pilkington. Fitzwilliam and Pilkington were knights in the king's household.[58] In all, eight of the fifteen dismissed in November 1470, were reappointed. The practice of appointing the stewards of Pontefract and Knaresborough to the commission was continued. Sir James Harington had been granted the office of steward of Pontefract on 17 July 1471.[59] The earl of Northumberland had been appointed steward and constable of Knaresborough on 28 June of that year and named William Gascoigne as his deputy.[60] Both Harington and Gascoigne joined the commission on 24 February.

It is probable that the timing and composition of this commission was determined by preparations for the war against France. The commission of array issued for the Riding a fortnight later on 7 March, in connection with these preparations, was composed of all the J.Ps. appointed on 24 February with the exception of the *quorum*.[61] This would explain the addition to the commission of the peace of two other leading knights from the Riding, Sir William Plumpton and Sir Hugh Hastings. Plumpton was returning to the commission after an absence of twelve years, having finally made his peace with the Yorkist dynasty. Hastings, who was to represent the county in the parliament which assembled later in 1472, was the grandson of Edward, Lord Hastings of Fenwick.

After much delay, the expedition against France took place in the summer of 1475, but no blood was shed. In November of that year, when the king and his army had returned, the commissions of the peace throughout England were reviewed.[62] There was a general reduction in the number of J.Ps. appointed. The West Riding commission, which was renewed on 10 November, was reduced from twenty-three J.Ps. to sixteen. There is no evidence that any of those who left the commission had incurred the king's displeasure. Stanley, for instance, was no longer at Skipton and Harington had been appointed sheriff of Yorkshire on 5 November. Plumpton, Hastings, Saville and Gascoigne were also dismissed. The removal of these men would seem to be part of a general policy rather than a reflection on their capabilities as J.Ps. The only knights to retain their appointment were the two knights of the royal household, Sir Richard Fitzwilliam and Sir John Pilkington.

Four of those removed from the commission on 10 November 1475 were restored during the next six years. Plumpton was the first to be re-appointed, and he owed his restoration on 6 December 1476 to the good offices of the earl of Northumberland.[63] Gascoigne was the last, re-joining the commission on 14 August 1481. This renewal was issued at a time of war with Scotland which would explain why the four men who now joined the commission were all constables of particular castles in Yorkshire. Gascoigne was the earl of Northumberland's deputy at Knaresborough. Sir John Neville (of Liversedge) had been appointed constable of Pontefract on 26 July 1471.[64] Sir Robert Rither had been granted the office of constable of York castle on 18 November 1478.[65] Thomas Fitzwilliam had succeeded his father as constable of Conisborough and Tickhill, Sir Richard Fitzwilliam having died in 1478. The commission of 14 August remained in force for the rest of Edward IV's reign.

The return of members of the royal household and officers of the duchy of York in February 1472 had ensured a measure of continuity between the commissions of the 1460s and those of the 1470s. Apart from the restoration of Sir William Plumpton in December 1476, the influence of the earl of Northumberland and the duke of Gloucester was generally indirect, although it is hard to believe that the king did not take heed of their opinions. Sir John Pilkington, a knight of the body, became a member of Gloucester's affinity but did not owe his appointment as a J.P. to the duke's influence. It is quite possible that Sir James Harington and Sir John Neville were granted the offices of steward and constable of Pontefract in July 1471 on the duke's recommendation. Gloucester was then chief steward of the duchy of Lancaster.[66] It was their tenure of these offices, however, rather than the duke's direct persuasion, which secured their appointment to the commission in 1471 and 1481 respectively. The increased involvement of the more notable of the local gentry families in appointments to the commission of the peace was not peculiar to the West Riding.[67] The majority of knights and esquires included in the West Riding commission during Edward IV's second reign were holders of office within the administration of the duchies of York or Lancaster. Only after 1472 were the major offices of the duchy of Lancaster in the Riding mainly in the hands of the local gentry. In the 1460s these offices had been monopolised by the earl of Warwick and Marquis Montagu. They had appointed lawyers and lesser esquires as their deputies, of whom only Henry Sotehill had joined the commission.

Although the number of knights and esquires appointed to the commission varied considerably between 1471 and Edward IV's death in 1483, the size and composition of the *quorum* remained substantially unaltered. On 24 February 1472, two of the eight named in the *quorum* during the Readeption were dismissed, but the size of the *quorum* remained the same by the restoration of Brian Roucliff and William Saville. When Robert Gascoigne died in 1473, he was succeeded by Thomas Middleton, a lawyer in the service of both the earl of Northumberland and the duke of Gloucester. When William Bradford died in

1476, his place was taken by his own son, John Bradford. The only other alteration in the composition of the *quorum* between 1471 and 1483 concerned Henry Sotehill, who left the commission on 10 November 1475.

The West Riding commission was renewed three times in 1483: on 14 May, when the duke of Gloucester was declared protector of the realm during the minority of Edward V; on 26 June, when the duke seized the throne; and on 5 December as part of a general review of the commissions of the peace in England after the rebellion in the south that autumn. The commissions of the peace for the North and East Ridings were renewed on the same three dates, and there was a similarity in the appointments made to each commission.

The renewals of 14 May seem to have been an attempt by the duke to secure commissions of the peace in Yorkshire favourable to his interest. Since 1471, the territorial basis of his power in the north had been the north Yorkshire estates which had once been the property of the earl of Warwick.[68] Yorkshire was the county where the duke should have felt his position to be most secure, but the dates and composition of the commissions suggest that he was uncertain even here.[69] Three lords who were closely identified with the duke during the period in which he was protector were added to the Yorkshire commissions in May and June. On 14 May, Henry Stafford, duke of Buckingham joined all three commissions. At the same time, Richard, Lord FitzHugh, who had been a J.P. for the East Riding since 3 February 1482, joined those for the North and West Riding. John, Lord Howard was included in the commissions for each Riding from 26 June, the day on which he was created duke of Norfolk. The two new appointments of members of the local gentry made to the West Riding commission on 14 May were of men whom the duke apparently felt able to trust. Edward Redman was a lawyer in the duke's service and he joined the *quorum*. Sir Thomas Wortley had served in Edward IV's household and remained in the household during Richard III's reign. Wortley's departure from the commission seven months later, on 5 December, arose from the king's decision to employ him in important office outside Yorkshire. In particular, on 5 November, he had been appointed sheriff of Staffordshire.

Between May and December 1483, four of the seven knights who had served on the West Riding commission during the latter part of Edward IV's reign were removed from office. In May Sir Henry Vavasour and Sir Robert Rither were dismissed. It is probable that Gloucester felt unable to trust them. Neither was much employed by him when he was king, and Rither's return to the commission a month after Henry VII's victory at Bosworth on 22 August 1485 suggests that his departure in May 1483 had not been entirely voluntary. By contrast, the two knights who left the commisssion on 5 December were members of the royal household. Sir John Neville, constable of Pontefract and appointed a J.P. during the war with Scotland, could apparently be released from office now that the war was ended. Hastings, like Wortley, was employed in the local government of another county. In this case, the county concerned was Norfolk, where the Hastings family had held property since the beginning of the fourteenth century.

The renewals of the Yorkshire commissions on 5 December were, in part, influenced by the preparations for the establishment of a council in the north, and this may to some extent also account for the removal of Hastings, Neville and Wortley from the West Riding commission. Ordinances regarding the work of the council were issued in July 1484.[70] The council was to be concerned mainly with the government of Yorkshire and must in some measure have superseded the work of the commission of the peace in the county. It was a court with both civil and criminal jurisdiction.[71] The ordinances make it clear that the members of the council were, in part, to be drawn from the commissions of the peace. No 'mater of gret weght' was to be determined without the presence of members who were also J.Ps. As with quarter sessions, meetings were to be held every three months, although it was expected that all members of the council would attend each meeting if at all possible. The sessions were always to be held at York. Except in the case of a few lords, the identity of the councillors is unknown but Dr. Reid believed that Sir Richard Radcliff and John Dawney were probably among them.[72] Radcliff's appointment to all three Yorkshire commissions of 5 December would tend to support this, and the similar appointment of Sir Gervaise Clifton suggests that he too may have been a member. Both were prominent in Richard III's service. Radcliff was also steward of the lordship of Wakefield (in the duchy of York) and Clifton steward of the honour of Tickhill (in the duchy of Lancaster). The four stewards and one deputy steward of the major local estates of both duchies were now the only J.Ps. for the Riding drawn from the gentry[73] (apart, that is, from the lawyers appointed to the *quorum*). John Dawney joined the commission on 5 February 1485 at the same time as John de la Pole, earl of Lincoln, the king's nephew and head of the council. Lincoln's household, of which Dawney was treasurer, had been established at Sandal in the lordship of Wakefield.

As a result of Henry VII's seizure of the throne, the council ceased to exist in the form in which it had been constituted by Richard III.[74] For many years, the new king's régime remained open to challenge. In the first few years of the reign, until his authority became more firmly established, Henry VII relied on only a few of the lords and gentry of Yorkshire to perform the work of the commission of the peace. This was in part the result of the particular hostility of Yorkshire to the new régime. The commissions of the peace for each Riding were again considered quite separately. The first commission of the reign for the West Riding was issued on 22 September 1485, a month after Henry VII's victory at Bosworth. The quality and experience in office of the membership would have given the commission credibility, although it is impossible to say how effective it proved. In the appointment of lords and the members of the *quorum*, there was a measure of continuity between this and the last commission issued during Richard III's reign in February 1485. Ralph, Lord Greystoke, a J.P. for each

Riding since 1461, was re-appointed. So too was Richard, Lord FitzHugh, who had owed his initial appointment in May 1483 to support for the duke of Gloucester but who was now active in the service of Henry VII. They were the only lay lords appointed to the commission during the first year of Henry VII's reign. Until December 1485, Henry, fourth earl of Northumberland was in custody in the Tower. Like other kings before him, however, Henry VII found that the north of England was a difficult area to control without the support of the Percies, and Northumberland was restored to the three commissions of the peace in Yorkshire during November 1486. Appointed with him was George, fourth earl of Shrewsbury, who was declared of age on 7 November of that year.[75] Henry, Lord Clifford was not included in the West Riding commission until the renewal of 8 May 1496, and he probably owed his appointment then to renewed war with Scotland. He was the son of John, Lord Clifford, who had been attainted in 1461. The influence of his father and grandfather, Thomas, Lord Clifford (d.1455), had been confined almost entirely to the north-west of the Riding, although here he had been pre-eminent. As a result of the family's misfortunes in the civil wars, they had few, if any associates in the Riding by 1485. Henry, Lord Clifford was restored promptly enough to his father's lands and title in 1485, but he had little influence in the Riding at that date. This could explain why he was omitted from the commission of the peace for so long, but Henry VII seems never to have fully trusted him.[76]

The commission of 22 September marked the return of Sir Robert Rither and Sir Hugh Hastings and the first appointment of Sir John Saville, whose grandfather had been a J.P. for the Riding between 1467 and 1475. The few members of the West Riding gentry who were prepared to support Henry VII actively in the early years of his reign were given much work. On 25 September 1485, Rither, Hastings and Saville were appointed to the commission of array for Yorkshire which was issued to counter the threat from Scotland.[77] The previous day, Rither and Hastings had been commissioned to distribute the king's pardon in the northern counties.[78] On 5 November, Saville was appointed sheriff of Yorkshire and, in November 1486, he was succeeded by Rither.

Sir John Saville and Sir John Everingham were the only J.Ps. appointed in September 1485 who had not served on the commission before. Everingham, like Hastings, had been a knight in Richard III's household.[79] Sir John Saville seems to have been dissatisfied with his treatment by Richard III. In 1480 he had succeeded his grandfather as steward of Wakefield, an office which the latter had held for almost thirty-eight years.[80] In February 1484, Saville was appointed captain of the Isle of Wight.[81] This, however, was an office which he was not permitted to exercise through a deputy and, probably because of this, he was removed from the stewardship of Wakefield in November 1484 in favour of Sir Richard Radcliff. The likelihood that he may have resented the move south and the loss of the stewardship is suggested by the terms of a bond in which he had to pledge his future 'good and true behaviour' as captain and by his swift and active support for Henry VII.[82] By November 1485, Saville was a knight of the body in the king's household and within a few months of Henry VII's accession was also restored to the stewardship of Wakefield.[83]

At the beginning of his reign, Henry VII did not make the customary appointment to the commission of the steward of Pontefract. This was despite a close family connection with George, Lord Strange, to whom Henry VII granted the office on 21 September 1485.[84] Strange was the eldest son of Thomas, Lord Stanley, the king's stepfather.[85] The following year, on 12 September 1486, Strange was replaced as steward by Sir Richard Tunstall, a member of the king's household.[86] Tunstall did not join the commission until the renewal of 4 June 1489, which was prompted by the murder of the earl of Northumberland a few weeks before on 28 April.

There was little change in the selection of local gentry appointed to the West Riding commission between September 1485 and June 1489. There was, however, an increase in the membership of the *quorum*. The justices of assize, who had been omitted from the commission of 22 September, were restored in the second renewal of the reign which was issued before 21 August 1486.[87] Two other lawyers had been added to the *quorum* by June 1489, at least one of whom, William Saville, had previously served on the bench.[88] From the renewal of 4 June 1489, there was a marked increase in the involvement of the royal household in appointments to the commission, including the *quorum*. On 4 June, Sir Thomas Fitzwilliam, a king's knight, and Brian Sandford, an esquire of the body, were added to the *quorum*. This was Sandford's first appointment, but Fitzwilliam had been a J.P. for the Riding since the renewal of 14 August 1481.[89] The commissions of the peace of all three Ridings were renewed on 22 October 1489. Sir Henry Wentworth was added to each commission and was the only new appointment to that of the West Riding. Like Tunstall, who had joined the commission in June, Wentworth was a knight of the body and a member of the king's council. On 24 June Wentworth had also replaced the earl of Northumberland as steward of Knaresborough.[90] As a result of these additions the West Riding commission of the peace was composed of a *quorum* of ten members, two of whom were in the royal household, and four other knights, all of whom were in the king's household. The lords appointed to the commission were the two archbishops and George, earl of Shrewsbury, the only lay lord included.[91] Henry VII was sufficiently satisfied with its composition for the commission of 22 October 1489 to remain in force for almost four years.

The character of these appointments suggests little immediate connection with the decision made, following the death of the earl of Northumberland, to establish Thomas Howard, earl of Surrey as the king's lieutenant in the north. Although the earl of Surrey joined the East Riding commission on 22 October 1489, he was not appointed to those of the North and West Ridings until 20 May 1493 when there was a general review of the commissions of the peace in response to the threat of an invasion in support of the pretender, Perkin

Warbeck. The earl is known to have attended quarter sessions for the West Riding on 27 March 1496, when the indictments considered were especially serious.[92] His administration, which was based in the East Riding, affected the membership of the commissions of the peace in all the northern counties. Sir John Cheyne and Sir Richard Pole, neither of whom was native to Yorkshire, joined the West Riding commission with the earl of Surrey on 20 May 1493.[93] Richard Cholmley joined the West Riding commission on 8 May 1496, as did William Senhouse, abbot of St. Mary's York, who is known to have worked with the earl.[94] Cholmley was then treasurer and lieutenant of Berwick, and revenue for the defence of the town was drawn from a large number of northern estates in the king's hands, including the West Riding property of the duchy of York. On 13 November 1500 Cholmley was appointed surveyor-general of these estates.[95] The tenure of these offices would explain why, unlike Cheyne and Pole, he retained his appointment as a J.P. after the departure of Surrey from the north in 1499. Brian Sandford, appointed to the *quorum* on 4 June 1489, was removed from the *quorum* but not the commission on 26 February 1501, at the time of the first renewal of the commission following Surrey's departure. Sir Thomas Fitzwilliam had remained a member of the *quorum* until his death in 1498.

The West Riding commission of 22 October 1489 had lasted for almost four years. That of 20 May 1493 remained in force for three years. From 1496 an increasing number of local gentry were appointed to the commission. Amongst these were members of the royal household such as Sir Thomas Wortley, Sir Thomas Darcy, later Lord Darcy, and Sir Thomas Tempest, all of whom were knights of the body at the time of their appointment. After the earl of Surrey's departure in 1499, however, the most notable development in appointments to the commission was the inclusion of a number of knights and lawyers from one particular part of the Riding, the area around Wakefield. Sir John Saville had been a J.P. since 1485. On 26 February 1501 he was joined by Sir William Calverley, whose estates lay just north of Wakefield, and by two lawyers from that area, Thomas Grice and William Amyas. With their appointment, three of the four lawyers named in the *quorum* who were native to the Riding were from Wakefield. During 1502 Saville's neighbours, Sir John Neville and Sir William Mirfield, joined the commission. On 26 June, a month before his appointment to the commission, Neville had replaced Saville as steward of Wakefield.[96] The appointment of these men, within two years of Surrey's departure, suggests a deliberate attempt by the government to concentrate the administration of the Riding in one area. By the reign of Henry VIII, Wakefield was becoming 'something of an administrative capital for the Riding.'[97]

Any conclusions suggested by the study of the appointments made to the commission of the peace for one particular area must be tentative, since so little is known of the actual work and effectiveness of the commission during the fifteenth century. Throughout the entire period under study, there was only one renewal of the West Riding commission, that of 17 February 1485, in which no alteration was made in the personnel appointed. The Yorkist dynasty showed the most frequent concern for the composition of the West Riding commission. There were twice as many renewals during the period of Yorkist rule as during the comparable periods of the adult reign of Henry VI and the reign of Henry VII.[98] There was, however, little variation in the total number of gentry families involved in appointments to the commission during each of these three periods.[99] After 1471, the families involved were generally of a higher social standing and of greater wealth. The leading knights of the Riding were primarily interested in securing appointment as sheriff of Yorkshire or election as knight of the shire for the county. Between 1437 and 1471, fourteen West Riding knights held these offices; four held both. Seven joined the commission of the peace. Between 1471 and 1509, however, of the twelve knights from the Riding known to have held these offices, ten were appointed to the commission.[100] The increased involvement of the leading families was not peculiar to the West Riding and was the result of deliberate policy on the part of Edward IV and his successors. By the end of Edward IV's reign, the J.Ps. drawn from the local gentry, and not of the *quorum*, were mostly the major estate officials of the duchies of York and Lancaster. Only after the death of Warwick and Montagu in 1471 were the chief offices of the duchy of Lancaster held mainly by the gentry. Richard III reduced the number of gentry appointed to the commission until, by the renewal of 5 December 1483, the only J.Ps. apart from the *quorum* were the stewards of the two duchies. During the reign of Henry VII, the stewards continued to form an important part of the membership of the commission, especially after the appointment of Tunstall and Wentworth in 1489.

The magnates generally seem to have had little direct influence on appointments to the commission. The increasing involvement of the royal household, however, was a major development of the period. Of the gentry appointed during the adult reign of Henry VI, only John Hastings had been a member of the royal household, and he does not appear to have owed his appointment to the commission to his position as a king's esquire. Edward IV began to include men whose first allegiance was to the house of York, especially when he was faced with continued resistance in the north and with the widening breach between himself and the earl of Warwick. He maintained this factional policy even after 1471. In November 1475, the two knights of the king's household were the only knights to retain their appointment. Four of the five knights appointed on 5 December 1483 were certainly members of Richard III's household. During the first fifteen years of Henry VII's reign, members of the royal household were prominent in appointments to the commissions of the peace in Yorkshire, as also to other major offices of county government. The inclusion in the *quorum* of two members of the royal household from 1489 was conterminous with the ten-year lieutenancy of the earl of Surrey. During this decade, as in the reign of Richard III, appointments to the commission were determined by the king's policy towards the government of the north of

England, rather than by purely local considerations, and this resulted in the inclusion of men with little personal interest in the Riding or even in Yorkshire. From the late 1490s, and especially during 1501 and 1502, there was a greater willingness to appoint members of the local gentry who were not necessarily holders of local office or members of the royal household. This must have been deliberate policy, since most were drawn from one area of the Riding. There was little substantial alteration in the composition of the commission during the remainder of the reign. For the last ten years of Henry VII's reign, therefore, the commission was again mostly in the hands of local gentry.

Notes

1. For a full discussion of the duties of the commission of the peace, see B.H. Putnam, 'The Transformation of the Keepers of the Peace into the Justices of the Peace, 1327–1380', *TRHS*, fourth series, XI (1929), 19–48; *idem, Proceedings before the Justices of the Peace in the Fourteenth and Fifteenth Centuries* (London, 1938), pp. xix–xxxiv; R.Sillem, 'Commissions of the Peace, 1380–1485', *BIHR*, X (1932), 81–104.
2. The right to exclude the sheriff was the essence of this franchise: M.T. Clanchy, 'The Franchise of Return of Writs', *TRHS*, fifth series, XVII (1967), 64. In the West Riding these estates included all the property of the duchy of Lancaster, the lordship of Wakefield which was part of the duchy of York, and, from July 1442, all the estates of the archbishopric of York.
3. J.Ps. of the West Riding were commissioned to assist in raising loans for the king on 19 March 1439 and 30 March 1442: *CPR, 1436–41*, p. 250; *1441–46*, p. 61. J.Ps. were responsible with the sheriff for holding inquisitions to determine who was liable to pay the subsidy on aliens. Some of these inquisitions survive among the exchequer records (PRO, E179). J.Ps. were also involved in the collection of the graduated tax voted in 1449 (*CPR, 1446–52*, p. 169). If the normal methods of collecting lay subsidies proved inadequate, the J.Ps. might be commissioned to take the responsibility for collection, for instance on 1 August 1483 and 21 January 1489 (*CPR, 1476–85*, p. 394; *1485–94*, p. 242).
4. This power was first granted in 1484 (*SR*, II, pp. 478,512).
5. B.H. Putnam, *Proceedings*, p. liv.
6. *Ibid.*, p. xxviii.
7. John Kemp, archbishop of York, joined the West Riding commission on 7 November 1431. It became the usual practice thereafter to include the current archbishop.
8. R.L. Storey, 'Liveries and Commissions of the Peace, 1388–1390', in *The Reign of Richard II: Essays in honour of May McKisack*, ed. F.R.H. Du Boulay and C.M. Barron (London, 1971), p. 150.
9. B.H. Putnam, *Proceedings*, p. lxxix.
10. *Plumpton Correspondence*, ed. T. Stapleton (Camden Society, IV, 1839), p. 33.
11. The only certain evidence of this is the removal of the sheriff in a renewal of the commission issued during his year of office. Of the nine J.Ps. of the West Riding who were selected as sheriff of Yorkshire between 1461 and 1509, five were excluded from commissions issued during their year in office. All were re-appointed to the commission. The change after 1461 may be a result of legislation passed during the first parliament of Edward IV's reign, which removed from the sheriff the power to proceed to any further process on indictments presented at the tourns and required him to forward these to the J.Ps.
12. B.H. Putnam, *Proceedings*, p. lxxxi.
13. *Ibid.*, p. xxv.
14. *Ibid.*, p. lxxxvii.
15. The shortest interval between renewals of the West Riding commission was 22 November and 6 December 1476. The longest was that between 23 November 1443 and 4 May 1448.
16. R.L. Storey, 'Liveries and Commissions of the Peace', p. 139. Two knights were to be appointed with the two justices of assize and no more than four others.
17. *Ibid.*, p. 138.
18. There are few extant records of the proceedings of quarter sessions held in any county during the fifteenth century. There are none for the West Riding for the period between 1392 and 1597. Some indication of the work of the commission and of individual J.Ps. can be gathered from the records of gaol deliveries, of the assizes, and of the central courts, especially king's bench and chancery. Fragments of information regarding the attendance of individual J.Ps. at

quarter sessions can be gathered from indentures for the payment of their wages. From 1388, J.Ps. had been entitled to 4s. for each day's attendance. As the sheriff was responsible for the payments, references to these occur, though not with any consistency, on the pipe rolls. A few of the original indentures can be found in PRO, E101. As only those of the rank of knight and below were allowed a wage, these indentures give no indication of the attendance of lords.

19. The four with major estates in the Riding were Richard, duke of York; Henry Percy, second earl of Northumberland; Thomas, Lord Clifford; and the archbishop of York. William de la Pole, earl of Suffolk was chief steward of the duchy of Lancaster north of Trent and Richard Neville, earl of Salisbury was steward of Pontefract. The remaining three lords were Humphrey, earl of Stafford, Ralph, Lord Cromwell and John, Lord Scrope of Masham.

20. The honour of Tickhill was of least importance in the history of the riding as most of the estates lay in the neighbouring county of Nottingham.

21. The chief stewards, Roger Flore and Walter Hungerford, were appointed to the commissions of the peace for certain counties from November 1417.

22. R. Someville, *History of the Duchy of Lancaster*, I (London, 1953), p. 240.

23. *Ibid.*, p. 513.

24. *Ibid.*, p. 524.

25. Quarter sessions in the West Riding during this period were held at Leeds, Pontefract, Doncaster, Wetherby, Wentbridge, Tadcaster, Selby and Skipton.

26. PRO, E101/598/42; 614/44.

27. On 27 November 1442, Sir Christopher was granted the office of bailiff of Staincross, the area north of Sheffield: PRO, DL37/10/5. On 12 February 1443, Sir John secured the farm of the manor of Laverton for a period of seven years, his brother acting as a mainpernor (*CFR, 1437–45*, p. 252). Sir John's will was written at Sheffield on 8 September 1446 (*Testamenta Eboracensia*, ed. J. Raine, II [Surtees Society, XXX, 1855], pp. 252 4).

28. A.J. Pollard, *John Talbot and the War in France, 1427–1453* (Royal Historical Society, 1983), p. 89.

29. Somerville, *Duchy of Lancaster*, I, p. 425.

30. R.A. Griffiths, 'Local Rivalries and National Politics: the Percises, the Nevilles, and the Duke of Exeter, 1452–55', *Speculum*, XLIII (1968), 589–632.

31. Waterton joined the commission on 8 November 1436. Thomas Harington was the eldest son of Sir William Harington of Hornby (Lancashire) and Brierley (West Riding). Sir William had been a J.P. for the Riding continuously from 20 July 1424 until his death in February 1440. The renewal of 12 October 1440, when Thomas Harington joined the commission, was the first to be issued after Sir William's death.

32. Hastings had joined the royal household by Michaelmas 1441 (PRO, E101/409/9 f. 36v). He was still in the king's household in 1451 (PRO, E101/410/6 f. 39).

33. This is clear from the indentures for the payment of wages (which specify the number of days within a given period when each J.P. attended quarter sessions); from the surviving inquisitions concerning the assessments for the alien subsidy; and from appointments to various *ad hoc* commissions issued for the Riding.

34. See, for instance, S.M. Wright, 'A Gentry Society of the Fifteenth Century; Derbyshire, *c.* 1430–1509' (Birmingham Ph.D. thesis, 1978), p. 150.

35. Those who retained their appointments were Sir William Plumpton, Sir Thomas Harington, John Hastings and, of the *quorum*, Henry Sotehill, Guy Fairfax and John Thwaites. This was the one commission issued during the period 1437–1509 which adhered to the limit fixed during the parliament of 1388.

36. CPR, *1452–61*, p. 518.

37. Sir John was in receipt of £6 13s. 4d, and his son Richard in receipt of £5, by Michaelmas 1443 (Petworth House Archives, MAC D 9/3).

38. W.A. Shaw, *The Knights of England*, II (London, 1906), p. 12.

39. *CPR, 1452–61*, p. 559.
40. The earl was ordered to leave Pontefract on 24 August (*CPR, 1451–61*, p. 610).
41. Edmund Fitzwilliam, Percival Cresacre and Nicholas Fitzwilliam. Edmund Fitzwilliam was constable of the duchy of York castle at Conisborough, but as this was an office previously held by both his father and grandfather, his tenure of the constableship cannot be taken as evidence of strong personal loyalty towards Richard, duke of York or his eldest son (F.M. Wright, 'The House of York 1415–1450' [Johns Hopkins Ph.D. thesis, 1959], p. 42).
42. J.S. Roskell, 'Sir James Strangeways of West Harlsey and Whorlton: Speaker in the Parliament of 1461', *Yorkshire Archaeological Journal*, XXXIX (1956–58), 455.
43. *CPR, 1452–61*, p. 651.
44. *CPR, 1461–67*, p. 115.
45. *CPR, 1467–77*, p. 549.
46. *CPR, 1461–67*, p. 49.
47. *Ibid.*, p. 479.
48. *CPR, 1467–77*, p. 111.
49. *CCR, 1461–68*, p. 20.
50. Yorkshire Archaeological Society, Wakefield Court Rolls, MD 225.
51. PRO, E101/410/9 f.36.
52. C.D. Ross, *Edward IV* (London, 1974), p. 119.
53. *CCR, 1461–68*, p. 452.
54. William Copley was a member of the Middle Temple; Robert Gascoigne a member of Lincoln's Inn; and William Saville a member of Gray's Inn.
55. On 28 January 1471, the property of John, Lord Clifford was granted to John, Marquis Montagu during the minority of Clifford's son, Henry (*CFR, 1461–71*, p. 291). The terms of the grant help to confirm the opinion that the attainders of 1461 were reversed during the Readeption.
56. The earl of Warwick had succeeded his father as chief steward of the duchy of Lancaster north of Trent and as steward of Pontefract. On 15 December 1461 he had been granted the stewardship of Knaresborough (Somerville, *Duchy of Lancaster*, I, pp. 514, 524). On 20 March 1466 the two stewardships had been granted to Warwick's brother, John Neville, then earl of Northumberland (PRO DL37/35/4; 35/28).
57. *CP*, XI, p. 706.
58. Pilkington was knighted after the battle of Tewkesbury and appears to have become a knight of the body immediately (Shaw, *Knights of England*, II, p. 14: *CPR, 1467–77*, p. 307).
59. Somerville, *Duchy of Lancaster*, I, p. 514.
60. *Ibid.*, p. 524.
61. *CPR, 1467–77*, p. 349: C.L. Scofield, *The Life and Reign of Edward the Fourth*, II (London, 1923), p. 31.
62. The commissions for all counties were renewed between 30 October and 1 December.
63. *Plumpton Correspondence*, p. 33.
64. Somerville, *Duchy of Lancaster*, I, p. 515.
65. *CPR, 1476–85*, p. 127.
66. Gloucester was appointed on 4 July 1471 (Somerville, *Duchy of Lancaster*, I, p. 422).
67. See Wright, 'A Gentry Society of the Fifteenth Century', p. 156.
68. See M.A. Hicks, 'Descent, Partition and Extinction: the "Warwick Inheritance"', *BIHR*, LII (1979), 116–28, for the arbitrary apportionment of the estates of the earl of Warwick and his wife.
69. Several of the dismissals were of knights most closely associated with the earl of Northumberland: in the North Riding Sir William Eure and Sir John Pickering, and in the East Riding Sir Marmaduke Constable. Neither Vavasour nor Rither, however, can be connected with the earl at this date.
70. R.R. Reid, *The King's Council in the North* (London, 1921), p. 504.

71. *Ibid.*, p. 64.
72. *Ibid.*, p. 67.
73. These were Sir James Harington, steward of Pontefract; Sir Gervaise Clifton, steward of Tickhill; Sir Thomas Fitzwilliam, steward of Conisborough; Sir Richard Radcliff, steward of Wakefield, and Sir William Gascoigne, deputy to the earl of Northumberland as steward of Knaresborough. All except Fitzwilliam were knights of the body in Richard III's household.
74. Reid, *King's Council*, p. 75.
75. CP, XI, p. 707.
76. M.A. Hicks, 'Dynastic Change and Northern Society: the Career of the Fourth Earl of Northumberland, 1470–89', *Northern History*, XIV (1978), p. 79.
77. *CPR, 1485–94*, p. 39.
78. *York Civic Records*, I, ed. A. Raine (Yorkshire Archaeological Society Record Series XCVIII, 1939), p. 125.
79. PRO, DL42/20 f. 8v.
80. *CPR, 1476–85*, p. 193.
81. *Ibid.*, p. 410.
82. The bond was dated 12 February 1485 (*CCR, 1476–85*, p. 419).
83. He was described as a knight of the body in a grant made to him on 30 November of the feodary of Pontefract (PRO, DL42/21 f. 64). He received exemption from the act of resumption passed during the first parliament of the reign in respect of a number of offices, including the stewardship of Wakefield (*RP*, VI, p. 353).
84. Somerville, *Duchy of Lancaster*, I, p. 514.
85. On 10 October 1485, Thomas, Lord Stanley was granted the office of chief steward of the duchy north of Trent (*ibid.*, p. 422). The principal interests of this family lay in north-west England, especially in Lancashire and Cheshire, and only Lord Stanley's brother, Sir William Stanley, had hitherto shown any interest in West Riding affairs (J.M. Williams, 'The Stanley Family of Lathum and Knowsley, *c.* 1450–1504: A Political Study'. [Manchester M.A. thesis, 1979], part 1).
86. Somerville, *Duchy of Lancaster*, I, p. 514. Tunstall was from Lancashire.
87. The commission is dated only 1 Henry VII but certainly followed that of 22 September.
88. The other was John Fitzwilliam. There were several esquires of this name then alive and it is impossible to be certain whether this was the same John Fitzwilliam who was appointed to the commission, but not the *quorum*, between 18 November 1479 and 5 December 1483.
89. Fitzwilliam had been the only knight to serve on the commission during the latter part of Richard III's reign and to retain his place in September 1485.
90. Somerville, *Duchy of Lancaster*, I, p. 524. Like Tunstall, Wentworth was not a native of Yorkshire; his family's estates were mostly in Suffolk.
91. The archbishop of Canterbury was first appointed on 8 March 1488. He was similarly included in the commissions for the other two Ridings.
92. PRO, KB8/3/1. The indictments concerned the illegal giving of liveries by Sir Thomas Darcy.
93. Cheyne and Pole had joined the East Riding commission on 20 February 1491 and the North Riding commission on 28 February 1493.
94. Reid, *King's Council*, p. 84.
95. *CPR, 1494–1509*, p. 233.
96. *Ibid.*, p. 277.
97. R.B. Smith, *Land and Politics in the England of Henry VIII: The West Riding of Yorkshire, 1530–46* (Oxford, 1970), p. 157.
98. There were fifteen renewals of the West Riding commission during the adult reign of Henry VI, one was issued during the Readeption. Under the Yorkist dynasty, the commission was renewed twenty-nine times and, in the reign of Henry VII, seventeen times.
99. Eighteen West Riding families were involved in appointments to the commission of the peace during the adult reign of Henry VI. In the period of Yorkist rule twenty-two families were

involved and in the reign of Henry VII, eighteen families. Members of only three families served on the commission in all three periods: the family of Fairfax of Steeton, as a result of the legal careers of Sir Guy and his eldest son, Sir William, and the families of Hastings of Fenwick and Fitzwilliam of Aldwark (Edmund, Sir Richard and Sir Thomas).

100. The true figure may be higher because the identity of the two knights of the shire for Yorkshire is known for only four of the eleven parliaments which assembled between 1471 and 1509.

7

Resources and Retaining in Yorkist England: William, Lord Hastings and the Honour of Tutbury

Ian Rowney
King Edward VI College, Nuneaton

'A man of great sense, virtue and authority' was how the French chronicler, Philippe de Commynes, described Edward IV's chamberlain, William, Lord Hastings.[1] This was evidently an opinion shared by many, including both of Commynes's masters, Charles of Burgundy and Louis XI. Both gave Hastings extravagant gifts and a pension (in Louis's case this amounted to 2,000 crowns). Merely to say that this generosity matched Hastings's influence, while true, is ultimately unhelpful. On what was his position based? Historians often measure magnate influence in the later middle ages in terms of landed wealth, royal patronage, and a goodly supply of client gentlemen. Given the ephemeral nature of the last two of these in particular, Hastings's record of sustained success in Yorkist England is unsurpassed. Power was hard to win, harder to keep. Yet this was not merely an age of livery and maintenance, when to attain and maintain power one had only to retain powerful allies. As Dr. Richmond recently remarked, 'Fifteenth-century England is not like some twentieth-century mechanical toy called perhaps "Connection": press a button marked William, lord Hastings, eighty odd names appear, and you have won the central Midlands[2].' It is true that the bulk of Hastings's estates and affinity lay in the Midlands and that he held several important crown offices there, but this does not in itself prove that he was able to exploit his position. There were undoubtedly limitations on his freedom of action from other, possibly more entrenched, interests in the area, while he in turn had more pressing responsibilities elsewhere. Thus, the extent of his authority is impossible to discern from a bald list of properties and appointments. We need to seek the man at work.

William was born in 1430 or 1431, the eldest son of Sir Leonard Hastings, a retainer and close associate of Richard, duke of York. The son followed the father in York's service with considerable success. In 1455 William was appointed sheriff of Warwickshire and Leicestershire, and in the following April he received a life grant of the keeping of the ducal forests and chases in Shropshire.[3] Hastings repaid his patron by accompanying him to the fiasco at Ludford and his son to Towton. He emerged from the factional bloodletting of 1459–61 as William, Lord Hastings, councillor and chamberlain to Edward IV. The Hastings inheritance, as outlined in Sir Leonard's will of 8 October 1455, contained major estates in Yorkshire and Leicestershire with others in Warwickshire and Northamptonshire.[4] In the 1460s William acquired wider interests in the east Midlands from grants of Lancastrian forfeitures (including Ashby de la Zouche), and appointments as steward to his brother-in-law, Richard, earl of Warwick, in Leicestershire, Northamptonshire and Rutland, and as royal steward and surveyor of Fotheringay.[5] Such were the rewards for 'backing a winner' and being thought reliable enough to be advanced in a district which, though nowhere near the richest in England, was of considerable strategic important.

Although Hastings headed the trustees into whose hands control of the badly-governed Nuneaton Priory was granted in September 1462[6], there is no evidence that his interests were expanding westwards at that time. Indeed, why should they have done, given that this would have brought him into rivalry with other loyal intimates of Edward IV, namely, Warwick and the king's brother, George, duke of Claence? Warwick had emerged as the leading 'indigenous' magnate in the west Midlands after the eclipse of the Staffords with the death of Humphrey, duke of Buckingham in 1460. Clarence had had an inheritance carved out for him in 1465–6 from duchy of Lancaster lands: the honours of Tutbury and Duffield, and the lordships of High Peak and Castle Donnington, Although these included parts of Nottinghamshire, Leicestershire and north Warwickshire, and also Newcastle-under-Lyme, the bulk of Clarence's midland estates lay in Derbyshire and eastern Staffordshire. Under Clarence and his steward, Sir Walter Blount (later Lord Mountjoy and second husband of Anne, duchess of Buckingham), these lands were administered as one unit. Property was entered in the accounts under the headings 'Staffordshire lands', 'Derbyshire lands', and the lordship of Castle Donnington (a disparate group including Wirksworth and Ashbourne). Although the names Duffield, Castle Donnington and High Peak continued to be used, it is more convenient here simply to refer to the estates collectively as the honour of Tutbury (for such it was also frequently styled at the time). The steward of the honour had at his disposal a wealth of patronage with numerous leases and appointment, particularly in the Derbyshire Peak District and the Needwood forest of eastern Staffordshire.[7] Control of Needwood by stewards of the honour was due to their holding the office of master-forester there as a subsidiary appointment. The land was low-lying and possessed a soil derived from keuper marl, which, though difficult to work, made for excellent pastureland. The forest was divided into five wards (Barton, Marchington, Tutbury, Uttoxeter, and Yoxall), each of which was in the theory held by a hereditory forester-in-fee.[8] More important than these were the Duchy appointees: bailiffs, keepers for the wards, and parkers for the ten forest parks.[9] The Derbyshire estates consisted of four wards (Belper, Coalbrook, Duffield, and Holland), seven parks.[10], numerous petty bailiwicks, and the lordship of High Peak, which itself accounted for over forty per cent of the total Derbyshire charge.[11] There were also 'industrial' assets in the shape of mills, a millstone quarry at Roncliff, lead mines at Wirksworth, and alabaster and 'plaisterstone' deposits around Tutbury.

On 20 March 1472 Clarence appointed Hastings as chief steward of the honour of Tutbury.[12] The duke was far from having been forgiven by Edward IV for his treachery in 1469–71, and hoped for Hastings's support in his political rehabilitations. However, the king was determined to clip his brother's wings, particularly since Clarence's marriage to one of Warwick's daughters left him co-heir to the extensive Beauchamp-Neville inheritance. One of the aims behind the parliamentary act of resumption in December 1473 was to prevent Clarence from enjoying the dangerous pre-eminence resulting from any union of this inheritance with his existing Midland territories. The resumption of the honour of Tutbury (and other grants) also stemmed from Edward's need to settle some of his vast debts, and in June 1475 an order was issued that £500 a year was to be paid to John Elrington, treasurer of the royal household and one of the king's leading creditors.[13] Having removed Clarence, Edward settled the fate of the honour's estate officials in the spring of 1474 while visiting the district. On 30 March Hastings was re-appointed steward of the honour of Tutbury (which was taken to include Castle Donnington and Duffield); the stewardship of High Peak, curiously, only came to Hastings sometime later, on 3 August.[14]

With Hastings's appointment in 1474, there was undoubtedly a change of estate officials in the honour, and particularly in Needwood forest, where seven of the ten parkers and the keepers of two wards were replaced. John Agard of Foston, one of the honour's local administrative stalwarts, did take over as parker of Castlehay, but in general the new officials came from the royal household (over much of which Hastings presided as chamberlain). It is uncertain whether it was Hastings or the king himself who extended the rewards to such crown servants as Thomas Steel, John Reed, Edward Burton,[15] and Geoffrey Whitford, who were to remain absentee sinecurists in the honour until the end of the reign. Whitford, for example, became keeper of Barton ward, parker of Barton and Shirholt with rights to herbage and pannage, and farmer of Barton mill.[16] On the Derbyshire estates of the honour (where the offices were fewer and more prized by the

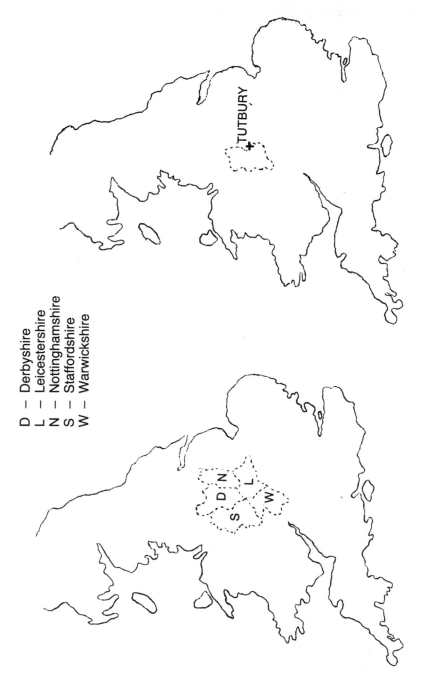

TUTBURY

D — Derbyshire
L — Leicestershire
N — Nottinghamshire
S — Staffordshire
W — Warwickshire

S D N
   L
   W

Map 1: The Central Midlands

Map 2: Places in the North Midlands of particular importance to Lord Hastings

local gentry), Thomas Nortrich, an official in the Chancery, took over Belper park and ward from John Fitzherbert on 29 June 1474, but in general the Fitzherberts' pre-eminence was respected.[17] A balance had to be struck between the need to avoid upsetting local sensibilities and a desire to reward household favourites. On occasions, Hastings's influence in an appointment cannot be doubted. Alexander Sidebotham, who became keeper of Holland ward in November 1475, was specifically described as his servant, while the advice of Hastings in the appointment of Hugh Berdesley as keeper of Hanbury park and Uttoxeter ward in the Needwood forest in February 1476 was again duly noted in the grant.[18] Hastings was also certainly behind the advancement of his own family. His brother, Richard, Lord Wells, became bailiff of Melbourne and the hundred of Gresley in Derbyshire, while kinsmen among the Ferrers family of Tamworth also received preferment.

The marriage of Anne, William's sister, and Sir Thomas Ferrers around 1448 had produced a close association between their families. In 1459 they were even held to have been responsible for the unlawful death of Robert Pierpoint, and had £40 awarded against them by Richard of York in an arbitration settlement.[19] Sir Thomas's brother, Ralph, was appointed dean of Tamworth in July 1479 after Hastings had been granted the deanery's advowson.[20] Another brother, Henry Ferrers (the sometime sheriff and M.P. for Kent), obtained a post in the king's chamber. Henry was also receiver of the honour of Tutbury. However, as he had been in that office since 1461, we must presume that either Hastings or Warwick had sponsored him before the honour was earmarked for Clarence, or else that his family was independently favoured by Edward (Sir Thomas having fought at Wakefield), or a mixture of both. Hastings's nephew, Sir John Ferrers, was granted an annuity of £10 from the honour on 28 October 1476, and was appointed parker of Agardsley and keeper of Marchington in the following May.[21] It is probable that Hastings also engineered Sir John's election as a knight of the shire in 1478 when (though still only the heir to his family's estates) he represented Staffordshire in the parliament summoned to attaint Clarence.[22]

Thus, at least three different groups eagerly awaited a share of the spoils of office. The local gentry looked to Hastings as their royal steward and surrogate overlord, crown servants in London and Westminster looked to him as the head of the royal household, and kinsmen saw him as the proverbial rich uncle. It is a measure of Hastings's achievement that he managed to accommodate the leading members of these groups and yet still reserve to himself considerable profit from the honour.

Between 1461 and 1483 Hastings retained ninety men and doubtless developed an unretained affinity several times that number. The retainers included gentlemen whose estates and interests took in much of south and central England, but it was centred on the Midlands. At least fifty-four men were closely associated with Derbyshire and the honour of Tutbury, with seventeen others hailing from adjacent areas of Staffordshire, Warwickshire and

Leicestershire.[23] Given the wide spread of Hastings's estates and responsibilities from north Wales to Calais, and of course in London, the prominence of the honour of Tutbury and its environs in the composition of the affinity is striking.

In a recent article describing the construction of the Hastings affinity in the honour and the incidence of his retainers among county and parliamentary officers, I suggested that he may have found the honour of financial rather than of political value.[24] It could hardly have been otherwise. Hastings had numerous other commitments, some of which, like the lieutenancy of Calais and his seat on the council, were far more time-consuming, lucrative or influential. Furthermore, Hastings had not been granted the estates of the honour, merely a temporary supervisory appointment. He was a stranger in a strange land, and his priority was to establish fruitful and effective working relationships rather than to put down roots. This helps to explain the prominence both of lawyers and administrators (such as the Agards, Eyres, Curzons of Croxall, and Rugeleys of Hawksyard) and of kinship networks in his retained local affinity. Ten families connected with Staffordshire and the honour had more than one member retained by Hastings,[25] with another four Derbyshire families (the Eyres, Knivetons, Longfords, and Sacheverells) in a similar position. The picture becomes increasingly complicated when one considers uncles, cousins and in-laws. For instance, Nicholas Montgomery of Cubley (d. 1494) had sisters married to the Agards and Meverells, progeny among the Bagots, Bassets, Gresleys, and Sacheverells, and was himself married to a Longford. The extended family, with its ready-made lines of communication and bonds of self-interest, afforded opportunities for the perceptive outsider to exploit. In the north Midlands this was accentuated by a local propensity for large families and in-breeding; almost everybody had married a Gresley! In short, Hastings 'bought' a clan rather than constructed an affinity.[26]

With what was the affinity 'bought'? The Hastings indentures differed from those between Humphrey, duke of Buckingham and the gentry of the area in the 1440s and 1450s; these detailed both the fees to be paid and the number of troops to be raised on ducal demand by client gentlemen. However, in only two instances is Hastings known to have offered a monetary fee in addition to good lordship, while the general vagueness of the contractual obligation indicates that we are hardly dealing with precise and permanent legal instruments. Hastings did not use the diplomatic of a military contract since he was not raising a private army, though some retainers did serve at Calais and on the 1475 campaign in France.

There were several reasons for the absence of monetary fees. Although there was no reason to suppose that Hastings would not be steward of the honour for many years, even for life, he was not laying the foundations of dynastic rule in the area, in the manner of the Staffords or Nevilles. Thus, it was unlikely that he or his family would benefit markedly from any sizeable financial investment. The local gentry had shown themselves to be fickle, apathetic or shrewdly wary (depending on one's viewpoint) in the struggles of 1455–71, and there was no reason to suspect any change of heart. Whatever loyalties the gentry did owe were to the stewardship as the fount of patronage, not to the individual steward. Thus, Hastings might have reasoned, whatever patronage they could reasonably expect from him should come from the issues of the honour and not from his private coffers. He was particularly unwilling to waste his own money retaining in the Midlands or anywhere else, given the expensive building programmes being carried out for him at Ashby de la Zouche in the 1470s and later to his fortified manor house at Kirby Muxloe. Work on the latter cost nearly £1,000 in the early 1480s and was still unfinished at the time of his execution.[27] Hastings substituted patronage from the areas under his control (something that he would have had to have given anyway to ensure their smooth administration) for cash payments from himself. In the week following his confirmation as steward of the honour on 30 March 1474, there were no fewer than sixteen new leases and farms of honour property, worth £233 a year.[28] Of these, grants worth £143 a year went to present or future retainers and their families. For example, the Fitzherberts leased for lead mines at Wirksworth for £27,[29] Nicholas Montgomery leased the mill, market tolls and certain properties at Uttoxeter for £30. Such grants, consolidating as they did the influence of the leading local families, produced a contented, if not pliable, county community.

Annuities, usually stated to have been awarded for good and praiseworthy services, were occasionally granted by the council of the duchy of Lancaster on the recommendation of its stewards or other principal officers. Throughout most of the period that Hastings was steward at Tutbury, the annuities charged upon the honour came to £163. The largest of these annuities was 100 marks payable to the College of St.Mary, Leicester. Hastings himself received £40. Only ten members of the local gentry received annuities from the honour:

Nicholas Longford	13 6s. 8d.	30 March	1474
Nicholas Montgomery	£10	30 March	1474
Hugh Egerton	£6 13s. 4d.	2 April	1474
George Stanley	£1 13s. 4d.	6 April	1474
Thomas Curzon	£5	25 July	1474
John Curzon	£5	10 November	1475
Ralph Sacheverell	£5	10 November	1475
John Ferrers	£10	28 October	1476
John Mountfort	£6 13s. 4d.	8 November	1481
Ralph Longford	£6 13s. 4d.	26 November	1481

Of these, five (the Curzons, Ralph Longford, Montgomery and Sacheverell) were later retained by Hastings, while Mountfort, Stanley and, of course, Nicholas Longford (Ralph's father, who died in 1481) were related to retainers.[30] The halving of the Longford annuity is perhaps evidence that Ralph was less of a force in local affairs than his father had been. Young Mountfort evidently succeeded to the other half of the old man's allowance. With Ferrers Hastings's nephew and Egerton his deputy steward in Newcastle-under-Lyme, it is clear that this source of patronage at least was under Hastings's sway. It might, therefore, be asked why he did not exploit this situation more fully and secure annuities for other local notables with whom he wished for a close association. The answer may partly lie in the growing concern that the king was showing towards the end of his reign over the profitability of crown lands.

Although at this time the clear charge on the honour averaged approximately £1,450, with deliveries of cash around £650- a very low proportion- there were significant annual fluctuations. For example, deliveries in 1476–9 were respectively £394, £571, £767, and £744, while the total charge lay between £1,516 and £1,574, with arrears of £11. The clear charge in the last three years of Hastings life jumped to between £1,193 and £1,450, having been little more than £800 a decade earlier.[31] Such unpredictability hardly facilitiated forward planning, and was presumably a significant reason for the king's dissatisfaction with the financial health of the honour. Early in 1479 Edward declared that the custom in the honour of Tutbury whereby bailiffs farmed their offices 'gretely hurted' the crown's interests and had to cease.[32] This was quickly followed by a ban on repairs in the honour that were paid for without due authorisation.[33] In July 1480 rentals were ordered to be renewed, though this took time to be effected, and in February 1482 Geoffrey Whitford is found complaining to the council of the duchy of Lancaster that he was unable to raise his full charge on the town of Barton-under-Needwood for lack of a decent rental.[34] It is unclear how much effect this all had on the issues of the honour. In January 1484, Richard III, who was dissatisfied with the administration of the honour, spoke of longstanding extortions and oppressions committed by the bailiffs, and also forbade any parker to hold the farm of herbage and pannage in his park.[35] However, the significance of these matters is unclear, coming as they did in his instructions to Marmaduke Constable, his new steward. Richard had earlier ordered Constable to ensure that no illegal 'liveries ne cognizance' were to be distributed in the honour and that able and 'well-disposed' persons were to be appointed to the bailiwicks.[36] Given his conflicts in 1483 with Hastings and Henry, duke of Buckingham (who was Hastings's immediate successor as steward), Richard was evidently not certain of the loyalty of the Staffordshire and Derbyshire gentry. Simon Stalworth's phrase that 'all the lord Chamberleyne men be come my lordys of Bokyngham menne' would have had ominous overtones for the usurper.[37] Therefore, Richard sought to weaken any resistance to him by widening the circle of those who enjoyed patronage from the honour. By Michaelmas 1484 many of the Edwardian estate officials had been replaced and the annuities paid amounted to over £450.[38] Compared with Richard, Hastings appears frugal, but then their needs were different. The honour was not Hastings's to exploit ruthlessly, and he was never the man so to abuse the trust of his beloved king, Edward. Hastings knew that lasting success depended on the ability to survive, and that was not something regularly associated with covetousness among the later medieval nobility. This is not to say that Hastings was completely disinterested in his administration of the honour, merely that he took care not to appear over-ambitious.

Hastings drew influence and much-needed revenue from his position within the honour of Tutbury. If one includes his interests in the High Peak and in Castle Donnington, Hastings's fees by the time of his fall totalled £50 5s. 2d. a year. To this may be added his annuity and the undoubtedly sizeable profits made from the self-awarded farms of agistment in thirteen of the honour's parks, for which he paid £39 11s. 6d.[39] His final perquisite arrived on 17 March 1483, when he leased the Derbyshire manors of Hartington and Shene, which a financially embarrassed John Pole had been forced to sell to the crown in 1478.[40] Hastings's direct association with the honour brought him annually at least £150 and possibly much more. It was also responsible for his acquisition of control of the inheritances of two of his retainers whose death had resulted in minorities.[41] Another retainer, Thomas Chaworth, felt obliged to award his good lord, Hastings, a life annuity of £20.[42]

The extension of Hastings's rule throughout the Midlands brought him numerous other offices and associations. In June 1471 he was made constable of Nottingham castle and steward of eight forests in Nottinghamshire.[43] In 1473 the town authorities at Derby chose him as their steward; it was shrewd move, since the good lordship of a magnate was useful if borough privileges were to be protected and extended. Hastings showed his mettle in this respect that very November, when he procured for Ashby de la Zouche permission to hold annually two five-day fairs.[44] In July 1474 Hastings acquired the wardship and marriage of George, earl of Shrewsbury, whom Hastings married to his own daughter, along with custody of the Talbot inheritance in Derbyshire, Nottinghamshire and Yorkshire in lieu of a debt of £1,667 owed him by the king.[45] Four years later, Hastings leased other Talbot properties, including Alton (Staffordshire), Monyash, Crich, Winfield and Thermerdon in Derbyshire, Sheffield, and sixteen estates in southern England for £300 a year during George's minority.[46] Control of these consolidated his position in the north Midlands. Hastings even extended his interests into Worcestershire, where in 1477 he leased the stewardship of the estates of George, Lord Bergavenny.[47]

This accumulation of offices in one region was not coincidental; it was a corollary of Hastings's control of the honour of Tutbury and of its pre-eminent status in the north Midlands. Given the welter of appointments and responsibilities he acquired, it is surprising that he did not experience a frequent clash of interests. For example, by 1471–2 he had become steward of Weston-on-Trent (Derbyshire), a large manor in the heart of the honour held by the abbey of St. Werburgh, Chester, and from which he drew a fee of £8 a year.[48] His loyalties, however, must have been divided when, in 1481, the abbot complained to the council of the duchy of Lancaster that officials of the honour had been interfering with the rights of the abbey there and, in particular, ruining the fishing.[49] With Hastings as steward for both parties in the dispute, we may presume that an equitable settlement or arbitration was arranged, though the precise outcome is unknown.

A further benefit that accrued to Hastings from his position in the honour was influence- or at least potential influence- over leading county appointments and elections in the north Midlands. Hastings did not monopolise the offices of local government by inserting retainers therein; quite the opposite. What evidence there is points to it having been 'business as usual' in such matters, with the favour of the steward of the honour of Tutbury (as expressed in an indentured contract) being little more than an optional extra. Between 1472 and 1483 there were four sometimes retainers appointed sheriff in Staffordshire (William Basset, John Aston, Nicholas Montgomery and Humphrey Stanley), five in Nottinghamshire and Derbyshire (William Basset, John Babington, Gervaise Clifton, Robert Eyre and Ralph Pole), and three in Warwickshire and Leicestershire (Richard Boughton, Thomas Entwistle and William Trussell). Of these twelve, only two, Clifton and Aston, are known to have been appointed before being retained. However, given that most of the others came from families which had supplied sheriffs, escheators and county commissioners for generations, it would be an oversimplification to see this as proof that Hastings's support was the crucial factor in their appointments. Evidence is needed that Hastings was advancing those who otherwise would not have attained such prominence, if we are to avoid concluding that he latched onto the established gentry leadership. Given his need to operate alongside such men, this would have been- and, indeed, was- a move of shrewdness not of weakness, a move which politicians of lesser ability and foresight might have emulated.

While Hastings was steward of the honour of Tutbury, his sometime retainers were returned to parliament from the Midlands on twelve occasions: four in 1472, six in 1478, and two in 1483.[50] In 1472 three of these members (Blount, Boughton and Trussell) are known to have been retained after their election, as was probably the fourth (Longford). In 1478, by which time Hastings had been able to settle in as steward, three of those elected (Mountfort, Moton and John Gresley) were his retainers. While the retention dates for two others (Thomas Gresley and Henry Vernon) are unknown, it is probable that they too had already been retained. Mountfort and Vernon were the retained members in 1483; there may have been others, for the names of most of those elected then are unknown. As with the sheriffs, many of these M.Ps. would have had a good chance of holding office without any intervention by Hastings. For instance, are we to believe that Sir John Gresley, having sat in at least four previous parliaments, really needed Hasting's patronage to be returned for the fifth time? Or that Henry Vernon, who led Derbyshire's

most powerful gentry family and whose forebears included numerous M.Ps. and
a speaker of the commons under Henry VI, could not engineer his own
election?

Yet one cannot entirely rule out Hastings's influence in county appointments.
Consider the implications to be drawn from the following extract from a letter
written in the mid-1470s to Sir William Plumpton:

> As for the message to my Lo. Chamberlain, what time labored to him that
> ye might be Justice of the peace, he answered thus; that it seemed by your
> labour and mine, that we wold make a jelosie betwixt my Lo. of Northum-
> berland and him, in that he shold labor for any of his men, he being
> present.[51]

If Hastings were sufficiently well placed to influence the commission in the West
Riding of Yorkshire (for that was the bench to which the writer was alluding),
how much more so for the Midlands where his interests and influence were
wider?

Ten sometime retainers of Hastings sat on the Derbyshire bench while he was
steward at Tutbury.[52] Henry Vernon, Ralph Fitzherbert and two leading Blounts
were obvious appointments to any Derbyshire commission. Four of the rest
(Robert Eyre, Lawrence Lowe, John and Ralph Sacheverell) were legal and
administrative 'dogsbodies', a sub-group of the lesser gentry on whose shoulders
the burden of county government lay. That Hastings had a say in the selection
of these particular individuals is in little doubt, as they hailed from a species not
noticeably rare in those parts. How far he sought the advice of others in making
this choice is, however, unknown. Eyre and Lowe had just been appointed when
Hastings took over and were retained subsequently. The Sacheverells' retention
preceeded their appointment.[53] Meanwhile, six retainers sat in Staffordshire:
Henry, Lord Grey of Codnor, John, Lord Mountjoy, William Basset, Humphrey
Stanley, Sir John Gresley and John Aston. From 1480 Sir John Ferrers was also
an appointee. In Warwickshire there were only two retainers on the bench: Sir
Simon Mountfort, who had been a regular appointee in the 1460s under
Clarence, and Richard Boughton (appointed as late as June 1482). To these
should be added Hastings's brother, Richard (1474–8), and their kinsman, Sir
Thomas Ferrers, though the Ferrers family has held a regular place on the
commissions of that county long before Hastings was a power in the land. In
Leicestershire, the Hastings heartland, only Robert Staunton and William
Moton among his retainers were appointed, though this does not mean that he
lacked support from the other justices of the peace. Quite the contrary: it merely
downgrades the significance of the indentured contract *in this instance*, and
certainly destroys any notion of 'haves' and 'have-nots' based on evidence of
retention alone. Surely we are not to believe that Edward IV's right-hand man
would suffer this region of special interest to him to be governed by men hostile
to him?

At the time of Hastings's execution, twelve of his retainers sat on the commissions of the peace of these four counties: six in Staffordshire, four in Derbyshire and two in Warwickshire. By the end of 1483, only two (Humphrey Stanley in Staffordshire and Sir Thomas Ferrers in Warwickshire) had been removed; indeed, Sir Gervaise Clifton had even been added to the benches of Derbyshire and Leicestershire. In Derbyshire Ralph Fitzherbert of Hastings's retained affinity had been appointed to the bench after his lord's demise, but death was to take him too before the close of that year. The sheriffs of Nottinghamshire-Derbyshire in 1483–5 and of Warwickshire-Leicestershire in 1484–5 were also ex-Hastings retainers. Yet merely to say that the Hastings affinity had a life of its own is to miss the point, for it implies an organic vitality and independent coherence that never actually existed. In reality, the Hastings affinity (though, as has been stated, no mechanical toy) was instead similar to some wayward marionette that had never really danced at the bidding of its operator. Now that its strings had been cut, it certainly danced no more, though its limbs and body could still be discerned by those with an eye for such things.

Hastings could hardly be called a resident lord in the area, and there is little evidence that he took much interest in local affairs other than dispensing financial patronage and exercising a sporadic influence on county appointments. However, he did act as a feoffee occasionally, for instance, for the Needwood family of lawyers, the Hills of Marchington, and for members of the retained Cockayne and Vernon families.[54] Furthermore, in the early 1480s, having become established to some extent in the area, Hastings twice arbitrated in local disputes. He was called in to decide on the ownership of over 800 acres of land in Great Clifton (Derbyshire) by two groups of retainers, the Fitzherberts and Cockaynes.[55] Whether Hastings was acting as a local magnate (of sorts) or as the head of his affinity is a moot point; probably it was a combination of both. On the other occasion, two unretained notables, the bishop of Coventry and Lichfield and the former exchequer official, Ralph Wolseley, enlisted his services in their long-running feud over enclosures in eastern Staffordshire. He eventually abandoned this case, not being able to afford to spend the necessary time and expense for its settlement.[56] It seems reasonable to assume that had Hastings lived longer, he would have developed more relationships along these lines, but it was not to be.

Though short-lived, the Hastings affinity served its purpose. Like other successful medieval institutions, its strength was that of the ploughshare not the sword, of the pruning hook not the spear. That Hastings recognized that this was so speaks volumes about the man and the changing weapons of statecraft. Yet what should be the idea on which to conclude this survey? We might say that Hastings oversaw the region without undue interference; that he developed a position of profit while avoiding the dangers of greed and over-ambition; that he financed an impressive affinity at negligible cost to himself; and that his was an affinity, moulded to the contours of gentry society, which represented and fostered stability rather than factional rivalry or social unrest. All this would be true, yet for Hastings (and for his king) of greater importance was that he discharged his duties with tact, efficiency and undivided loyalty. Like Edward, we would expect no less of him.

Notes

1. Philippe de Commynes, *Memoirs*, ed. M. Jones (Harmondsworth, Middlesex, 1972), p. 359. Charles the Bold of Burgundy had initially made Hastings a pensioner (for 100 *écus*) as early as 4 May 1461: BL, Harleian MS. 3881, fo. 15r. This is a volume of documents relating to the Hastings family covering several centuries.
2. C.F. Richmond, 'After McFarlane', *History*, LXVII (1983), 58.
3. BL, Harleian MS.3881, fo. 13ᵈ. Sir Leonard had a fee of £15 a year from the duke from 5 March 1435: *Ibid.*, fo. 13r.
4. *Ibid.*, fo. 13r. York was a feoffee for Sir Leonard.
5. *CPR, 1461–67*, pp. 103–4, 352, 354; HMC, *Hastings MS*, I, p. 302; *CPR, 1467–77*, p. 154.
6. VCH, *Warwickshire*, II, p. 68.
7. For an excellent short study of Needwood, see VCH, *Staffordshire*, II, pp. 349–58.
8. Respectively, the Griffith, Mynors of Blakenhall, Boughay, Mynors of Uttoxeter, and Wells families.
9. Agardsley, Barton, Castlehay, Henbury, Highland, Rolleston, Rowley, Shirholt, Stockley, and Tutbury.
10. Belper (or Ladypark), Holland, Maunshill, Morley, Postern, Ravensdale, and Shothill.
11. The bailiwick of the High Peak was, for obvious reasons, the only one which Hastings felt it worthwhile to administer personally.
12. HMC, *Hastings MS.*, I, pp. 302–3.
13. Elrington was owed £3, 729, and Tutbury was only one of several honours ordered to help pay this off.
14. PRO, DL37/43, nos.6 (Tutbury) and 34 (High Peak).
15. Burton was granted the parkership of Rowley in Needwood forest: PRO, DL37/43, no.13. More significantly for his position in Staffordshire was a grant of the wardship and marriage of Richard Lane, heir to estates in the west of the county: *CPR, 1476–85*, p. 62. He subsequently married Richard's widowed mother.
16. PRO, DL37/43, no.10; DL37/44, no.6; DL37/56, no.44. There were also other crown servants, Otto Radiche and Richard Fiche, whose appointments in the honour went back to 1461.
17. The Fitzherberts maintained their control of Coalbrook ward, the liberty in Derbyshire, and the parks of Holland, Maunshill and Shothill.
18. PRO, DL29/403/6469 (Sidebotham); DL37/44/23 (Berdesley). Berdesley took these offices over from John Reed.
19. HMC, *Hastings MS.*, I, p. 301. See also J.T. Rosenthal, 'Feuds and peace-making: a fifteenth-century example', *Nottingham Medieval Studies*, XIV (1970), 84–90; also Ian Rowney, 'Arbitration in gentry disputes of the later middle ages', *History*, LXVII (1982), 374.
20. *CPR, 1476–85*, p. 155.
21. Ferrers also served under Hastings at Calais.
22. Ferrers's election was the only Staffordshire one influenced by Hastings in 1478, despite a general reluctance on the part of the local gentry to be involved in the destruction of someone who had been a good lord to many in the area. For a fuller discussion of the Staffordshire elections in the 1470s, see Ian Rowney, 'The Hastings Affinity in Staffordshire and the Honour of Tutbury', *BIHR*, LVII (1984), 38–41.
23. See W.H. Dunham, 'Lord Hastings' Indentured Retainers, 1461–83', *Transactions of the Connecticut Academy of Arts and Sciences*, XXXIX (1955), 117–22. In these categories are the following: Derbyshire and Honour of Tutbury- Agard (x3), Aston, Babington, Basset, Blount (x2), Bonnington, Bradbourne, Bradshaw, Chaworth, Clifton, Cockayne (x2), Columbell (x2), Curzon (x2), Delves, Dethick, Eyre (x3), Fitzherbert, Gresley (x2), Grey, Griffith (only Sir Walter), Kniveton (x2), Leche, Leek, Longford (x3), Lowe, Meverell (x3), Montgomery,

Myners, Pole, Sacheverell (x2), Shirley (x2), Stanley (x2), Stathom, Thirkill, Vernon (x2), Willoughby; other areas of Staffordshire, Warwickshire and Leicestershire- Boughton, Burdet, Draycote, Entwistle, Harcourt (x2), Moton, Mountfort, Palmer, Peshale, Rugeley (x2), Staunton (x3), Trussell, Wistow.

24. Rowney, 'Hastings Affinity', p. 45.
25. The Agard, Blount, Cockayne, Curzon, Gresley, Harcourt, Meverell, Rugeley, Stanley, and Vernon families.
26. Although in Staffordshire Hastings did not generally recruit from areas outside the honour, there were only a few leading gentry families in the county community absent from his retained affinity, namely, the Bagots, Egertons and Mittons.
27. A.H. Thompson, 'The building accounts of Kirby Muxloe castle, 1480–1484', *Transactions of the Leicestershire Archaeological Society*, XI (1915), 193–345. For the licence of 17 April 1474 to fortify Ashby and other manors, see CCR, VI (1427–1516), p. 242. Hastings also spent 200 marks buying out a neightbour at Kirby in March 1474. (BL, Harleian MS, 3881, fo. 18d).
28. PRO, DL37/56, nos.35–51.
29. PRO, DL37/56, no.37. For other leases by the Fitzherberts of the lead mines around this time, see DL37/54, m.2r and DL37/66, m.1r.
30. The annuity to Stanley was undoubtedly connected with his appointment on 6 April 1474 as constable of Tutbury. (PRO, DL37/43, no.19).
31. There are conflicting figures for the cash deliveries. See both PRO, DL29/403/6469–73 and DL28/5/11.
32. PRO, DL5/1, fo. 24r.
33. *Ibid.*, fo. 24d. It was not that the repairs in themselves were unwanted or unnecessary, merely that money due to the crown was apt to go missing unless the proper channels were strictly used. In the 1480s there was actually a massive increase in expenditure on repairs in the honour, from around £30 a year to between £130 and £160 a year. Most of the money was spent on Tutbury castle or the honour's parks. See also J.R. Birrell, 'The forest economy of the honour of Tutbury in the fourteenth and fifteenth centuries', *University of Birmingham Historical Journal*, VIII (1962), 134.
34. PRO, DL5/1, fos. 57r. For the actual order to renew the rentals, see *ibid.*, fo. 41r. and DL42/19, fo. 74r. The second of these details how Hastings was to set about his task. Edward had claimed that because the rentals were out of date, 'the paiement of diverse and many of our rentes and autres have been canceled and withdrawen from us. And without the hastier remedie . . . it will grow unto us grete hurtes and damages.'
35. B.P. Wolffe, *The Crown Lands, 1461–1536*, (London, 1970), pp. 132–3.
36. Edward IV had issued a similar, though less strict, order shortly before his death. See *Ordinances for the Duchy of Lancaster*, ed. R. Somerville (Camden Society, 4 series, XIV, 1975), p. 28.
37. *The Stonor Letters and Papers*, ed. C.L. Kingsford (Camden Society, XXX, 1919), no. 331.
38. PRO, DL29/404/6476, mm.6r, 7r, 8. It may be significant that one of the first things that Henry Tudor did after his usurpation of the throne was to forbid John Agard (by then receiver of the honour) to pay any of the annuities granted by Richard (DL37/62, m.1d).
39. Birrell, 'Forest Economy', p. 121.
40. PRO, DL42/19, fos. 148–149r; DL29/403/6468.
41. Both of these occasions occurred in 1481; those involved were the Griffith and Trussell families. See S. Shaw, *The History and Antiquities of Staffordshire* (London, 1798–1801), I, p. 128; CPR, 1476–75, pp. 275–6. In Hastings's will, it was directed that the Trussell wardship and marriage be sold off to pay for the will's execution: BL, Harleian MS 3881, m.20d.
42. HMC, , *Hastings MS.*, I, p. 99.
43. CPR, 1467–77, pp. 310–11.
44. Dunham, 'Indentured Retainers' p. 290; CChR, VI (1427–1516), 241–2.

45. *CPR, 1467–77*, p. 460. See also BL, Harleian MS 3881, fo.19r, for an indenture between Hastings and the widowed countess of Shrewsbury in which she accepted the wardship settlement in return for a payment of 100 marks.
46. *CPR, 1476–85*, pp. 120–1.
47. HMC, *Hastings MS*, I, p. 271–2.
48. Staffordshire Record Office, D(W)1734/J.2004, m.3. Robert Staunton (£2 13s. 4d). and John Fitzherbert (6s. 8d.) also had fees from Weston.
49. PRO, DL5/1, fo. 52. The complaint was heard in the Michaelmas term 1481.
50. For a fuller discussion of this and the following paragraphs, see Rowney, 'Hastings Affinity', *passim*. 1472, James Blount and Nicholas Longford for Derbyshire, Richard Boughton for Warwickshire, William Trussell for Leicestershire; 1478, John Gresley and Henry Vernon for Derbyshire, Thomas Gresley for Stafford borough, Simon Mountford for Warwickshire, William Moton for Leicestershire, John Wistoe for Leicester borough; 1483, Henry Vernon for Derbyshire, Simon Mountfort for Warwickshire.
51. *The Plumpton Correspondence*, ed. T. Stapleton, (Camden Society, IV, 1839), p. 33.
52. Two others sat before 1471, Sir Thomas Stathom and Sir John Gresley.
53. The remainder consisted of Sir Nicholas Longford (1471–81) and Henry, Lord Grey of Codnor (1460–1, 1463–70, 1471–96).
54. Derbyshire Record Office D410m/33/276 and D231M/T277; I.H. Jeayes, *Descriptive Catalogue of Derbyshire Charters* (London and Derby, 1906), no.2398.
55. *CCR, 1476–85*, p. 273.
56. Rowney, 'Arbitration in Gentry Disputes', pp. 373–4.

8

Local Politics and the Good Parliament

A. Saul

Council for National Academic Awards, London

The Good Parliament sat from 28 April to 10 July 1376. It was remarkable for the severity of its attack on the king's ministers, for its refusal to grant Edward III a subsidy, for the introduction of impeachment, and for the spearheading of the assault on Latimer and his associates by the shire knights in the commons. Equally remarkable was the speed with which the decisions taken during the session were overturned. Many were reversed at the meeting of the great council in the autumn of 1376, whilst the parliament that met on 27 January 1377 confirmed pardons for most of those impeached and for many their restoration to previously held offices.

The 1376 parliamentary session has been much cherished by Whig historians who have seen it as an important rung on the ladder of constitutional development; not perhaps quite ranking with the Witan or Simon de Montfort, but significant enough. While exploring the constitutional dimension, Bishop Stubbs was careful to limit the significance of the session, pointing out that 'it asserted some sound principles without being a starting point of new history. It afforded an important illustration of the increasing power of the commons, but, as an attempt at real reform and progress it was a failure'.[1] Subsequent historians, for example, T.F. Tout and T.F.T. Plucknett, built on the work of Stubbs and emphasised such constitutional aspects of the session as impeachment and the role of the commons[2].

More recently the political dimensions of the Good Parliament have attracted greater attention. In 1959 Miss McKisack indicated the profound political *malaise* afflicting England in the years before the Peasants' Revolt[3], and in 1973 Dr Keen pointed to the political as well as the constitutional importance of impeachment, arguing that it 'opened to the commons a way to achieve what magnates had so often only achieved by force of arms, or the threat of it, the punishment of royal servants and agents whose malpractices had made them odious'[4]. In 1975 Dr Holmes firmly demonstrated the essentially political character of the proceedings of the Good Parliament. He took constitutional historians to task for 'indifference to actual historical situations' and suggested that they had 'denatured a great deal of medieval history'. He stressed the need 'to approach the events of April to July 1376 with less regard to the evolution of institutions' and instead to accentuate 'the aim of understanding the nature of the political crisis'[5].

Behind the discontent voiced at the Good Parliament, Dr Holmes traces three closely entwined themes: the conduct of the war with France, the political ambitions of Pope Gregory XI and the state of English crown finances.[6]. The session also saw the airing of two local issues: political and commercial rivalry in London and an urban dispute in East Anglia. In the network of international intrigue, financial malpractice and political corruption revealed in the Good Parliament, the quarrels among Great Yarmouth's burgesses and between the town and its neighbour, Lowestoft, are, perhaps not surprisingly, side issues, but they are illuminating since they demonstrate the tangled connection between national and provincial affairs and the tensions and difficulties that kings could experience when attempting to resolve local disputes. These feuds also show the need to recognise the potential complexity of local issues and to go beyond a simple juxtaposition of the local and the national.

In addition to the prosecution of Alice Perrers, the royal mistress, the principal charges in the Good Parliament revolved around financial corruption by a small group of royal ministers and advisers. William Latimer, the chamberlain from October 1371, and Richad Lyons, a London merchant, were accused of having issued licences for the evasion of the staple at Calais, with the consequent loss of revenue burdening the king with the cost of the town's defence. Brokerage of royal debts, to the loss of the crown, had been practised by Latimer and Lyons, who were also said to have made excessive profits from loans to the king, notably, though not exclusively, from a loan of 20,000 marks in August 1374. Lyons was stated to have imposed a tax of four pence in the pound on letters of exchange. Latimer was charged with extortion while captain of Becherel in Brittany, with having been responsible, through negligence, for the loss of the fortresses of Becherel and St Sauver, and with the illegal release of spies and prisoners. John Neville, steward of the household from November 1371 and Latimer's son-in-law, was denounced for the illegal brokerage of debts, for overcharging the king for his military sevices and for allowing his retinue to pillage Hampshire while *en route* for Brittany in 1372. A number of lesser fry and clients of Latimer and Lyons such as Henry de Medbourne, clerk, and two citizens of London, John Pecche and Adam de Bury, were enmeshed in the web of malpractice and intrigue[7].

The session also witnessed a serious challenge to the privileges both of Great Yarmouth and of its principal inhabitants. In this assault there were several

distinct but interlinked elements: an attack on two leading Yarmouth
burgesses, William Elys and Hugh Fastolf, a quarrel between the town's greater
and lesser burgesses, and an attempt by Lowestoft to curtail Yarmouth's trading
rights. In the case of William Elys, the accusations in the Good Parliament
specifically linked him with one of the session's central figures, Richard Lyons.
The explanation of why such local issues were discussed almost in the same
breath as mighty matters of international diplomacy and crown finances lies in
part in Great Yarmouth's changing fortunes as well as in the connection
between Elys and Lyons. In the 1370s Yarmouth faced severe economic
difficulties and had entered a period of depression which lasted into the
sixteenth century.[8] In 1334 Yarmouth was the fourth highest taxed among
England's provincial towns, and of the ports between the Severn and the Tyne
only London and York had greater assessments. Yet, in the 1377 poll-tax,
Yarmouth ranked eighteenth and in the subsidies of the 1520s twentieth[9]. In
the 1370s and 1380s the town complained repeatedly of depopulation, of the
burden of its tax and farm and of the high costs of defence. To judge by the
reactions of a monarchy well versed in dealing with such urban *cris de coeur*,
Yarmouth's complaints may well have been genuine enough.[10]. Certainly, of
the twenty leading towns in 1334 only Shrewsbury and Winchester, in terms
of tax assessments at least, had declined further by the 1520s[11].

Yarmouth's prosperity early in the fourteenth century was based on fishing
and shipping. The town's autumn fair was second in European importance only
to that at Scania, and its merchant fleet was heavily involved in the wool,
wine and salt trades. Economic vitality was matched by constitutional vigour.
Building on royal grants in 1277, 1305 and 1314, Yarmouth steadily secured
control of its autumn fair from the Cinque Ports. The king sought the advice
of its burgesses on trade, on defence and on naval affairs[12]. By 1350, however,
there were signs of economic distress at Yarmouth and plague alone will not
explain the town's misfortunes. By the 1370s the town's economy had been
undermined by the impact of the early stages of the Hundred Years' War on its
merchant fleet, by the decline of its herring industry[13] and by the repeated
silting of its access to the North Sea.

While Yarmouth's herring trade undoubtedly diminished in the second half
of the fourteenth century, it was by no means negligible. It is not possible for
the later years of the century to assemble anything approaching complete
statistics, but there is evidence of valuable individual shipments of herring
leaving the port. For example, in December 1392 four vessels sailed with
herring cargoes belonging to merchants from Bayonne and valued by the royal
customs staff at between £101 and £180[14]. Although – or perhaps because – its
value had been reduced, Yarmouth remained determined to control its herring
industry. In the early years of the century, its principal rivals in the trade had
been the Cinque Ports and London. After 1360 the chief threat came from
Lowestoft, and this was not so much the product of political circumstances, as

it had been in the case of the Cinque Ports and London, as of changing geographic conditions.

Through North Sea drift, the entrance of the river Yare to the sea not only silted but moved progressively southwards and closer to Lowestoft[15]. To maintain river access to Yarmouth for sea-going vessels[16], four separate harbour entrances were used between 1300 and 1410[17]. By the 1370s the entrance constructed soon after 1346 near Corton, approximately seven miles south of Yarmouth, had silted. Ships were unloading at Kirkley Roads, the stretch of sheltered coastal water from Corton to just south of Lowestoft, or at Lowestoft itself[18]. As a result, much of Yarmouth's trade, including the herring trade, was claimed by its burgesses to have been forestalled or diverted, with a consequent loss of local tolls.

In August 1372 Kirkley Roads were annexed to Yarmouth; the town acquired the right to levy customs there and the sale of fish or any other merchandise within seven miles of Yarmouth was prohibited[19]. This royal grant lay behind the protracted quarrel between Great Yarmouth and Lowestoft and was hotly contested by both parties. The grant was revoked in April 1376 and reissued temporarily in April 1378. The temporary regrant was made permanent in November 1378, only to be revoked in February 1382, regranted in February 1385, revoked in October of the same year and regranted in November 1386[20]. After 1386 Yarmouth controlled Kirkley Roads for the remainder of the century and reached an uneasy understanding with Lowestoft. Lowestoft men acted as farmers of Yarmouth's customs in Kirkley Roads and in 1401 an agreement was struck which gave Lowestoft a share in Yarmouth's herring trade.[21]. The dispute re-emerged in the fifteenth century.

When the Good Parliament opened in April 1376, Yarmouth's background was one of serious economic difficulty engendered by the decline of its principal industries and accentuated by the repeated failure of its harbour entrance. Its dispute with Lowestoft was well established, and if Lowestoft were to win control of Kirkley Roads then the ruin of Yarmouth could well have been complete. While clearly a great deal was at stake for both settlements, the dispute between them does not appear, on the surface, one that should have caused the crown much difficulty; certainly not the kind of problem that the complex pattern of grant and revocation of the August 1372 privileges suggests. In its own right, the quarrel between Yarmouth and Lowestoft was not of major significance, but it does show how local issues could entwine with, and be exacerbated by, political events at the centre.

The two Yarmouth burgesses specifically mentioned in the Good Parliament and its aftermath were William Elys and Hugh Fastolf. Elys was impeached for malpractice as farmer of the petty custom at Yarmouth and as deputy to Richard Lyons, farmer of the poundage there.[22] Fastolf does not appear in the record of the 1376 session, but that for the Hilary Parliament of 1377 states that he 'was impeached by malice and hate of some of his neighbours, his ill-wishers, both by various bills put forward and by clamour at the end of the last parliament, for various extortions, misprisions, champerties, maintenance and oppression done by him'. He had subsequently been cleared of all accusations by a number of inquisitions held in East Anglia.[23] Both men came from leading Yarmouth families. The Elyses were established in the town in the second half of the thirteenth century and regularly served as bailiffs from the 1330s onwards. Nine members of the family held that office and three were members of parliament for Yarmouth in the fourteenth century. William himself was bailiff seven times between September 1359 and September 1379 and M.P. in 1366, 1368, 1376, 1378 and 1380[24]. While firmly retaining their Yarmouth roots and commercial interests, the family invested in land in Norfolk and Suffolk. William dealt in wine, wool, cloth, grain and salt, and his rural property included Soham Hall. His trading links abroad involved the Low Countries, France and Germany[25]

William Elys served frequently in the royal customs service, which he presumably found advantageous given his own participation in sheep farming and in the wool trade[26]. William was appointed deputy to the king's butler at Yarmouth in 1363 and served as customs collector in the port from November 1375 until February 1382[27]. It was the customs service that brought William his links with the royal court. For part of his service as collector, William acted as agent for Richard Lyons, who had been assigned the customs as security for loans to Edward III. William also held the farm of the cloth custom at Yarmouth with Sir George Felbrigge for twenty years from 1362[28]. William's gentry connections extended beyond this commercial link with Felbrigge, and Nicholas Dagworth stood surety for him after his impeachment in 1376[29].

Hugh Fastolf came from an even better established and distinguished Yarmouth family. Between 1280 and 1391 ten Fastolfs served as bailiff and Hugh held the office nine times between September 1354 and September 1376. In the fourteenth century, Fastolfs served as Yarmouth's M.P. on eleven occasions, with Hugh being the town's representative in 1354, 1361, 1366, 1373 and 1377[30]. Like the Elyses, the Fastolfs retained their commercial roots in Yarmouth but invested very heavily in the East Anglian countryside; Hugh had property in nineteen villages and land well in excess of 1,000 acres[31] He also had very strong links with London and moved there, probably early in the 1380s, following marriage, his second, to the widow of a London grocer. He became deeply involved in the political life of the capital, serving as both alderman and sheriff[32]. Hugh was a shipowner and dealt in herring, wine, wool, cloth, salt, grain and ale. In London he joined the Grocers' Guild[33] Hugh Fastolf's gentry links were particularly well developed. Robert Cayley stood surety for him and he was involved in enfeoffments to use with Sir Roger de Boys, Sir Walter Bygod and Sir Robert Salle[34] He had business connections with the countesses of Pembroke and Norfolk and with the duke of Norfolk. Hugh's brother, John, married the daughter of a landower, was esquire to the earl of Warwick and entered the royal household. John's son, John Fastolf K.G., found service with the duke of Norfolk before joining the duke of Bedford[35].

In addition to his business interests, Hugh Fastolf worked extensively for the crown for over thirty years. Much of his early service was connected with the sea: serving as a ship's captain, acting as deputy to the admiral, raising retinues for service at sea and organising supplies.[36] He was engaged in the royal customs service at Yarmouth as collector and as controller[37]. In the 1360s, '70s and '80s he worked extensively in county administration, for example, serving on commissions of the peace, of inquiry and of *oyer* and *terminer* and acting as tax collector[38]. Fastolf was used more widely in, and received more from, royal service than any other Yarmouth burgess in the fourteenth century. His main rewards seem to have come not from wages but from royal grants: for example, in 1363 the wardship of the lands of John Holbrook, in 1377 the keeping of the alien priory of Panfield and Wells, and in 1387 the farm of the manor of Lowestoft[39].

Hugh Fastolf was undoubtedly a more eminent figure in county life than William Elys, but their backgrounds were not dissimilar. If Hugh had the better gentry connections, William was more closely attuned to the intricacies of royal finance. Through patronage and commercial networks, both men could trace links to John of Gaunt[40]. Both were indisputably bastions of the upper ranks of Yarmouth's burgess society. In the mid-1370s this burgess society was split by political discord, probably caused, and certainly accentuated, by economic pressures. The town's herring industry was dominated in the fourteenth century by a small group of burgess families, including the Elyses and the Fastolfs. This was clearly demonstrated during royal attempts to enforce the statute of herrings in the 1350s. While the industry flourished it was always possible for the lesser burgesses to make a living, but this became more difficult as the herring trade struck hard times. By the 1370s the problems of the industry were acute and the lesser burgesses bitterly resented the grip held by Yarmouth's leading families. What appeared to incense the lesser burgesses further were the connections of the town's rich with London merchants, which gave to some of the capital's fishmongers a share in the trade from which many of Yarmouth's own inhabitants increasingly felt themselves excluded.[41]. Not unexpectedly, in the context of medieval urban life this led to violence[42].

This violence came to a head in 1375 and 1376 and related investigations lingered on into 1377. Its immediate cause seems to have been connected with the grain rather than the herring trade, though the precise details are unclear. On 18 March 1375 a group of townsmen, apparently attempting to fix the price of corn in Yarmouth market, made 'confederaciones' to resist the bailiffs, two of whom were Hugh Fastolf and William Elys. The following day, the town court could not be held because the bailiffs were out pacifying the crowds.[43] In July Walter Sibille, a London fishmonger, accused a group of twenty-five townsmen, predominantly from the lower ranks, of assault, of driving him from the town and of stealing corn which he intended to ship to Bordeaux; in March he had been licensed to export five hundred quarters of wheat from Yarmouth. In

September 1375 the king took bonds for good behaviour from twenty-eight townsmen, four of whom were among Sibille's attackers. Sibille secured the imprisonment in Newgate of one of those involved, Geoffrey Pulle, but apparently made little headway in the case against him. On 13 July 1376 a group of Norfolk men, including Sir Ralph de Poleye, knight of the shire for Norfolk in the Good Parliament, secured Pulle's release from prison and a summons was issued to Walter Sibille and Hugh Fastolf to appear before the Council to explain their conduct. Fastolf had not only been bailiff in 1375, but he was also a frequent business partner of Sibille.

In the spring of 1376 the dispute between the greater and lesser burgesses was heard in the Good Parliament. A petition from the poor commons of Yarmouth sought redress for 'the various hardship, wrongs and oppressions done to them against their franchise by the great men of the town'. A further petition from Yarmouth's lesser burgesses claimed that the town's leading inhabitants bought up all the herring coming to the port, thereby improverishing their fellow townsmen and denying them their right to free trade[45] Parliamentary action by the lesser burgesses apparently did little to improve their position and seems to have attracted even greater hostility from their powerful neighbours. On 11 September 1376, the king, following strong rumours of unlawful assemblies in the town, ordered the bailiffs to take action to prevent disorder. In October thirty-four burgesses were identified as rich and powerful oppressors of the poor and had to give bonds for their good behaviour. This list of burgesses reads like a 'Who's Who' of Yarmouth society and their sureties included Walter Sibille[46]. The final outcome of this dispute is not known.

The accusations against William Elys, and possibly also those against Hugh Fastolf, stemmed not simply from political discord within Yarmouth. William Elys was impeached in 1376 as part of the general attack by the commons on financial and court corruption. The charges against him related to malpractice in the customs service at Yarmouth, where he was joint farmer of the cloth custom and agent for Richard Lyons. Lyons had been assigned the customs revenue at London, Yarmouth, Boston and Hull as security for the loan of 20,000 marks made in August 1374 and which was the subject of special investigation in the Good Parliament[47]. The principal charge against Elys involved the illegal levying of customs from a group of Scots merchants on board a Prussian vessel. The ship had been caught by storms in Kirkley Roads and had been driven ashore. William, it was said, claimed that the goods belonging to the Scots merchants had been landed and consequently levied import duties[48]. Evidence against Elys was given by two Lowestoft men, John Botild and William Cooper, who seem to have been only too willing to use national politics to further local interests, and in their case local interest was synonymous with self-interest. While claiming in their evidence to be able to show how herring could be made cheap, to the nation's advantage, both had been involved in several incidents over trading rights and customs dues in Kirkley Roads.

Following the assignment to him of the customs revenue at Yarmouth, Richard Lyons had sought to ensure its effective administration. Revenue collection at Kirkley Roads was particularly troublesome and Lyons petitioned Edward III concerning evasion of customs there. Among those accused was John Botild who, Lyons claimed, 'carried away rhenish wine and various other merchandise from the said Road without payment of the custom and subsidy'. Lyons argued that Botild and his confederates had prevented him from collecting dues in the Roads for two and a half years. When an investigation was ordered, Botild's defence was that he had already paid the customs on the wine to William Elys. Another of the accused, Lawrence Rochendale, claimed that William Elys, out of malice, on two occasions had refused to accept customs dues offered to him. Also charged with Botild were Richard Perles and William Donmowe of Lowestoft[49].

Whatever the merits of Lyon's petition, the king does not seem to have been satisfied with the collection of customs at Yarmouth. In 1375 collection in the port was apparently put in the hands of the Ipswich collectors and Yarmouth men were not appointed again until 1377[50]. The cloth custom remained in the hands of the farmers, William Elys and Sir George Felbrigge, and they obtained in February 1376 a judicial commission to investigate smuggling[51]. Following his impeachment and conviction, William Elys was imprisoned in the Tower, whence he secured his release in August 1376. He did not, however, obtain a pardon until April 1377 and then only following a thorough investigation and the further examination of Botild and Cooper in the parliament that met in January 1377[52].

In addition to the proceedings against Elys and the presentation of petitions by Yarmouth's lesser burgesses, the Good Parliament saw an attempt by Lowestoft to secure the reversal of the 1372 grant which annexed Kirkley Roads to Yarmouth. This annexation was bitterly resented and hotly contested by Lowestoft[53], whose inhabitants sought to avoid the tolls levied by Yarmouth in the Roads. For example, John Botild, Elys's accuser in 1376, was alleged to have bought secretly in October 1372 £50 worth of herring from an Ostend fisherman in Kirkley Roads and to have attempted to move them secretly at night. When apprehended, Botild claimed to have caught the fish himself[54]. In the Good Parliament, Lowestoft's attempt to break Yarmouth's hold on the Roads was supported by seven neighbouring counties *et autres de la commune*. The counties claimed that the grant of the Roads and the prohibition of fish sales within seven miles of Yarmouth had forced up the price of herring to the general harm of the country.[55] The complaints of Lowestoft and its allies were successful. The annexation of Kirkley Roads to Yarmouth was revoked and the bailiffs and commonalty were ordered to appear before the king on 4 July 1376 to give up the 1372 charter for cancellation[56].

In the spring and summer of 1376 the political fortunes of Great Yarmouth and its leading inhabitants seem to have reached their nadir. The town lost control of Kirkley Roads, and thus of what remained of its trade and the ensuing tolls; William Elys, a bailiff of Yarmouth and its M.P., was placed in the Tower, and the conduct of Hugh Fastolf, also a bailiff, was under investigation. The town's lesser burgesses had received a sympathetic hearing in parliament and Lowestoft's petitions had been supported by a substantial number of English counties. However, just as the major judgements of the Good Parliament were rapidly overturned, so the political fortunes of Great Yarmouth and its principal burgesses quickly revived. There was no change in the backkgrounds of the men ruling Yarmouth, both William Elys and Hugh Fastolf continued their political and administrative careers, and in 1378 Kirkley Roads were once more annexed to the town.

It seems clear that both Lowestoft and the lesser burgesses of Yarmouth used the political crisis in the spring of 1376 to advance their own causes. It seems equally clear that they had substantial, though unspecified, support in the commons, perhaps from those who saw their complaints as yet another means of adding to the discomfiture of John of Gaunt and the court party. The reversal of the major decisions of the Good Parliament stemmed from Gaunt's resurgence, especially from the early autumn of 1376 onwards. There is some evidence to suggest that in the 1376 crisis, Gaunt may have acted as patron for Yarmouth and its leading burgesses, although whether out of a positive desire to help the town or whether simply because Yarmouth's enemies in the commons were also his is uncertain.

During his impeachment, William Elys received firm support from his business partner, Sir George Felbrigge. Elys argued that the carriage of customs revenue from Yarmouth to Felbrigge in London had been threatened by John Botild and William Cooper who, he had believed, had been lying in wait at Wickam Market. Felbrigge entered a petition that Botild was a notorious smuggler whose evidence should not be believed. Botild and Cooper claimed, in giving testimony against Elys, that Felbrigge and Elys had procured their imprisonment to prevent their appearance in parliament.[57] Felbrigge was a substantial Suffolk landowner, holding part of his estates from John of Gaunt. He was well connected with the court and undertook much work for the crown. He was on the jury at Alice Perrer's trial for maintenance and was part of the court of chivalry hearing the case between Lords Lovell and Morley. He frequently served as a justice of the peace in Suffolk and undertook diplomatic missions to Calais, Flanders and Milan[58]. The success of his bid for the farm of the Yarmouth cloth custom may have been part of his reward for such service. Nicholas Dagworth, who stood surety for Elys after his impeachment, was a loyal servant of the court who had been used in 1375 and early 1376 to bolster William of Windsor in Ireland[59].

In the case of Yarmouth's dispute with Lowestoft, the intervention of John of Gaunt may have been more direct. The possible re-annexation of Kirkley Roads to Yarmouth was discussed in April 1378 at a meeting of the royal council attended by Gaunt. Yarmouth was granted control of the Roads until the next parliament, and in the meantime commissions of inquiry were to be set up. In the 1378 parliament there was continued hostility to Yarmouth's privileges, but this time a petition from the commons for cheap fish brought a regrant of Yarmouth's 1372 charter[60]. Walsingham had no doubt that Gaunt's influence was responsible and suggested that Yarmouth had bought his support[61]. Neither can it have been to Yarmouth's disadvantage that Walter Sibille formed part of the investigating team in 1378[62]. The town may have had more general support from some of London's fishmongers in its struggle against Lowestoft[63].

Constitutional historians have attempted to present the Good Parliament as an event in an evolutionary process, as part of an historical continuum. It is important that those investigating its political dimensions and significance should also seek to place the session in its context. In many important respects, the problems faced by Edward III in the Good Parliament were similar to those that had dogged his father and which were to afflict his grandson. An unsuccessful war, an unsure foreign policy, a country reluctant to grant taxes, a hostile parliament, a court weakened by factionalism and the absence of a strong hand at the helm were recurrent features. That there was a political crisis in 1376 is beyond doubt, but it was not isolated and in its essentials it was not unique, and that is as true of the local as of the national issues. In many instances, medieval English kings never solved local disputes; at best they kept them within bounds. Such disputes had a marked tendency to erupt when the king was weak or was threatened by other pressures. The quarrel between Yarmouth and Lowestoft, in 1376 was part of a centuries-old attempt by the town to control its herring trade. Whether the struggle was against the Cinque Ports, London or Lowestoft, it frequently rose to a peak during periods of national political tension when the crown's attentions and energies were diverted elsewhere. For example, trouble between Yarmouth and the Cinque Portsmen was particularly violent in the years immediately after Bannockburn[64], and the town's feud with London reached a climax between 1326 and 1330[65].

The dispute over Kirkley Roads should not be seen simply as a local issue: it also formed part of the general wrangling over mercantile policy which occupied so much parliamentary time after 1350, particularly under Richard II. Almost every session brought a reversal of the decisions of its predecessor[66] The Kirkley Roads affair dragged on because neither Edward III nor his grandson could readily find a solution to the conflict of interests involved at both national and local levels. If the king needed taxation, he had to listen to the demands of the shires for cheap food and of the merchant community for free trade. If he wished for loans, he responded to those who could provide them, often London financiers. In the Good Parliament many of these interests were present. The royal attitude to Kirkley Roads was governed in 1376, and frequently on other occasions, not so much by the strength of the cases presented by the immediate protagonists as by the influence of a particular interest group at a particular time.

At the local level there were two pressing concerns for the king: the capacity of Yarmouth to meet its financial commitments to the crown, as in 1372 and 1378[67], and its ability to respond to the needs of national defence. Although its shipping contribution to royal fleets had fallen from the high levels of the first half of the century, Yarmouth remained a major defensive centre between the Thames and the Wash. It was no accident that Kirkley Roads were put under Yarmouth's jurisdiction temporarily in 1385, and permanently in 1386, when Richard II feared the real possibility of a French invasion. The king hoped that with this grant the town would be able to support not only its farm and tax but also the cost of repairing its walls and strengthening its fortifications[68].

Tout emphasised 'the solidarity of the whole parliament in the common cause of restoring order and sound rule' in 1376[69], but it seems more probable that the Good Parliament witnessed not so much an attempt to destroy privileges as a drive to participate in them by those presently excluded. For example, Botild and Cooper attacked alleged malpractice at, and by, Yarmouth to advance their own fortunes, and much of Walworth's spleen against Lyons stemmed from his own unsuccessful bid for the Calais wool custom[70]. Just as Lowestoft and Yarmouth's lesser burgesses used the demands of the knights of the shire for cheap food to secure their own ends, so London merchants sought advantage from the king's need for money. Some in the capital had common interest with Elys and Fastolf, whilst others sought to harry those tainted with curial corruption. Neither in London nor in parliament was there unity of interest or continuity of policy, and it is against this background that the repeated changes in control at Kirkley Roads should be seen[71].

While royal mercantile policy may have lacked continuity, there were considerable political links between the Good Parliament and the Peasants' Revolt. The hostility to Gaunt and his associates, which was so much a feature in 1376, extended into 1381. The Savoy was burnt and Gaunt's lands, friends and servants were attacked in London and the provinces. Property belonging to Richard Lyons was sacked in Suffolk[72] and Lyons himself was killed by the insurgents in Cheapside. The rebels both in Norfolk and Suffolk demonstrated the continuing hostility to Yarmouth and its privileges. On 18 June 1381 a significant section of the Norfolk rebels, who had assembled at Norwich, marched on Yarmouth. Under Sir Roger Bacon, second-in-command in the east of the county, they were joined by a large number of Suffolk men. Despite its walls and gates, the town offered no resistance and the rebels entered with banners flying. Yarmouth surrendered its charter, which was torn in two: Bacon kept one half for his leader, Geoffrey Litster, and despatched the other to John Wraw, chief of the largest rebel group in Suffolk. The political aspects of the Peasants' Revolt in eastern Norfolk are paticularly marked with Litster apparently seeking to establish an administration of his own. At Yarmouth the rebels not only engaged in the common activities of prison breaking and of murdering Flemings, but they also established their own customs service and set about collecting revenues at Kirkley Roads[73].

It was not just Yarmouth's privileges that excited the attention of the rebels. Within the town, property belonging to William Elys and Hugh Fastolf was attacked. How far this was simply the work of the insurgents in unclear. Given the unpopularity of Elys and Fastolf with Yarmouth's lesser burgesses in 1376, it is not unlikely that the rebels had inside help. Whether internal support for the rebels influenced the decision of the bailiffs to offer no resistance to their entry is not known. Rural property belonging to Elys was also looted during the Peasant's Revolt, and sheep and customs revenue were stolen[74].

Emnity towards Hugh Fastolf seems to have been widespread. In addition to attacks on his tenements at Yarmouth, the Norfolk rebels robbed his property at Caister and their Suffolk counter-parts looted his manor at Bradwell, from where they were said to have taken goods worth £400. In London, his house in the parish of St Dunstan in the East was invaded, his wife beaten, and money, weapons, wine and ale were stolen. It was made clear to his wife that had Hugh been at home he would not have lived long[75]. The assaults on Fastolf are illustrative of the variety of rebel motivation in 1381. Hostility to him in East Anglia stemmed from a number of factors, from the general unpopularity of Yarmouth's privileges, from his role in Yarmouth's internal politics and from his participation in county administration. His work, over a long period, in raising naval contributions and in purveyance cannot have endeared him to the rural and coastal communities of Norfolk and Suffolk. The seal to his unpopularity was almost certainly his appointment in March 1381 to the commission enforcing the collection of the third poll tax in Norfolk. The threats and theft in London seem to have been entirely separate from events in East Anglia and to have arisen from a private property dispute[76].

Yarmouth's involvement in the Good Parliament, though a side issue to the main events, is interesting because it shows clearly not only the links between local and national issues but also the complexity of those links. It is not simply that an internal dispute among the town's burgesses and a quarrel with a neighbouring settlement, Lowestoft, became embroiled in the struggle for influence with, and over, an enfeebled Edward III. Although some Yarmouth men had connections with the court, others sought the help of those trying to limit the power of Gaunt, Latimer and their associates. While some of the town's burgesses had business contacts with London financiers and found their support valuable, London merchant society itself was divided. Richard Lyons and Walter Sibille, for differing reasons, were not universally popular within their own communities, the one through his links with Gaunt, the other through his membership of the Fishmongers' Guild. It is possible that Yarmouth's leading burgesses had the support of Gaunt and it seems probable that Lowestoft was helped by his critics. The outcome of the Good Parliament, as it affected Yarmouth and Lowestoft in their rival claims for control of Kirkley Roads, rested not so much on the force of the arguments they put forward as on the influence of the groups supporting them.

The Kirkley Roads affair also has a longer term significance. It formed part of a protracted series of disputes involving Yarmouth's struggle to control its own trade, particularly the herring trade. The crown found it impossible to bring about anything more than temporary respites and short-term solutions. When the monarchy was weak, or its attention diverted, these disputes had a marked tendency to erupt, frequently violently. Just as the dispute with Lowestoft became involved in national issues in 1376, so Yarmouth's other quarrels became enmeshed in broader policy matters. As Edward III responded to pressure rather than argument in the Good Parliament, so more generally decisions relating to Yarmouth and its privileges often revolved around the vagaries of mercantile legislation or the needs of war. The events of 1376 illustrate clearly the continuity of many themes in the political life of later medieval England and this phenomenon is as pronounced at the local as at the national level. In the short-term, there is the common hostility to Yarmouth in 1376 and in 1381; in the longer term, the involement of Yarmouth and Lowestoft in the Good Parliament is not without parallels with the participation of Yarmouth and the Cinque Ports in the quarrels between the crown and Simon de Montfort. Perhaps just as national and local issues are entwined so it is dangerous to isolate constitutional change from underlying and long-term political themes.

Notes

1. W. Stubbs, *The Constitutional History of England* (3 vols., 4th. ed., Oxford, 1886), II, pp. 448–55.
2. T.F. Tout, *Chapters in the Administrative History of Medieval England* (6 vols., Manchester, 1920–33), III, pp. 290–308; T.F.T. Plucknett, 'The Origin of Impeachment', *TRH*, 4th series, XXIV (1942), 47–71, and 'The Impeachments of 1376', *TRHS*, 5th series, I (1951), 153–64.
3. M. Mckisack, *The Fourteenth Century* (Oxford, 1959), p. 422.
4. M. Keen, *England in the Later Middle Ages* (London, 1973), pp. 263–4.
5. G. Holmes, *The Good Parliament* (Oxford, 1975), pp. 2–3.
6. *Ibid.*, pp. 7–100.
7. *Ibid.*, pp. 63–69, 108–10.
8. A. Saul, 'English Towns in the late middle ages: the case of Great Yarmouth', *Journal of Medieval History*, VIII (1982), 75–88.
9. W.G. Hoskins, *Local History in England* (2nd ed., London, 1972) pp. 238–39.
10. E.g., in 1372, 1377, 1378, 1385 and 1386: CCR, *1354–60*; p. 231; CCR, *1341–1417*, pp. 224–45, 254–56, 305; CPR, *1381–85*, p. 504; PRO, SC8/117/5844.
11. Hoskins, *Local History*, pp. 238–39.
12. Saul, 'English towns in the late middle ages', p. 77.
13. A Saul, 'Great Yarmouth and the Hundred Years War in the fourteenth century', *BIHR*, L11 (1979), 105–15; 'The Herring Industry at Great Yarmouth, 1280–1400', *Norfolk Archaeology*, XXXVIII (1981), 33–43.
14. PRO, E122/149/27.
15. H. M. Evans, 'The Sandbanks of Yarmouth and Lowestoft' *Mariner's Mirror*, XV (1929), 261–63; J.A. Steers, *The Coastline of England and Wales* (2nd ed., Cambridge 1964), pp. 346, 380.
16. It was frequently necessary to trans-ship cargoes. For example, in 1377 small boats took grain out to the royal fleet waiting off-shore, and in 1373 Hugh Fastolf used lighters to get wine into Yarmouth from his ship in Kirkley Roads. PRO,E101/20/7; CPR, *1370–74*, p. 307.
17. In the fifteenth century the best advice for navigating the approaches to Yarmouth at night was to wait until morning. *Sailing Instructions for the circumnaviation of England and for a Vovage to the Straits of Gibralter*, ed. E. D. Morgan (Hakluyt Society, LXXXIX, 1889), p. 11.
18. A. Saul, 'Great Yarmouth in the Fourteenth Century. A study in Trade, Politics and Society' (Oxford D.Phil thesis, 1975), pp. 38–40, 162–63.
19. CChR, *1341–1417*, pp. 224–25.
20. RP, II, p. 330; III, p. 49; CChR, *1341–1417*, pp. 225, 305; CPR, *1377–81*, p. 188; CPR, *1381–85*, pp. 105, 540; CPR, *1385–89*, p. 73.
21. CPR, *1399–1401*, p. 428; H. Swinden, *The History and Antiquities of the Ancient Burgh of Great Yarmouth* (Norwich, 1772), p. 643.
22. RP, II, p. 327–28.
23. *Ibid.*, p. 375.
24. Saul, 'Great Yarmouth in the Fourteenth Century', pp. 265–69.
25. *Ibid.* pp. 230, 368, 375; CPR, *1361–64*, p. 495; CPR, *1364–67*, p. 82; CPR, *1381–85*, p. 197.
26. He was licensed to export 100 sacks in 1374 and 400 in 1375 (CFR, *1369–77*, pp. 276, 329–30; CPR *1381–85*, p. 197).
27. William probably died in January or February 1382. His final account as collector ended on 1 February, when he was succeeded in that office by his son John. John Hacon was appointed deputy to the king's butler on 6 February 1382 (PRO, E356/14 m.31; CPR, *1361–64*, p. 312; CPR, *1381–85*, p. 103).
28. In 1362 both men recognised the farm's potential for efficient collectors, being willing to pay

some eighty per cent more than the cloth custom had yielded the previous year. Felbrigge relinquished the farm in 1399 and the following year the royal collectors raised £50 less than the £200 that Felbrigge had paid (Saul, 'Great Yarmouth in the Fourteenth Century', pp. 104–5).

29. CCR, 1374–77, pp. 437–38.
30. Saul, 'Great Yarmouth in the Fourteenth Century', pp. 264–69.
31. Ibid., pp. 230, 234, 375.
32. R. Bird, The Turbulent London of Richard II (London, 1949), pp. 55, 94, 96, 144.
33. Saul, 'Great Yarmouth in the Fourteenth Century', pp. 225–26, 369; Bird, Turbulent London, p. 96.
34. Saul, 'Great Yarmouth in the Fourteenth Century', pp. 231–32; E.L.T. John, 'The Parliamentary Representation of Norfolk, 1377–42' (Nottingham M.A. thesis, 1959), pp. 304–16.
35. Saul, 'Great Yarmouth in the Fourteenth Century', pp. 236–37.
36. E.g. PRO,E101/27/1, 30/28, E364/11 m.6; Saul, 'Great Yarmouth in the Fourteenth Century', pp. 58, 77, 127, 232.
37. Collector from March 1361 to April 1367 and controller from November 1351 to November 1354 (PRO,E356/5 m.19; 8 m.53, 54).
38. Saul, 'Great Yarmouth in the Fourteenth Century', pp. 55, 283–85.
39. CFR, 1356–68, p. 270; CFR, 1369–77, p. 336; CFR, 1377–83, p. 22; CFR, 1383–91, p. 192.
40. See below pp. 164–65.
41. Saul, 'The Herring Industry at Great Yarmouth', pp. 38–39.
42. Although, with the exception of serious disturbances in 1272, 1302–3, 1358–59 and 1375–76, Yarmouth was relatively free from internal political violence. (Saul, 'Great Yarmouth in the Fourteenth Century', pp. 244–47).
43. PRO, E163/5/15; Norfolk Record Office, Great Yarmouth Court Roll 1374/75, m.10.
44. CPR, 1374–77, pp. 81, 157, 160; CCR, 1374–77, p. 431; Saul, 'Great Yarmouth in the Fourteenth Century', pp. 171–72, 246–47; Holmes, Good Parliament, p. 118.
45. RP, II, pp. 352–53.
46. CCR, 1374–77, pp. 415, 470.
47. Holmes, Good Parliament, pp. 73, 1099.
48. RP, II, p. 327.
49. PRO,SC8/10378, 79.
50. Although the Yarmouth collectors continued to account at the Exchequer (CFR, 1369–77, p. 307; CFR, 1377–83, p. 7; PRO,E356/8 m.54; 14 m.31).
51. CPR, 1374–77, p. 311.
52. PRO, SC8/660; 661; RP, II, pp. 374–75; CCR, 1374–77, p. 438; CPR, 1374–77, p. 455; Tout,
     Chapters, III, p. 317.
53. The full chronology of the dispute between Yarmouth and Lowestoft can be found in Select Cases Before the King's Council, 1243–1482, ed. I.S. Leadham and J.F. Baldwin (Selden Society, XXXV, 1918).
54. Swinden, Great Yarmouth, pp. 614–15.
55. RP, II, pp. 330, 332, 334.
56. CCR, 1374–77, pp. 432, 434.
57. RP, II, p. 328; PRO, SC8/10404.
58. W. Copinger, The Manors of Suffolk. Notes on their History and Devolution (7 vols., Manchester and London, 1905–11), III, 87; John of Gaunt's Register, 1379–1383, ed. F.C. Lodge and R. Somerville (2 vols., Camden Society, 3rd Series, LVI and LVII, 1937) I, p. 94; CFR, 1356–68, p. 352; CPR, 1388–92, pp. 137, 139, 342, 525; PRO,E364/12 m.6; 13 m.5; 16 m.4.
59. CCR, 1374–77, pp. 437–38; Holmes, Good Parliament, pp. 96–97.
60. CPR, 1377–81, p. 188; RP, III, pp. 49, 222, CCR, 1341–1417, pp. 254–55.
61. Chronicon Angliae, 1328–88, Auctore Monacho Quodam Sancti Albani, ed. E.M. Thompson (RS, 1874), p. 95.

62. In 1379 Sibille and his fellow Londoner, John Horn, fitted out at their own expense a small fleet to protect the east coast fisheries from foreign attack. *CIM, 1–12 Richard II*, no. 84; *RP*, III, p. 63; *Chronicon Angliae*, p. 170.
63. L.F. Salzman, *English Industries of the Middle Ages* (2nd ed., Oxford, 1923), p. 261.
64. *CPR, 1313–17*, pp. 140, 142, 514, 520, 576; *CCR, 1313–18*, pp. 95, 367; *RP*, I, p. 332; PRO, SC8/E434 and 2380.
65. Saul, 'Great Yarmouth in the Fourteenth Century', pp. 159–61.
66. G. Unwin, *Finance and Trade under Edward III* (Manchester, 1918), pp. xxxvi–vii, 237.
67. *CCR, 1341–1417*, pp. .224–25, 254–56; PRO, SC8/5136, 13188, 5844.
68. *CPR, 1381–85*, p. 540; *CCR, 1341–1417*, p. 305.
69. T.F. Tout, 'The English Parliament and Public Opinion, 1376–88' in *Historical Studies of the English Parliament*, ed. E.B. Fryde and E. Miller (2 vols., Cambridge), 1970, I, 305.
70. *The Anonimalle Chronicle, 1333–1381*, ed. V.H. Galbraith (Manchester, 1927), p. 86.
71. Bird, *Turbulent London*, p. 1; Unwin, *Finance and Trade*, pp. xxii–iii.
72. C. Oman, *The Great Revolt of 1381* (2nd ed., Oxford, 1969), p. 103.
73. E. Powell, *The Rising in East Anglia* (Cambridge, 1896), pp. 32–33; Oman, *Great Revolt*, pp. 117–18.
74. *CPR, 1381–85*, p. 197; Powell, *Rising*, pp. 32–33.
75. Oman, *Great Revolt*, pp. 108–9; Powell, *Rising*, pp. 32–33; *CPR, 1381–85*, pp. 30–31.
76. *CFR, 1377–83*, pp. 248–49; *CPR, 1381–85*, pp. 30–31.

9

A Collector of Apocryphal Anecdotes:
John Blacman Revisited

Roger Lovatt
Peterhouse, Cambridge

What credence can we give to the account of Henry VI provided by John Blacman in his *Collectarium Mansuetudinum et Bonorum Morum Regis Henrici VI?*[1] This question has recently been raised in particularly pointed form by the publication of Dr Wolffe's re-appraisal of the king which opens with, and in a sense rests upon, a comprehensive assault on Blacman's credibility.[2] The *Collectarium* is dismissed as mere hagiography, a series of trivial and apocryphal anecdotes, quite at odds with other contemporary evidence, and providing a totally false picture of the king which must be completely discounted in any modern, critical biography. The status of Blacman's work is also of consequence for broader reasons. We have no other extended account of the king's personality from an apparently contemporary hand. In a sense Dr Wolffe acknowledges this fact by placing his attack on the authority of the *Collectarium* right at the beginning of his book, making it the foundation for what follows. The character of the king and its impact on the course of his reign clearly pose difficult, and currently controversial, questions, as is evidenced by the very different answers recently provided by Dr Wolffe and Professor Griffiths.[3] However, if Blacman's account is to be taken at its face value, he is indeed an informed witness. He claimed to have been intimate with the king over a long period. He participated in many of the king's central interests. He moved readily within the circle of the king's closest associates and was able to call on their recollections when he came to write the *Collectarium*. His credentials are impressive and it matters to what extent they can be impugned. In a recent essay, I attempted to say something about Blacman's career, his milieu and his links with the king, and also to place his characterisation of the king within the general framework of contemporary spirituality.[4] In this paper I want to concentrate on the more precise issue of assessing the authority of the *Collectarium*.

The most radical criticism of the authority of the *Collectarium* has taken the form of denying Blacman's authorship. In a strict sense, even if this suggestion could be proved it would not of itself demonstrate that the work was entirely untrustworthy. It would merely mean that it had a different author. Nevertheless, such an attack does go to the heart of an important issue because the details of Blacman's career provide some of his most persuasive credentials as the king's biographer. In assessing the veracity of the *Collectarium*, it matters that its author was at Eton for some eleven years from 1443 until 1454. It also matters that his patrons and associates were men as familiar with Henry VI as Henry Sever, the royal almoner; Bishop Carpenter, another royal chaplain; Robert Wodelarke, the king's devoted servant in Cambridge; and, above all, William Waynflete, of all Henry's bishops perhaps the one closest personally to him.[5] So what evidence is there to suggest that Blacman was not the author? Two lines of argument are adduced. Firstly, it is pointed out that, although Blacman is said to have been the king's spiritual director or confessor, there is no record of his name amongst the various lists of royal chaplains.[6] However, at no point in the *Collectarium* does Blacman in fact claim to have been the king's confessor or chaplain in any official sense. This claim was actually made, not by Blacman, but by his editor, M.R. James.[7] It is therefore not surprising that his name does not appear in any official list of royal chaplains. What Blacman does tell us is that from time to time he said mass in the king's presence and also apparently held spiritual conversations with him.[8] Neither activity presupposes any formal, household appointment. They suggest simply that Blacman was a priest moving within the king's immediate circle. This is exactly what is indicated in any case by his Eton fellowship. What is more, there is additional and informed contemporary evidence that Blacman did occupy precisely such a position. Later in his life, one of Blacman's *confrères* at the Witham Charterhouse wrote a short account of him, verifiable in all of its other details, in which he is described as *minister rege*, or priest to the king.[9] So he was, no more and no less.

The second argument against Blacman's authorship is derived from the words used on the title page of Copland's edition, where the *Collectarium* is described as *ex collectione Magistri Joannis Blakman*. It is held that this phrase does not amount to an unequivocal assertion of Blacman's authorship and may signify no more than that the work was found amongst his papers.[10] In itself such an argument is scarcely conclusive in any direction. The most natural sense of these words might suggest that they merely echo the title *Collectarium*, which is itself an accurate description of the work. For it is exactly a gathering of reminiscences about the king, some by Blacman himself, some by various named informants and others without attribution. From this point of view, Blacman can indeed perhaps best be regarded as in part a compiler rather than as the author of an entirely original text. But he would not be alone amongst medieval writers in this respect.

However, the authorship question does not hinge on ambiguities such as these. There is a range of arguments in favour of Blacman's hand which do not depend on Copland's attribution, accurately circumstantial in detail though it is, and which seem cumulatively quite decisive.[11] In essence, these consist of a series of affinities, or parallels, between the contents of the *Collectarium* and what we know of Blacman himself. The work bears his fingerprints, as it were, and they are everywhere. For example, it shows a particular interest in the affairs of Eton. One of its most vivid passages dwells on the king's close interest in his new foundation, twice quoting Henry's own words, and stressing his concern to find suitable teachers and pupils, as well as his anxiety lest the boys should be corrupted by the proximity of the court. Such intimate knowledge would be natural in one who was himself a fellow of Eton at the time. Likewise, although few of the occurrences mentioned in the *Collectarium* are localised, it is significant that two of them – including one directly involving its author – are described as having taken place at Windsor.[12] In the same vein, although the main purpose of the work is the portrayal of character and it shows little concern for the recording of events or the establishment of any chronology, it is remarkable how much of its material is based on incidents which took place between 1443 and 1452.[13] Yet these are exactly the years when Blacman was closest to the king, that is, while he was a fellow of Eton. Again, some of these fingerprints are fragmentary yet strikingly precise. In one of Blacman's books there is an annotation in his own hand, drawing attention to Henry VI's habitual oath, 'forsooth and forsooth'. On no less than three occasions the *Collectarium* also mentions Henry's use of this same oath, and dwells on the matter as an illustration of his modesty of speech. Not only is this coincidence so particular as to be in itself, one might almost say, a conclusive indication of Blacman's authorship, but there is in fact independent, external evidence that this was indeed an expression commonly used by the king.[14]

Others of these fingerprints are apparent in the general character of the work. They are unmistakeable both in the central theme of the *Collectarium* and also in what the work tells us of the environment in which it was composed. Far from being a portrayal of bland, anodyne sanctity, the *Collectarium* casts Henry in the precisely detailed role of a paradigm of contemporary lay piety. His devotional life is a specific exemplar of late-medieval spirituality.[15] However, what matters in this context is the range of affinities between what is described in the *Collectarium* and what we know of Blacman's own spiritual life. Some of these affinities are matters of detail, although perhaps the more persuasive for that. As an aspect of Henry's devotion to the suffering humanity of Christ, the *Collectarium* records how the king had an image of the Five Wounds placed before him at mealtimes. Amongst contemporary *dévots*, this would immediately be identified as the emblem of the Bridgettine community at Syon, the most distinguished religious house to be founded in late-medieval England. Blacman's own library included two volumes of the *Revelations* of St Bridget. When the *Collectarium* described Henry as an *imitator* of Christ, this was not a common-place but a term of art, and it serves as a reminder that Blacman owned a text of the *Imitatio Christi*, a comparatively rare book in England at the time. Or, again, the *Collectarium* dwells on the king's devotion to St Anselm (not a popular cult in mid-fifteenth-century England) and to St Dunstan. Blacman's library con-tained no less than six works attributed to Anselm as well as a volume of saints' lives which almost certainly included an account of Dunstan.[16] Equally, it is important to consider the general character of the king's religious life as portrayed in the *Collectarium*. His was a spirituality imbued with the physical manifestations of devotion, dwelling on the wounds of the Crucifixion, enjoying revelations from the saints and corporal visions of the Assumption, and intensifying adoration of the Real Presence to the point of visualisation. This concrete, emotionally overwrought piety represents a precise strain in contem-porary English spirituality, a strain exemplified by the writings of Richard Rolle and, conversely, one resisted by Walter Hilton and the author of *The Cloud of Unknowing*. It is as striking that Blacman should have owned two of Rolle's works, the *Emendatio Vitae* and the *Incendium Amoris*, as that his comprehensive library of modern spiritual literature should have contained nothing from the pen of Walter Hilton.[17] Time and again the king's piety, as described in the *Collectarium*, finds a distinctive echo in Blacman's own devotional life. Biog-rapher and subject are as one, and these resonances are so distinctive as to embody a formidable case for Blacman's authorship.

The same conclusion can be drawn from reconstructing the environment in which the *Collectarium* was written. In general, it seems that its author did not move readily amongst the nobility, nor was he familiar with political, diplomatic or military affairs. His interests lay with the king almost as a private person, with his character and behaviour, and particularly with his devotional and charitable activities. But this picture can be given more precision, because casual references in the *Collectarium* enable us to people the author's milieu. Some-times he describes his informants in general, though still revealing, terms such as the king's 'privy servants', many who were 'once of his household', or 'some in his confidence to whom he was used to reveal his secrets'.[18] Elsewhere these figures assume more definite shape when the author specifically identifies his sources or mentions other people by name. The result is the emergence of a homogeneous group whose careers strikingly coincide with Blacman's own. They might be characterised as the king's *familiares*, that is, his non-noble, personal associates, churchmen and graduates, often linked with Eton and King's. They include Bishop Aiscough (the king's confessor, a benefactor of Eton and one of the commissioners to draw up the first statutes for King's College), Bishop Waynflete (provost and benefactor of Eton), Bishop Carpenter

(royal chaplain and feoffee of Eton), Bishop Moleyns (keeper of the privy seal
and another feoffee of Eton) and William Towne (a foundation fellow of King's
College who declined the opportunity to succeed Blacman as warden of King's
Hall in 1457). To these can be added a similar group who were with the king
when he was pursued and finally captured in July 1465. They consisted of Sir
Richard Tunstall, the king's chamberlain; Thomas Mannyng, formerly the
king's secretary and dean of St George's, Windsor; and John Bedon, another
Oxford theologian.[19] In other words, the people whom Blacman would have
known as a fellow of Eton, or later at Cambridge, do indeed figure in the pages of
the *Collectarium*. Similarly, the work reflects many of the concerns of this group,
making little reference to other matters. There are no false notes, no bogus
attempts to gain credence, but rather a strong sense of circumstance and
homogeneity. The world of Blacman and the world of the *Collectarium* are all of
a piece.[20]

The authority of the *Collectarium* has also come to be seen as dependent in
large measure on the date of its composition. The line of reasoning is a
straightforward one. If the work was composed after 1485, and particularly in
the 1490s, then it can be dismissed as a mere product of Tudor propaganda,
compiled – like the Windsor *Miracula* – simply as a *pièce justificative* in the official
campaign for Henry VI's canonisation.[21] Before turning to this issue, it is worth
stressing that any solution to the dating problem is not nearly so consequential
as this proposition suggests. The argument rests on the assumption that evidence
produced in support of a canonisation process is *ipso facto* to be discounted. Have
the Bollandists laboured in vain for two hundred and fifty years? Are we to doubt
that St Thomas Cantilupe had a taste for lamprey pie simply because our only
evidence for this fact is a deposition made at the canonisation enquiry, even
though the deponent had been Thomas's personal servant on and off for thirty
years?[22] To be sure, the exegesis of hagiographical material requires particular
subtlety and sensitivity, but it should no longer need to be stressed that
information contained in canonisation processes is to be approached like any
other historical evidence, to be weighed and tested, sometimes found wanting
and sometimes reliable. To discard such material on principle is as gullible as to
accept it at face value. The *Collectarium* may be telling the truth, or it may not.
The purpose for which it was written is only one clue to the resolution of that
dilemma. What is more, it is mistaken to regard the date of 1485 as representing
a watershed in this respect. The Tudors did not invent the cult of Henry VI.
Rather they took over for their own purposes a cult which was already
flourishing. It is clear that many people were hoping for the canonisation of
Henry VI well before Bosworth Field, and a work written before that date might
be as hagiographical in purpose as one written later.[23] It is as unsafe to argue that
the *Collectarium* can be discounted if it was written after 1485 as it is to suggest
that it must be trustworthy if it was composed earlier. Nevertheless, the date of
the work must represent one consideration in assessing its status, and here I must

immediately acknowledge that I was too hasty in stating in my earlier study that Blacman was buried in January 1485. This assertion may rest upon a misapprehension and, for the moment at least, it is best to regard the date of his death as uncertain.[24]

There are three passages in the *Collectarium* which appear to give substance to the view that it must have been compiled during the reign of Henry VII. The first occurs in the Prologue, where Blacman refers to Henry VI as having been twice crowned as 'the rightful heir' of both England and France.[25] It is pointed out that such a statement would have been treasonable if it was made between 1471 and 1485, and therefore that the *Collectarium* cannot have been written before Henry VII came to the throne.[26] Would that the issue were quite so straightforward. In general, the fact that a statement is treasonable does not of itself indicate when it was uttered. Men did make treasonable remarks in the fifteenth century, especially concerning the succession dispute. Equally, it remains true that Henry was twice crowned as rightful heir to the two kingdoms, at least in the eyes of those who officiated at the coronations, regardless of any opposing legitimist theories. There are also some more specific considerations which suggest that this accusation of treason may not carry such weight as appears at first sight. In particular, if the *Collectarium* was compiled in Richard III's reign then its dynastic background was equivocal. It is a commonplace that Richard's régime was insecure and that the need to attract support was his dominant political motive. In order to discredit the memory of Edward IV, and win the backing of his brother's enemies, Richard deliberately pointed the contrast between his own assumed position as the defender of morality and orthodoxy and the viciousness of his brother. To this end Edward's marriage was attacked as an adulterous union, his mistress was forced to do penance as a whore in the streets of London, and his government was publicly characterised as motivated by sensuality and concupiscence with 'every good maiden and woman standing in dread to be ravished and defouled'. According to some reports, Richard was even prepared to vilify the reputation of his own mother by asserting that his brother was illegitimate.[27] This search for allies bordered on the reckless and may in fact have gone further than mere denigration of his predecessor. Certainly, where Edward had been hostile towards Henry VI's greatest monument, King's College, Richard was lavish in his generosity.[28] It was perhaps in the same spirit that Richard decided to translate Henry's body to a more fitting tomb at Windsor, despite the irony of its presence in the Yorkist mausoleum next to the grave of Edward IV. The translation might be interpreted as an act of dynastic reconciliation by which Richard could hope to capitalise on a flourishing cult and even bid for Lancastrian support. Against such a background of dynastic opportunism, it is difficult to be quite so categorical about the treasonable implications of Blacman's words.

The second of these 'dating' passages occurs towards the end of the work, where Blacman refers to 'the long series of miracles' performed at Henry's grave.

It is argued that the recorded miracles in the Windsor *Miracula* do not become numerous until 1484 and hence that reference to a 'long series' must imply a date well into the 1490s for the composition of the *Collectarium*.[29] The problem here arises over the concept of 'recorded miracles'. The surviving record of the miracles was apparently initiated by the canons of Windsor soon after Henry's body was translated to St George's from Chertsey Abbey in 1484. But the Windsor *Miracula* does not provide a comprehensive account of all the miracles that took place between 1471 and 1500. On the contrary, it has little to say about the 'Chertsey' period from 1471 to 1484 and deals mainly with the 'Windsor' years from 1484 to 1500. In part this reflects the circumstances in which the work was compiled.[30] Soon after the king's body came into their possession, the canons began to collect the depositions of *miraculés* who visited the Windsor shrine. Their vernacular statements, which were later edited and translated to form the Latin *Miracula*, naturally concentrated on miracles which had some association with Windsor, sometimes because they had taken place recently, after the king's body was moved from Chertsey, or perhaps because a particular miracle was associated with a vow to undertake the Windsor pilgrimage. In other words, one reason why the recorded miracles largely date from 1484 onwards is that the formal record was begun by the canons in 1484. However, there are further complexities. There is evidence that the *Miracula* was also produced with the polemical intention of denigrating the earlier history of the cult and ensuring that this potentially lucrative devotion remained centred on Windsor. In one deposition, which was almost certainly made as early as 1484 or 1485, the canons recorded evidence discreditable to the Chertsey community, suggesting that they were dismissive of the cult and anxious to rid themselves of any links with it.[31] This same accusation was repeated by the canons in 1498 when they found themselves faced with two other competing claims for the king's body from the abbot of Chertsey and the abbot of Westminster. The canons fought their corner before the royal council, drawing particular attention to the hypocrisy of the abbot of Chertsey who, so they argued, had earlier shown an indecent haste to be rid of the body by breaking the ground for its exhumation with his own hands.[32] The verdict of the royal council went in favour of Westminster, but there are signs that the canons were not prepared to accept the decision, and in any case it had not been enforced when the Latin text of the *Miracula* was completed, probably in 1500.[33] Hence the purpose of the compilation was not simply to provide evidence of miracles for the canonisation process but also to strengthen the canons' claim to the body by demonstrating the efficacy of the 'Windsor', as opposed to the 'Chertsey', cult.[34] In a word, the recorded miracles largely seem to date from the period after August 1484 partly because the surviving record was not begun until then and partly because the compilers of this record had an interest in belittling the previous history of the cult.

In fact, there can be no doubt that belief in Henry's sanctity was widespread long before his body was translated to Windsor. The cult seems to have first developed as early as 1472–3 and by the end of the decade was already sufficiently popular to alarm the authorities. A statue of Henry VI in York Minster soon came to be venerated as though the king's sanctity was established. The statue was removed, and in October 1479 the archbishop of York condemned the veneration as being in contempt of the church and also in disparagement of Edward IV.[35] Similarly, only a year later Edward himself enlisted the aid of the London Mercers' Company to prevent the 'grete usage' of pilgrimages to Chertsey.[36] Subsequently, even Henry VII, who was certainly not sympathetic to the claims of the monks of Chertsey, testified in a petition to the papacy to the miracles worked while the king's body was buried there and to the crowds of pilgrims who were consequently attracted to the abbey, Indeed, the Windsor *Miracula*, albeit inadvertently, tells the same story for it shows that the Windsor pilgrimage enjoyed its greatest popularity during the years immediately after Henry's body was moved there, that is in 1484, 1485 and 1486.[37] The conclusion seems inescapable that the popular – as opposed to the official – cult was already at its most vigorous by the time the translation took place. In these circumstances, it is clear that one could well refer to a 'long series of miracles' in, say, 1480, and there are no grounds for assuming that such words could not have been used before 1490.

Finally, it is held that the *Collectarium* must have been composed after 1485 because it contains 'a clear reference to the downfall of the House of York'.[38] Before turning to this issue, it is worth recalling that it was precisely the vagueness of these remarks concerning the dynastic question – and not their clarity – which led M.R. James, its most recent editor, to infer that the work must have been written *before* Henry VII's accession. In fact, the issue is not at all straightforward, and Blacman does not refer in so many words to the downfall of the Yorkists. What he does say is much more ambiguous. He states that Henry was murdered so that 'others might, as was then the expectation, peaceably possess the kingdom'.[39] This is opaque to a degree and the words merit close scrutiny. What is immediately noticeable is that no names are mentioned, no Yorkists and no Tudors. This omission is in itself sufficiently inexplicable, particularly if it is assumed that the work was in some way officially sponsored. If the Tudors had come to the throne, why is this fact not acknowledged in unequivocal terms? One is forced to conclude that what is not said is more significant than what is said. In reality, the words may well imply the exact opposite, their oracular quality of itself indicating that the Tudors had not yet succeeded.

So what do these words mean? The implication is that those who murdered Henry had not achieved their expectation of peaceably possessing the kingdom. Two possibilities suggest themselves. The first is that they refer to the overthrow of Edward V and the usurpation of Richard III; that is, the direct line of Edward IV, who was responsible for Henry's murder, did indeed lose the kingdom. But, if the *Collectarium* was written in Richard III's reign, it would be advisable to phrase so sensitive an observation in decent obscurity. The second, and more likely, possibility arises from Blacman's use of the word 'peaceably'. He does not say that those who murdered Henry do not possess the kingdom; rather he says that they do not peaceably possess it. The difference is crucial. The statement simply means that the usurper's rule is disturbed, and so indeed was the case. Many people who had originally welcomed Edward IV's accession as promising an end to disorder subsequently complained that their hopes had been dashed. The same disenchantment might equally well have been voiced after 1471. The murder of Henry, following so soon after the death of his son Edward, could be expected to bring political conflict to an end since there was no obvious Lancastrian claimant left alive.[40] However, the extent of Edward IV's subsequent failure to maintain order, despite the orthodox view to the contrary, has recently been well stressed. 'England', we are told, 'was not a noticeably more law-abiding country in 1483 than it had been in 1461.'[41] The parliaments of 1472–5 and 1483 both complained about endemic violence. There was serious disorder throughout the Welsh border during the 1470s and in Lancaster at the end of the decade. In particular, the west country was chronically disturbed in the 1470s, to say nothing of the abortive rebellion of October 1483, and, if the *Collectarium* was compiled, as seems likely, while Blacman was a member of the west country charterhouse of Witham, it would be entirely accurate for him to reflect that the promise of an end to disorder inherent in justifying Henry's murder had indeed not been fulfilled.[42]

In reality, the references to the dynastic issue in the *Collectarium*, far from suggesting that the work was composed after 1485, indicate exactly the opposite. On no less than four occasions the matter is mentioned. Each time the sentiments are either backward-looking or opaquely non-committal. Besides the remark already discussed, Blacman refers briefly at the beginning of the work to Henry's royal descent and to his double coronation, but then adds with meaningful reticence that he will say nothing further about the issue as it is 'plainly known to all'. Henry's own statements, as recorded in the *Collectarium*, indicate resignation and retrospection. In captivity he is recorded as saying that he does not greatly care about his earthly kingdom and that 'our kinsman of March thrusts himself into it as is his pleasure'. Elsewhere he is quoted as reflecting on the fact that both his father and his grandfather had been king, that he himself had been crowned with unanimous support, and that he had subsequently worn the crown for forty years.[43] Despite such persistent prompting, at no point does the *Collectarium* add any comments on the events of 1485. If, as is sometimes argued, the work was an exercise in officially sponsored propaganda, some such reference to the Tudor succession would have been axiomatic. Blacman's account has been likened as propaganda to John Rous's *Historia Regum Angliae*, but the difference is decisive. As was fitting and inevitable, Rous dedicated his work in fulsome terms to Henry VII, in the same way that Polydore Vergil was later to do to Henry VIII.[44] But nowhere in the

Collectarium is there an unambiguous reference to the Tudors. It is a silence that speaks volumes for the date of the work.

There are other silences which are equally meaningful in this regard. At one point Blacman refers to the miracles taking place at Henry's grave without making any mention of the removal of his body to Windsor. The wording is unaccountably laconic if the translation had already taken place. Elsewhere Blacman stresses the way in which Henry VI cared for his two youthful half-brothers, Edmund and Jasper Tudor. Indeed, he is a unique authority for this period in their lives. But there is no reference to the crucial dynastic role of Edmund, as would surely have been obligatory after 1485. On two occasions Blacman talks of the death of Henry VI. Apart from stating that he was murdered, no details are given concerning the manner of his death or who was directly responsible for it.[45] It is a reticence entirely explicable in Edward IV's reign, and perhaps even more in that of his brother, but incomprehensible subsequently. Similarly, although the *Collectarium* dwells at length on Henry's virtues, in the circumstances of its own day it actually has very little to say about any strictly miraculous events associated with the king. The tone is quite different from that of the *Miracula* in being more modest and personal, and clearly implies that the work was written before any formal canonisation process had been undertaken. Certainly it is difficult to believe that a work as disorganised and inconsequential as the *Collectarium* could ever have been intended to form part of any official dossier. Its structure is of a piece with its status. It is a random, informal collection of disordered reminiscences.

There are difficulties in establishing a precise chronology for the composition of the *Collectarium*. The work is repetitious; men who are known to have been dead by 1471 are unaccountably mentioned as though they were still alive; and the last chapter has the appearance of an afterthought.[46] The process of composition may well have been protracted and unsystematic. For the moment, it is no longer possible to solve these problems by the simple establishment of a *terminus ad quem* in the date of Blacman's death. Nevertheless, it is certain that he was sixty-six years old in 1474, and would have been about seventy-seven in 1485.[47] On these grounds alone, an earlier date must be highly likely. It seems inconceivable that he could have written the work, as is sometimes suggested, in the later 1490s. However, the date does not depend on such considerations alone. There is ample evidence from other sources that it was completed before 1485.

In assessing the authority of the *Collectarium*, it matters that it was indeed compiled by John Blacman simply because of the closeness of his known associations with the king and also, it should be stressed, his access over a considerable period to informed sources.[48] Equally it matters that the work cannot be dismissed as mere Tudor propaganda. But these conclusions do not entirely resolve the central problem. That is, can the *Collectarium* be believed? Is it no more than a series of apocryphal anecdotes? Or, if we look carefully, does it represent a genuine, if partial, recollection of Henry VI by a man who had once lived at his court and looked upon him? The answer, as one might expect, is not straightforward. First of all, we must be aware of the limitations of Blacman's account. As he made clear at the outset, his purpose was 'to treat of some matters to the praise of God and of . . . King Henry' and to 'set forth somewhat concerning the many virtues of that king'.[49] The work was not intended to be a comprehensive biography, still less a chronicle of the times. It is a brief character sketch, focussed particularly on the king's religious life and perhaps even more precisely on his observance of the Ten Commandments. It has nothing directly to say about public affairs. Blacman does not tell us what we want to know, but what he wants us to know. In this respect, if not in others, he is reminiscent of those earlier royal biographers, the priest of St David's and the monk of St Bertin. Equally, as Blacman himself implies, the work is not carefully planned. It appears episodic, disordered and even jejune. Some of this appearance may be deceptive; it is the art that conceals art. In any case, the real value of the work lies not in its sophistication but in its immediacy.

Equally we must not expect to find in the *Collectarium* an unbiassed, even-handed account of the king, warts and all. As its author admits, the work is partial and tendentious; its central concern is the king's 'many virtues'. Hence, it has been argued that the *Collectarium* must be disregarded because it has so little to say about Henry's many political failures.[50] One immediate response might be that it is not concerned with political matters, nor with Henry's failures. But this is a mere debating point. The reality is both more subtle and more interesting. No sensitive, attentive reading of the *Collectarium* could come to the conclusion that the work ignores Henry's defects as a monarch. Although Dr Wolffe bases his view of Henry VI on the premise that the *Collectarium* is entirely untrustworthy, the paradoxical fact is that it provides ample support for many of his criticisms of the king. Hence, Blacman's monarch is prone to indiscriminate largesse, especially towards the members of his household. He is reluctant to enforce the full rigours of the law. He shows an erratic attitude to public affairs which ranges from indifference, through censorious meddling to obsessive enthusiasm. He is a king who does not seem to mix readily with his aristocracy, who is alienated from their manner of life and fails to provide them with any form of leadership. He is self-absorbed, indifferent towards conventional royal obligations such as accessibility and display, more concerned with matters of the spirit than with those of the battlefield. All of this is clear in the *Collectarium*.[51] There is no disagreement over the facts but over their interpretation. For Blacman, the king's public vices are redefined as private virtues. His largesse becomes charity, and his readiness to issue pardons becomes mercy. His dislike for the ways of his nobility is an austere, modest piety, and his self-absorption is a mind withdrawn from the things of this world. It is worth dwelling on a specific instance of this process of redefinition and the consequent misapprehension it can provoke. According to Dr Wolffe, one illustration of the inadequacy of the *Collectarium* is provided by the fact that it makes no mention of Henry's mental incapacity. Yet this is simply not true. Blacman describes Henry as being at times 'not conscious of himself or of those about him, as if he were a man in a trance'. This is an entirely accurate description, in brief, of the acute withdrawal that seems to have been the main symptom of Henry's mental breakdown. But the plain meaning of Blacman's words can be missed simply because he redefines the king's condition as one of spiritual rapture, 'on the verge of heaven, having his conversation in heaven'.[52] Such misunderstandings largely arise from the fact that, rightly or wrongly, Blacman simply does not accept traditional notions of good kingship, and chooses to justify Henry on quite different grounds. He is concerned, one might say, with the tension between private and public moralities. Not only does he reinterpret public vices as private virtues, but he transposes the dictum about a successful king having much ado to be saved by implying that political failure (or, at least, its causes) might be a prerequisite for personal salvation. In a word, we are directed to consider Henry as a man and not as a king. Moreover, this is not some eccentric whimsy on Blacman's part. The *Collectarium* is characteristic of the individualistic, private, self-regarding and often world-weary piety of the later middle ages. At its most sober, this is to be seen in the *Imitatio Christi*, at its most exuberant in the life of Margery Kempe. It is well exemplified in the popularity of that least collectivised of monastic orders, the Carthusians, and in the general shift away from monastic foundations towards the endowment of chantries. It is a view which Blacman articulated in so many words in his own devotional commonplace book (in itself a typical, and common, product of the individualistic spirituality of the period). Contemplating entry into the Carthusian order, he dwelt at length on the need to die to this world in order to gain life in the next. In other words, not only must we read Blacman with that particular sensitivity and attention which is appropriate to hagiographical sources, but we must interpret the *Collectarium* in the light of its author's own preoccupations. If we do so, the picture of bland sanctity fades away and these various layers of precise meaning begin to emerge.[53]

There are two other general considerations to be borne in mind in assessing the authority of the *Collectarium*. In August 1453 the king suffered a mental breakdown. Although he recovered to some extent at the end of 1454, it seems that this recovery was never complete and that he may even have had a relapse two years later.[54] Partly for this reason, there was in the 1450s a marked change in the king's manner of life. He seems to have become increasingly withdrawn. His interest in – and capacity for – public business diminished; the establishment of the court was reduced, and more and more time was spent living in monasteries. Even the king's itinerary was transformed. As a young man he seemed reluctant even to leave the Thames Valley; he now remained in the midlands, remote from the central organs of government.[55] In other words, the study of Henry's character presents us, not just with the normal problems of change over a period of twenty-five years of active kingship, but with a decisive break, a watershed. What was true of the king in 1445 was not true in 1455, or even less in 1470. However, Blacman's work lacks any clear chronological framework, and this problem is exacerbated by the fact that his information about the king spans a generation, from the late 1430s to 1471. Hence, we have to exercise great care in establishing which Henry he is describing. Some of the details of his portrayal are clearly drawn from the years after 1453. It is, therefore, important to stress that they cannot be refuted by adducing evidence from the 1440s. For example, there is one passage in the *Collectarium* where Blacman speaks of the king as a man of few words who was in the habit of eating his meals in complete silence.[56] It is not difficult to show that, before 1453, Henry was often sociable and forthcoming. Conversely, there is evidence independent of that of Blacman to suggest that subsequently he became noticeably taciturn.[57]

There is also another sense in which there was more than one Henry. It is sometimes argued that Blacman's favourable picture of the king is unacceptable because it is so much at odds with other contemporary views. Blacman's words are often capable of more than one interpretation. Nevertheless, the political failures of the reign inevitably led to attacks on Henry himself and it is not difficult to produce a catalogue of contemporary criticisms of the king, even though some of this evidence – notably that of the approvers in the 1440s – is itself not above suspicion.[58] The king's political inadequacies were clear and they did not go unremarked. However, that is only part of the story. Henry was a controversial figure and the hostile judgements have to be placed alongside the more favourable. These range from Piero da Monte's enthusiastic account of the young king in 1437 to Bishop Russell's sober reflections of 1486.[59] They also include those who rejoiced at Henry's recovery from his illness: Richard Andrew, his secretary, who founded a chantry for him in the unpropitious year of 1476, as well as some of the other early devotees of the cult. There is good evidence of Henry's loyalty to his close associates, from his childhood nurse to the duke of Suffolk, and Blacman is not the only one to have reciprocated these feelings.[60] Henry's enemies tended not to speak the same language as his friends, but we must not ignore the fact that he was capable of inspiring strong personal affection.

These ambiguities are well illustrated in the *Tractatus de regimine principum*, a treatise on the duties of a king which was written for Henry, perhaps in the late 1430s. The work lists many of the qualities which contemporaries sought in a ruler and has therefore been taken as a yardstick against which to measure, and discredit, Blacman's views.[61] However, the result is far from clear-cut. It is easy to show that Henry failed to live up to the precepts of the *Tractatus* that a king should dispense patronage equitably, enforce justice and take wise advice. But the work is noticeably delphic concerning the king's military responsibilities. On the one hand, it argues that the king must be prepared to lead his army personally in battle in order to defend his rights in France. On the other, a whole section of the work is devoted to the blessings of peace, and the author's conviction that the negotiations for peace must be pursued at any price has even led to the suggestion that he was a member of Suffolk's party. Equally, what is distinctive in the *Tractatus*, as opposed to the merely conventional, is the stress laid on the king's private devotional life and the importance attached to his patronage of learning and the universities. As its editor justly remarks, the *Tractatus* envisages 'a religious, saintly and rather unwordly king', an ideal strikingly close to that described in the *Collectarium*.[62] Blacman may well be prejudiced but others shared his prejudices. He cannot simply be dismissed as egregious and deluded.

These are some of the general considerations which have a bearing on the authority of the *Collectarium*. At the same time, Blacman also retails a number of more specific facts about the king and, in the nature of things, these can more readily be tested. However, it is important to recall that the *Collectarium* is a brief biographical sketch, only some twenty pages long. It is not a chronicle of the reign and factual information is recorded only in so far as it illustrates some feature of the king's character which Blacman wishes to emphasise. Sometimes he is clearly mistaken. He misunderstood the negotiations between the king and the executors of Cardinal Beaufort, although his remarks are a confused recollection of the actual financial complexities rather than a total fabrication.[63] His comments on the king's dislike of hunting are difficult to accept entirely at face value.[64] He has a bizarrely improbable tale to tell about the victualling of the king's army in the north in the 1460s.[65] There is, at the least, a conflict of evidence about Henry's treatment in captivity.[66] On the other hand, a prolonged study of the *Collectarium* has produced an increasing number of cases where laconic, and even improbable, remarks made by Blacman can be authenticated from other sources. Within the general context of stressing the king's mercifulness, he provides an accurately circumstantial account of the pardon granted to the associates of the duke of Gloucester in 1447, and of the similar pardon offered to the Yorkist lords in 1459 before Ludford Bridge. In the same vein, Blacman correctly records the (more suprising) way in which Henry subsequently forgave the soldier who wounded him in the neck at St Albans, and was even apparently reconciled to Edward IV himself.[67] Similarly, there is evidence to substantiate his remarks concerning the care which the king took over the education of his two half-brothers, Jasper and Edmund Tudor.[68] Blacman indicates that the king was at times reluctant to concern himself with public affairs. He is undoubtedly speaking here of the years after 1453 and the parliament rolls for 1455 tell exactly the same story. There are even some grounds to justify Blacman's assertion that the burden of taxation imposed during Henry's reign was comparatively light.[69]

Naturally, many of Blacman's statements concern detailed aspects of the king's spiritual life, but here again they can frequently be verified from independent sources. This is the case with his account of the king's devotion to the cult of the Holy Cross, and with Henry's related decision to insert a row of crosses around the rim of the royal crown.[70] Blacman dwells on Henry's sabbatarianism. We know that during the years of Henry's personal rule the court never travelled on Sundays, even during the crisis of Cade's rebellion.[71] Equally, Blacman's repeated stress on Henry's regular practice of private, often non-liturgical, prayer is supported by other testimony.[72] Similarly, Blacman emphasises not only Henry's chastity but his extreme prudishness. His words are echoed almost verbatim by Piero da Monte, who spoke of the young Henry as avoiding 'the sight and conversation of women, affirming these to be the work of the devil', and detesting scurrilous games and obscene conversation.[73] The example which Blacman gives to demonstrate Henry's attitude describes his shock when he visited Bath and saw naked men taking the waters. This story has been discounted only recently, but it is in fact well attested. Henry visited Bath in August 1448. In 1449 the diocesan, Bishop Bekynton, acting on a report which had reached his ears, ordered that in future those taking the waters must be decently clothed.[74]

Many of these matters are trivial; in the *Collectarium* itself they serve merely as illustrative detail. Their importance lies in the way that they substantiate Blacman's account, or – as in the case of his knowledge of Henry's manner of speech – confirm his intimacy with the king. Other matters are more important, either because they are controversial or because they reveal important facets of the king's personality. One such concerns the king's habits of dress, a purely antiquarian issue at first sight but in fact an aspect of Henry's attitude towards the public *persona* of monarchy. Blacman describes the king's humility as manifesting itself in an exceptionally plain and modest manner of dress. Conversely, it has been argued that this is at odds with other contemporary evidence. The king's household accounts show that he regularly spent money on rich clothes. He greeted the French envoys in 1445 wearing cloth of gold and contemporary representations also show him as dressed in fitting style.[75] We are brought up against two issues here. The first is simply that Blacman must be read with care. What he actually says is that Henry *customarily* dressed plainly, not that he always did so. In fact, elsewhere he speaks of the king as 'decked with the kingly ornaments and crowned with the royal diadem', or as putting on a hair shirt at crown wearings 'so that pride . . . such as is apt to be engendered by pomp, might be repressed'.[76] He simply cannot be interpreted as suggesting that the king never wore rich clothes. Secondly, there is again the problem of which Henry is being described. In 1471 the king was paraded through the streets of London in an attempt to attract support. The policy failed because he made such a pathetic showing, being dowdily dressed in a long blue gown. The image may have been unimpressive but it became emblematic. In two of the earlier miracles described in the Windsor *Miracula* Henry is recorded as appearing in visions dressed in a comparable blue gown.[77] We see here the growth of a legend from a seed of truth, and in Blacman the same seed may well be present.

A similar argument on a broader basis applies when it is claimed that Blacman gives the impression of a shabby, indigent and dull royal court. Again, a careful reading of the work does not substantiate this conclusion. Blacman speaks of bare-breasted dancing girls brought before the king, of the 'pomp' of formal state occasions when the king wore his crown, and of rich gifts being made to the king. He refers to the courtiers' habit of bringing hawks into church with them, and he implies that the life of the court was luxurious and corrupting.[78] The point is not that all this did not happen. It did, but the king distanced himself from it or expressed his disapproval.

One of the main features of Henry's character to emerge from the *Collectarium* is his distinctive combination of piety and learning. This needs to be stressed, partly because it provides the background to the foundations of Eton and King's, but also because it has recently been argued that these foundations do not in fact correspond with the account of the king's motives given by Blacman. His picture is certainly clear. At two points he stresses Henry's habit of reading the Scriptures, a distinctive and sensitive matter at the time and scarcely a normal pastime among medieval kings of England. Elsewhere, he refers to Henry as kneeling before his missal and silently accompanying the priest in saying the prayers, epistle and gospel of the mass.[79] This account of the king is amply substantiated.[80] We have another picture of Henry, probably in 1458, sitting alone with his books and meditating on the Scriptures, and Henry's own copy of the Bible in English still survives.[81] A primer was bought for the king's use as early as 1427 and he was able to say some of the services by the age of six. In 1437 da Monte observed that the king was in the habit of reading the offices every day, and one of the first symptoms of his recovery from his illness in 1454 was his capacity to say matins and evensong.[82] This mentality is exemplified by his particular regard for two of his predecessors, Alfred and Edward the Confessor. He tried to obtain Alfred's canonisation and his devotion to the Confessor, which is specifically noted by Blacman, was even more fervent.[83] Formal state crown-wearings took place on the two feasts of the Confessor as well as the traditional occasions of Christmas, Easter and Whitsun. Not only was Henry's son named after the Confessor, but he was born on the feast of Edward's translation and, in all probability (as contemporaries noticed), he was conceived on the feast of Edward's Deposition. It was entirely in character that Henry should have chosen to be buried alongside the Confessor.[84] Alfred was a royal patron of learning; Edward, as seen in the fifteenth century, the most pious of English kings. For Henry piety and learning went hand in hand, intermingled, as it were opposite sides of the same coin. His attitude appropriately echoes that of one of his favourite saints, Anselm, *fides quaerens intellectum*.

So, in so far as Henry's foundations are criticised for not showing a 'renaissance interest' in learning for its own sake, this is a criticism which he would have accepted. As Blacman stresses more than once, the colleges were founded 'to enlarge the house of God and His worship' but also 'for the maintenance of a number of scholars'.[85] Piety and learning are indivisible. Blacman's words are an accurate account of the king's motivation and of the foundations themselves. It is true that Henry stipulated that, if the endowment of Eton should prove inadequate, then the educational functions should be sacrificed to the religious, but this was seen as an unlikely eventuality. In any case, William of Wykeham made a similar stipulation at New College, and Archbishop Chichele instructed the fellows of All Souls that, if their studies conflicted with their obligation to pray for the souls of the faithful departed, then their studies should give way.[86] Neither man can properly be regarded as half-hearted in his concern for the advancement of education. In fact, the element of piety and especially the chantry function are central to all late-medieval educational foundations. Any inclination to see Henry as egregiously atavistic in this respect can be corrected by contemplating the extensive spiritual obligations which a very different character, the future Richard III, laid on the four fellowships which he endowed some thirty years later at Queens' College.[87]

In similar vein, it is suggested that the foundations of Eton and King's are in some way diminished because their statutes are based on those of Winchester and New College.[88] In the abstract this is a curious argument. It implies that an educational foundation has merit only in so far as it differs from its predecessors. However, there are more profound issues at stake. The colleges of medieval Oxford and Cambridge were not totally dissimilar and it was natural that their statutes should have much in common. The statutes of Peterhouse are in part modelled on those of Merton; Clare on Michaelhouse; and those of God's House, which was actually one of the most innovatory of all fifteenth-century colleges, are very similar to those of Clare.[89] The true importance of Eton and King's (and even their originality) lies elsewhere. Eton was simply the first public grammar school to be founded by a king of England, and the king's action seems to have quickly encouraged others to follow suit.[90] In the same way, King's was the first fully independent college to be founded by a king in either university. The readiness of medieval kings to grant substantial privileges to the two universities has often hidden the fact that financially they were much less generous. In this respect, King's embodies a radical departure.[91] Similarly the establishment of so magnificent a royal foundation in Cambridge, rather than Oxford, marks a decisive stage in the changing balance between the two universities which was so central a feature of their history in the fifteenth century.[92] Finally, it is important to emphasise the effect which the establishment of King's had on the collegiate landscape in Cambridge. At the time when the foundation was being planned, the existing colleges maintained perhaps about eighty-five fellows. The appearance of King's, with its projected establishment of seventy fellows, would not only have almost doubled existing collegiate provision for the support of scholars but also represented an important early step in the evolution of a collegiate university.[93] It is often said that if all the Cambridge colleges had been dissolved in 1400, the effect would have been negligible. This would be much less true after the foundation of King's.

Lastly, it is argued that Henry's increasingly grandiose conceptions for his two colleges not only involved regular changes of plan which delayed their completion, but eventually produced magnificent foundations which were at odds with Blacman's picture of Henry as a man of humble, modest piety. It is true that Henry's plans, particularly for Eton, altered radically and, partly as a result, the buildings of both colleges were still unfinished by 1461.[94] However, that is not the end of the matter. In the first place, it was not unusual, or surprising, for founders of colleges to alter their original plans as circumstances changed. This was the case right from the outset, as the history of the two earliest Oxford and Cambridge colleges, Merton and Peterhouse, makes clear. Similarly, in the next century, the early histories of Oriel and Clare demonstrate in their different ways how transient the original intentions of a founder might be.[95] Secondly, and more importantly, it is necessary to distinguish between buildings and their occupants. The besetting problem of medieval collegiate foundations was not the inadequacy of their buildings (which often took centuries to complete) but the inadequacy of their endowments, which made it impossible for them to support their full quota of scholars. In 1400 the eight Cambridge colleges were nominally intended to maintain 137 fellows, but poverty meant that the real figure was about eighty. Both Gonville Hall and Trinity Hall could have contained twenty fellows but rarely exceeded four. From this point of view, both Eton and King's were a rapid and complete success. The full quota of seventy scholars was reached at Eton by 1447 and at King's by 1451.[96] In this regard, if not elsewhere, the king acted with both speed and effectiveness.

The related charge of ostentation comes oddly from those who are quick to attack Henry's general lack of kingly qualities, but again Blacman's account of the foundations rings true. For him, they are indeed 'noble' colleges 'endowed with large lands and revenues', but the purpose of this magnificence was (as their foundation deeds amply testify) 'to enlarge the house of God and His worship'.[97] The king's personal modesty is irrelevant. It is in any case unthinkable that such royal foundations, the first of their type, should have been meanly conceived. When Henry's father founded a Charterhouse it was a 'triple' house, a community of forty rather than the usual thirteen, with a church twice the normal Carthusian size.[98] When he founded Syon it was as one of the wealthiest abbeys in England. What is more, the fashion for substantial collegiate building had been set more than sixty years previously by William of Wykeham. The commons complained of the cost of Henry's colleges, and no doubt the building work was expensive, but it is worth stressing that they were endowed largely, not from the king's own resources, but from the lands of dissolved alien priories.[99]

This paper has ranged widely but it might appropriately conclude by returning to a central theme, the unity of author and subject in the *Collectarium*. Henry VI owned a copy of the *Vitae Patrum*, and so did Blacman.[100] What did they make of these sayings of the eastern Fathers? Perhaps they noticed that the eastern church retained a more vivid sense of the view of Jesus taken by some of His contemporaries: 'He is beside himself' and 'He hath a devil and is mad', and of the words of St Paul, 'we are fools for Christ's sake'.[101] But this tradition was not entirely lost to the west. St Bernard could speak of himself and his brethren as being like God's jesters and tumblers standing on their heads, and William of St Thierry recognised that Bernard taught a 'new wisdom' which made all worldly wisdom mad. St Francis said 'God wants me to be a new fool'. He stripped naked in the presence of his bishop; he would pick up a stick, play it as though it were a viol and sing to Christ. The great Spanish mystic Ramon Lull called himself Ramon the Fool.[102] The fool of God abandons the ways of this world and delights in its mockery. It is his joy to be treated as mad. We catch something of this in the life of Margery Kempe, but she could rebuke the archbishop of Canterbury, the son of an earl, to his face and be sent away with a kind word.[103] When Blacman records that Henry was so distracted during his devotions that he allowed his hat to fall to the ground, we are unwise to dismiss this as trivial anecdotage.[104] The more we read of Henry's political inadequacies the more difficult it is to understand why so incapable a king was allowed to reign for so long, especially after 1453. No doubt there were many reasons. Perhaps one was that contemporaries knew that holy folly was a charism.[105] Hence the problem of understanding Henry's reign becomes not just a problem in political history but one in the history of spirituality. Hence, also, an account of him written within this tradition may, if properly interpreted, tell us much about the king and his times.[106]

Notes

1. The standard edition is now *Henry the Sixth: A Reprint of John Blacman's Memoir*, ed. and trans. M.R. James (Cambridge, 1919), referred to henceforth as Blacman.
2. Bertram Wolffe, *Henry VI* (London, 1981), ch. 1, referred to henceforth as Wolffe.
3. Ralph A. Griffiths, *The Reign of King Henry VI* (London, 1981).
4. Roger Lovatt, 'John Blacman: Biographer of Henry VI' in *The Writing of History in the Middle Ages: Essays Presented to R.W. Southern*, ed. R.H.C. Davis and J.M. Wallace-Hadrill (Oxford, 1981), pp. 415–44.
5. *Ibid.*, pp. 419–30. Waynflete was provost of Eton from 1442 to 1447.
6. Wolffe, p. 6.
7. Blacman, p. xv.
8. *Ibid.*, pp. 13, 15–16.
9. This account of Blacman was added to one of the books which he gave to the Witham Charterhouse; see Bodleian Library, MS. Laud misc. 152, f. 1ʳ. It was written in Blacman's lifetime and is in the hand of a monk of the house, the 'Witham Librarian' who accessioned Blacman's gifts. It gives precise and accurate details about Blacman's career, namely, that he was an M.A. of Oxford, had been precentor of Eton and was a *redditus*, rather than a professed monk, of Witham. The original is now partly illegible; for an inaccurate text, see Blacman, p. 60.
10. Wolffe, p. 6. For a description of Copland's edition, see Blacman, pp. vii–ix. It is worth adding that Blacman was not a well-known figure and there would be no point in falsely attributing the work to him in order to give it added authority.
11. It is too hasty to claim (Wolffe, p. 6) that the attribution to Blacman is 'solely based' on the testimony of Copland's edition. The title-page of the edition describes Blacman as bachelor of theology and later monk of the London Charterhouse (Blacman, p. viii).
12. Blacman, pp. 12, 15–16.
13. For example, the reminiscences of Bishop Aiscough, which must date from *c.* 1446–50; the king's visit to Bath in 1448; the negotiations with the executors of Cardinal Beaufort, *c.* 1447–52; Waynflete's elevation to Winchester in 1447–8; the pardons granted to the associates of the duke of Gloucester in 1447; and the material concerning the early years of Eton and King's (Blacman, pp. 4–5, 8, 10, 11, 12, 17).
14. Bodleian Library, MS. Laud misc. 152, fo. 31ᵛ; Blacman, pp. 8, 16, 17; *Henrici VI Angliae Regis Miracula Postuma*, ed. P. Grosjean (Brussels, 1935), pp. 188*, 191*, 193*. The coincidence of recollection in these three separate witnesses is striking. Also, see below, n.25.
15. Lovatt, 'John Blacman', pp. 440–45.
16. Blacman, pp. 13, 18, 21. Three lists of Blacman's books are in Bodleian Library, MS. Laud misc. 154, flyleaf, fos. 1ʳ–2ᵛ, and have been printed (inaccurately and in conflated form) in Blacman, pp. 55–9, and in E.M. Thompson, *The Carthusian Order in England* (London, 1930), pp. 317–21. His copy of the *Imitatio* appears as *Musica Ecclesiastica* and his volume of saints' lives is entitled *Collectiones Sanctorum Somerseteorum*. For the exclusive contemporary readership of the *Imitatio*, see Roger Lovatt, 'The *Imitation of Christ* in Late Medieval England', *TRHS*, XVIII (1968), 97–121. For the distinctiveness of devotion to the cult of St Anselm at this period, see R.W. Southern, *St Anselm and his Biographer* (Cambridge, 1963), p. 341.
17. On this dispute, see Michael Sargent, 'Contemporary Criticism of Richard Rolle', *Analecta Cartusiana*, 55, i (1981), 160–205.
18. Blacman, pp. 13–14, 16, 20; also pp. 4, 10, 12, 15, 18 for similar references to his sources.

19.   *Ibid.*, pp. 4, 11, 13, 15, 21.
20.   Account should also be taken of the clear similarities of expression between the *Collectarium* and Blacman's meditations, written in his own hand in BL, MS. Sloane 2515, fos. 3ʳ–5ʳ. Blacman's style and vocabulary are so distinctive that these similarities provide something of a 'stylistic fingerprint' to supplement, and strengthen, the historical arguments deployed above.
21.   Wolffe, pp. 5–6, 12, 21.
22.   These depositions survive in Vatican Library, MS. Vat. Lat. 4015; see also *St Thomas Cantilupe, Bishop of Hereford: Essays in his Honour* ed. M. Jancey (Hereford, 1982), p. 197.
23.   *Miracula*, ed. Grosjean, pp. 42*–6*, 67*–8*; and below pp. 178–79.
24.   Lovatt, 'John Blacman', p. 429 and n.4; Wolffe, pp. 5–6 and n.6. The last specifically dated appearance of Blacman was in 1474, when he was a *redditus* of the Witham Charterhouse and described himself as having 'seen sixty-six winters' (Bodleian Library, MS. Laud misc. 154, fo. 2ᵛ) *Redditi* were entitled to the spiritual benefits of professed monks and hence their *obits* should be, and normally are, listed among the *professi* in the *chartae* of the Carthusian General Chapter; but there seems to be no mention of an *obit* for Blacman in the *chartae* for the English province during the years 1474–81; see Lambeth Palace MS. 413. On other grounds, it is likely that Blacman died *c.* 1483–4, when he would in any case have been about seventy-five. Unfortunately, the *chartae* for the English province do not appear to survive for the years 1482–1503. *Clerici redditi* could for an adequate reason leave the Order and it is possible that Blacman had done so at the time of his death. However, for the moment it would seem that he was not buried at Eton or, for that matter, at his other college of Merton. See A.J. Bott, *Monuments in Merton College Chapel* (Oxford, 1964). I am indebted to Dr Michael Sargent for his help with this note.
25.   Blacman, p. 3. In fact, one of Blacman's own books also contains a note drawing attention to Henry's two coronations and also to his legitimate descent from the kings of the West Saxons; see Eton College MS. 213, fo. xᶜ. For a somewhat similar coincidence and its implications, see above, p. 174.
26.   Wolffe, p. 6.
27.   *RP*, VI, pp. 240–42; *The Great Chronicle of London*, ed. A.H. Thomas and I.D. Thornley (London, 1938), pp. 231–3; Dominic Mancini, *The Usurpation of Richard III*, ed. C.A.J. Armstrong (2nd ed., Oxford, 1969), p. 94.
28.   R. Willis and J.W Clark, *The Architectural History of the University of Cambridge* (4 vols, Cambridge, 1886), I, pp. 473–5; *British Library, Harleian MS.433*, ed. R. Horrox and P.W. Hammond (Richard III Society, 1979–), II, p. 207.
29.   Blacman, p. 19; Wolffe, p. 6. In fact, about a dozen, and not 'one or two' (*loc. cit.*), of the miracles recorded in the Windsor *Miracula* seem to have occurred before Henry's body was translated. However, the central point about the chronology of the recorded miracles clearly stands.
30.   *Miracula*, ed. Grosjean, ch. 2.
31.   *Ibid.*, pp. 111–12; also pp. 21*, 152*, 235*–6*.
32.   *Ibid.*, pp. 181*–2*.
33.   *Ibid.*, pp. 194*–8*; also J.W. McKenna, 'Piety and Propaganda: The Cult of King Henry VI' in *Chaucer and Middle English Studies in Honour of R.H. Robbins*, ed. B. Rowland (London, 1974), p. 82.
34.   For attempts by the canons of Windsor to 'monopolise' the cult, see *Miracula*, ed. Grosjean, pp. 101, 111–12, 115–16.
35.   *Ibid.*, pp. 157*–8*, quoting the full text of the admonition from Archbishop Booth's register. Prayers inspired by Henry and datable to the 'Chertsey' period occur in Bodleian Library, MS. Don.e.20, ff. 1–4; see also *Trevelyan Papers*, I, ed. J.P. Collier (Camden Society, Old Series, LXVII, 1857), pp. 53–60. There is a so-called prayer of Pope Sixtus IV (1471–84) to Henry VI in BL, MS. Harley 5793, fo. 1. For comment on these, and other, prayers, see *Miracula*, ed. Grosjean, pp. 237*–41*, 246*, 249*–50*. There are also representations of Henry VI in

books of hours which may well date from before 1484, for example, Fitzwilliam Museum MS. 55, fo. 141ᵛ. The loss of a bone from Henry's right arm, which would seem to have taken place when his body was translated, can also probably be interpreted as the early appropriation of a relic. See W.H. St John Hope, 'The Discovery of the Remains of King Henry VI in St George's Chapel, Windsor Castle', *Archaeologia*, LXII, (1910–11), 533–42.

36. *Acts of Court of the Mercers' Company*, ed. L. Lyell and F.D. Watney (Cambridge, 1936) p. 139; other references to the Chertsey pilgrimage are in H. Harrod, 'Extracts from Early Wills in the Norwich Registries', *Norfolk Archaeology*, IV (1855), 338, and *Miracula*, ed. Grosjean, pp. 73, 111–12.

37. *Ibid.*, pp. 176*–8*, 67*–72* Wolffe, p. 357 n.28. On early miracles associated with Henry VI, see also, *Ingulph's Chronicle of the Abbey of Croyland*, trans. H.T. Riley (London, 1854), p. 468. This passage does clearly seem to refer to the 'Chertsey' period.

38. Wolffe, p. 6. It is also argued that Blacman's statement that Henry is rightly included among the register of saints must imply that the *Collectarium* was composed in 'the middle or later years of Henry VII's reign', presumably after the canonisation process had been officially initiated (Wolffe, p. 6; Blacman, p. 3). However, it was common for medieval *dévots* to anticipate a formal canonisation and to write or act imprecisely in this expectation. There are other examples even in the case of Henry VI (*Miracula*, ed. Grosjean, pp. 157*–8*, 10–11). Many were hoping for Henry's canonisation well before 1485; equally he never was formally canonised, either in Henry VII's reign or later. Hence, Blacman's remark must always have been in the nature of a pious, undefined aspiration, and it cannot be made to bear so precise a gloss as to its date.

39. Blacman, pp. 19, 45.

40. John Warkworth, *A Chronicle of the First Thirteen Years of the Reign of King Edward the Fourth*, ed. J.O. Halliwell (Camden Society, Old Series, X, 1839), p. 12. For the expectations aroused by Henry VI's death, see C.L. Kingsford, *English Historical Literature in the Fifteenth Century* (Oxford, 1913), p. 375.

41. C. Ross, *Edward IV* (London, 1974), pp. 405–12.

42. C. Ross, *Richard III* (London, 1981), pp. 105–17. Blacman himself came from the diocese of Bath and Wells, and the ordination lists of the bishops of Bath and Wells show that many of his *confrères* at Witham were also west-countrymen. Dorset's Exeter rebellion must have left its mark on the house.

43. Blacman, pp. 3, 19, 21.

44. Wolffe, p. 5. Other early Tudor propagandists, such as Bernard André or Pietro Carmeliano, were equally anxious to make their loyalties, however transient, overwhelmingly explicit. In such cases, an adulatory tone was *de rigueur*, and discretion unthinkable. The often repeated assertion that Blacman's work was 'probably written at the behest of Henry VII' (Wolffe, *loc. cit.*) seems to rest on no surer a foundation than a remark made some two centuries later by Archbishop Sancroft who, in turn, appears to have based his assertion on nothing more precise than his knowledge that the canonisation process had been initiated by Henry VII (Blacman, p. xi, and see the copy of the *Collectarium* now in the Bodleian Library).

45. Blacman, pp. 3, 8–9, 19.

46. *Ibid.*, pp. 7, 13, 14, 18, 20, 21.

47. See above, n. 24.

48. It is misleading to claim that the only sources Blacman mentions by name are drawn from Henry's 'later life after his deposition' (Wolffe, p. 6). During the period 1443–54 while he was at Eton, and perhaps for the next few years while at Cambridge, Blacman was in a position to be his own witness, as he makes clear on several occasions (Blacman, pp. 4, 13, 15–16). Equally he had access to the testimony of Bishop Aiscough (clearly identified in the *Collectarium*, although not by name), who was chaplain to the king by 1436 and later his confessor for many years, and of William Towne (specifically named by Blacman), who must have moved in circles close to the king since at least 1441 when he was appointed a

foundation fellow of King's College (Blacman, pp. 4–5, 13; A.B. Emden, A *Biographical Register of the University of Cambridge to 1500* [Cambridge, 1963], pp. 28, 592–3). He also appears to draw on the (attributed) recollections of William Waynflete, who was familiar with Henry, and with Blacman, from 1442 when he became provost of Eton. Other sources explicitly identified by Blacman are Thomas Mannyng, who certainly did remain with Henry after 1461 but had been his chaplain since 1451 and his secretary from 1455 to 1460, and Sir Richard Tunstall, who was also with Henry in the 1460s but was already a member of his household by 1453. See Blacman, pp. 11, 15, 21; A.B. Emden, *A Biographical Register of the University of Oxford to A.D. 1500* (3 vols., Oxford, 1957–9), II, pp. 1216–7; *RP*, V, p. 318. Both men may well have been Blacman's informants for the king's doings after 1461 but could equally well have provided authoritative evidence about the 1450s. In fact, as Professor Griffiths has rightly remarked, 'Blacman's information came from sources spread over more than a generation' (*Reign of Henry VI*, pp. 3–4, 7 n.9).

49.   Blacman, pp. 3–4.
50.   Wolffe, pp. 12–21.
51.   Blacman, pp. 5, 6, 7, 8, 9–11, 15–16, 17–18 and *passim*. Also, Lovatt, 'Blacman', pp. 435–9.
52.   Wolffe, p. 12; Blacman, p. 16. There are accounts of Henry's symptoms in *RP*, V, pp. 241–2, and *The Paston Letters*, ed. J. Gairdner (6 vols., London, 1904), II, pp. 295–6. A similar range of meaning, and consequent possibility of misunderstanding, is inherent in Blacman's characterisation of Henry as 'simplex' (p. 4). See Wolffe, pp. 19, 306; and, for a corrective, A. Gransden, *Historical Writing in England, II, c.1307 to the Early Sixteenth Century* (London, 1982), pp. 497–8. Also, Griffiths, *Reign of Henry VI*, p. 776.
53.   BL, MS. Sloane 2515, ff. 3ʳ–5ʳ; Lovatt, 'Blacman', pp. 438–44.
54.   For comment on Henry's condition in 1460, see *Ingulph's Chronicle of the Abbey of Croyland*, trans. H.T. Riley (London, 1854), pp. 420, 424, and also, in general, Griffiths, *Reign of Henry VI*, pp. 717–8, 775–6.
55.   *RP*, V, p. 285. For the reduction of the household in 1464, see *PPC*, ed. N.H. Nicolas (Record Commission, 1834–7), VI, pp. 220–33, and contemporary comment in *An English Chronicle of the Reigns of Richard II . . . and Henry VI*, ed. J.S. Davies (Camden Society, Old Series, LXIV, 1856), p. 79. See also, Wolffe, p. 283 and pp. 305, 361–71 (royal itinerary).
56.   Blacman, p. 13; compare p. 15.
57.   See, for example, Henry's gracious reception of the French embassy in 1445, or his positively loquacious behaviour at Coventry in 1451. *Letters and Papers Illustrative of the Wars of the English in France*, ed. J. Stevenson (2 vols. in 3, RS, 1861–64) I, pp. 87–148; *Coventry Leet Book*, ed. M.D. Harris (4 parts, EETS, 1907–13), pp. 263–6. For the taciturnity that was a central symptom of Henry's illness, see above n.52; and later, *Miracula*, ed. Grosjean, pp. 185˙–6˙, and *Incerti Scriptoris Chronicon Angliae*, ed. J.A. Giles (London, 1848), part 4, p. 47.
58.   Wolffe, pp. 12–21, esp. pp. 16–18. For a corrective, see Griffiths, *Reign of Henry VI*, pp. 241, 265 n.51.
59.   J. Haller, 'Piero da Monte, Ein Gelehrter und päpstlicher Beamter des 15 Jahrhunderts, seine Briefsammlung', *Bibliothek des Deutschen Historischen Instituts*, XIX (1941), 43–5. Piero da Monte may well have had an axe to grind (Griffiths, *Reign of Henry VI*, p. 235), as of course did Henry's opponents, but that is not the point at issue. Da Monte's perception of Henry as more like a monk than a king is precisely echoed by Blacman, pp. 4, 13. For Russell's views, *Ingulph's Chronicle*, p. 468; compare a comment of the late 1450s, *The Brut*, ed. F.W.D. Brie (EETS, 1906–8), II, p. 527, and the view of a roll-chronicle compiled before 1485 (John Rylands Library, Latin MS. 113, quoted by Griffiths, *Reign of Henry VI*, p. 7 n.11). All of these judgements are strikingly similar, in microcosm, to Blacman's account.
60.   *Paston Letters and Papers*, ed. N. Davis (2 parts, Oxford, 1971–6), part 2, p. 108; *The Fabric Rolls of York Minster*, ed. J. Raine (Surtees Society, XXXV, 1859), p. 301; *CPR, 1452–61*, pp. 462–3, for annuities restored to his nurses by Henry as late as 1458. Henry's loyalties to his servants, and their response, have perhaps not been studied in sufficient depth. For general

comment, see Wolffe, pp. 37, 223, 228, and Griffiths, *Reign of Henry VI*, pp. 252, 309, 394, 638–9, 678–82. For Suffolk's response, see *Paston Letters*, ed. Gairdner, II, pp. 142–3.

61. Wolffe, pp. 13–15.
62. *Four English Political Tracts of the Later Middle Ages*, ed. J–P. Genet (Camden Society, 4th series, XVIII, 1977), pp. 40–173, esp. pp. 41–5, 104–18, 151–6.
63. Blacman, p. 10. Compare K.B. McFarlane, 'At the Deathbed of Cardinal Beaufort', *Studies in Medieval History Presented to F.M. Powicke*, ed. R.W. Hunt, W.A. Pantin, R.W. Southern (Oxford, 1948), p. 422.
64. Blacman, p. 18. Strictly speaking, Blacman does not say that the king disliked hunting entirely but that he disliked the actual killing of innocent beasts, a rather different – and not uncommon – attitude. Certainly Henry hunted as a young man. See *Monasticon Anglicanum*, ed. W. Dugdale (re-ed. J. Caley etc., 6 vols. in 8, London, 1817–30), III, p. 113n; *John Benet's Chronicle*, ed. G.L. and M.A. Harriss (Camden Society, 4th series, IX, 1972), p. 184; and Griffiths, *Reign of Henry VI*, p. 250. Later in life the queen seems to have been the more enthusiastic, and it may be that this is simply another problem of chronology (see above pp. 183–84); *Letters of Queen Margaret of Anjou*, ed. C. Munro (Camden Society, Old Series, LXXXVI, 1863), pp. 100–1, 131, 137, 141. See also, C.L. Scofield, *The Life and Reign of Edward IV* (2 vols., London, 1923), II, p. 159.
65. Blacman, p. 20.
66. Blacman, pp. 17–18; Compare Wolffe, pp. 338–9. On the other hand, Henry's appearance on his release gives some support to Blacman's account (Warkworth, *Chronicle*, p. 11; *Great Chronicle of London*, p. 215).
67. Blacman, pp. 17, 18, 19; CPR, *1446–52*, p. 68; *Benet's Chronicle*, p. 193; *The Brut*, p. 513; RP, V, pp. 348–9. For events after St Albans, see Griffiths, *Reign of Henry VI*, pp. 747–8, and C.A.J. Armstrong, 'Politics and the Battle of St Albans, 1455', BIHR, XXXIII (1960), esp. 51–63. Henry's forgiveness of Edward is implied by J. de Waurin, *Anchiennes Cronicques d'Engleterre*, ed. E. Dupont (3 vols., Paris, 1858–63), III, pp. 210–14. In general, Griffiths, *Reign of Henry VI*, pp. 249, 364, 595, 822, 850 n. 319. Henry could be unyielding when his personal authority was at stake, but even in some of the most notorious cases (e.g. Thomas Carver) conviction was followed by pardon.
68. Blacman, pp. 8–9. Between 1437 and 1442 the two brothers were placed in the care of the abbess of Barking, Katherine de la Pole, Suffolk's sister. For the spiritual (and social) distinction of this house, see E. Power, *Medieval English Nunneries* (Cambridge, 1922), pp. 42, 571–2, and A.I. Doyle, 'Books Connected with the Vere Family and Barking Abbey', *Transactions of the Essex Archaeological Society*, XXV (1958), 222–43.
69. Blacman, pp. 15–16, 9; RP, V, pp. 284–90. On taxation, see Griffiths, *Reign of Henry VI*, pp. 378–82, 786, and Wolffe, pp. 308–9, although whether this is to be credited to Henry's forbearance is another matter.
70. Blacman, p. 6; J. Capgrave, *Liber de illustribus Henricis*, ed. F.C. Hingeston (RS, 1858), pp. 131–2; and also Lovatt, 'Blacman', pp. 434–5 and n.1.
71. Blacman, pp. 14–15; Wolffe, pp. 34, 232.
72. Blacman, pp. 4, 5, 6, 7, 14–15; *Miracula*, ed. Grosjean, pp. 185*, 188*, 189*, 190*, 191*, 192*. This testimony concerning Henry's prayerful behaviour in Westminster Abbey has been questioned (Wolffe, p. 9), but there seems no reason to doubt its essential truth. The witnesses were old, sometimes infirm, men giving evidence about events which had taken place some forty years previously, and they were frank about their uncertainty over details. However, there was widespread agreement about Henry's actions. Two witnesses (not one: Wolffe, p. 9) agreed that he prayed for a considerable time, and a third said that he prayed both at the shrine of Edward the Confessor and at his father's grave. Furthermore this information was gratuitous, having no relevance to the point at issue, namely, where Henry should be buried. The testimony is also persuasive on account of the accurate circumstantial details concerning Henry's behaviour, such as his taciturnity and his form of oath. It is further

confirmed by the discovery on the floor of the Confessor's chapel of the scratch made by the mason, on Henry's instructions, to mark the site of his proposed tomb. See L.E. Tanner, *Recollections of a Westminster Antiquary* (London, 1969), pp. 110–11, and also McKenna, 'Piety and Propaganda', p. 81. It might be added that although Henry did not initiate any really major building programmes in the royal palaces, he did have altar closets, or oratories, constructed at Sheen and Havering. See H.M. Colvin, *The History of the King's Works* (6 vols., London, 1963–73), II, pp. 959, 1000. For Henry's observant piety in 1460, see *Ingulph's Chronicle*, p. 420.

73.   Blacman, pp. 7–9; J. Haller, 'Piero da Monte', pp. 43–5.
74.   Blacman, p. 8; Wolffe, p. 7; *The Register of Thomas Bekynton, Bishop of Bath and Wells, 1443–1465*, ed. H.C. Maxwell-Lyte and M.C.B. Dawes, I (Somerset Record Society, XLIX, 1934), pp. 116–7.
75.   Blacman, p. 14; Wolffe, pp. 9–11; Griffiths, *Reign of Henry VI*, pp. 6, 8 n.16, 250, 269 n.100.
76.   Blacman, pp. 4, 14.
77.   *Great Chronicle of London*, p. 215; *Miracula*, ed. Grosjean, pp. 99–100, 188.
78.   Wolffe, p. 11; Blacman, pp. 4, 7, 8, 10, 12, 14.
79.   Wolffe, pp. 8–9, 135–45; Blacman, pp. 5, 6, 13, 15.
80.   As, also, is Blacman's aside (p. 15) that Henry was in the habit of reading chronicles. *RP*, V, pp. 375–6; *Registrum abbatiae Johannis Whethamstede*, ed. H.T Riley (2 vols., RS, 1872–3), I, pp. 338–9.
81.   *Ibid.*, I, p. 295; Bodleian Library, MS. Bodley 277.
82.   Griffiths, *Reign of Henry VI*, p. 53; J. Haller, 'Piero da Monte', pp. 43–5; *Paston Letters*, ed. Davis, II, p. 108.
83.   *Official Correspondence of Thomas Bekynton*, ed. G. Williams (2 vols., RS, 1872), I, pp. 118–19; Blacman, p. 20. Again, Blacman's remark is far from a bland commonplace; the cult of the Confessor enjoyed little general popularity in fifteenth-century England. See B. Harvey, *Westminster Abbey and its Estates in the Middle Ages* (Oxford, 1977), pp. 43–5.
84.   *Liber Regie Capelle*, ed. W. Ullmann (Bradshaw Society, XCII, 1959), pp. 18, 64; Wolffe, p. 261 and n. 99; *Miracula*, ed. Grosjean, p. 185* *et seq.*
85.   Wolffe, p. 145; Blacman, pp. 11–12.
86.   *Statutes of the Colleges of Oxford* (Royal Commission, 1853), I, Statutes of New College, rub. 68; Statutes of All Souls College, preface, and cap. 23.
87.   W.G. Searle, *The History of the Queens' College* (Cambridge Antiquarian Society, IX, 1867), pp. 89–92; in general, F.Ll. Harrison, 'The Eton Choirbook', *Annales Musicologiques*, I (1953), 151 *et seq.*
88.   Wolffe, p. 145.
89.   H. Rashdall, *The Universities of Europe in the Middle Ages*, ed. F.M. Powicke and A.B. Emden (3 vols., Oxford, 1936), III, pp. 295–8, 303–4, 314–15.
90.   N. Orme, *English Schools in the Middle Ages* (London, 1973), pp. 198–201.
91.   Before the foundation of King's College, the royal government provided about £175 a year for King's Hall, and £100 a year in total to the Franciscan and Dominican houses in Oxford and Cambridge. By 1460 the annual income of King's College was more than £1,000. See A.B. Cobban, *The King's Hall within the University of Cambridge* (Cambridge, 1969), pp. 202–6; *CPR, 1301–7*, p. 239; *VCH, Cambridgeshire*, III, p. 379. What is more, King's Hall was a 'closed' college whose members were directly nominated by the king, that is, 'an outlet for royal patronage' and in this respect quite different from King's College (Cobban, *King's Hall*, pp. 21–2, 151–4). Equally, the annual grants to the friars of Oxford and Cambridge were in the nature of alms as much as support for education. For the self-regarding grants to scholars made by an earlier, not uncultivated, king, see F. Pegues, 'Royal Support of Students in the Thirteenth Century', *Speculum*, XXXI (1956), 454–60.
92.   For different facets of this complex change, see A.B. Cobban, 'Origins: Robert Wodelarke and St Catharine's', in *St Catharine's College, Cambridge, 1473–1973*, ed. E.E. Rich, pp. 11–32, and

T.H. Aston, 'The Medieval Alumni of the University of Cambridge', *Past and Present*, 86 (1980), 11–27.

93.   Cobban, *King's Hall*, pp. 44–45.
94.   Wolffe, pp. 8–9, 138–45.
95.   *The Early Rolls of Merton College*, ed. J.R.L. Highfield (Oxford Historical Society, New Series, XVIII, 1964), pp. 21–27, 52–4; VCH, *Cambridgeshire*, III, pp. 334, 340–41; A.C. Chibnall, *Richard de Badew and the University of Cambridge* (Cambridge, 1963), pp. 11–44; VCH, *Oxfordshire*, III, p. 119.
96.   Cobban, *King's Hall*, pp. 44–45; H.C. Maxwell Lyte, *A History of Eton College* (4th ed., London, 1911), p. 20; VCH, *Cambridgeshire*, III, p. 379.
97.   Wolffe, pp. 138–45; Blacman, pp. 11–12.
98.   J. Cloake, 'The Charterhouse of Sheen', *Surrey Archaeological Collections*, LXXI (1977), 145–98.
99.   RP, V, pp. 217–8. The building accounts for King's College have been lost but an annual grant of £1,000 was allocated for the purpose from the revenues of the duchy of Lancaster. Some £15,000 had been spent on the building of Eton by 1461. See R. Willis and J.W. Clark, *The Architectural History of the University of Cambridge* (4 vols., Cambridge, 1886), I, pp. 353, 380–405; VCH, *Cambridgeshire*, III, pp. 388–9. For the endowment of King's, see *ibid.*, pp. 379–80.
100. King's College, MS. 4; Bodleian Library, MS. Laud misc. 154, fo.2, mistakenly transcribed as *Uter patrem* in Thompson, *Carthusian Order*, p. 321.
101. Mark 3:21; John 10:20; 1 Corinthians 4:10.
102. J. Saward, *Perfect Fools* (Oxford, 1980), pp. 58, 61, 84, 91–2.
103. *The Book of Margery Kempe*, ed. S.B. Meech and H.E. Allen (EETS, 212, 1940), pp. 36–7.
104. Blacman, p. 6; Wolffe, p. 7.
105. Reluctance to resist, or replace, Henry had many facets; for some general reflections, see Griffiths, *Reign of Henry VI*, pp. 628, 684, 797–8, 807, 821, 856–7, 863–9, and Wolffe, pp. 278–80, 319, 323.
106. I would like to express my gratitude to Professor R.A. Griffiths for his detailed assistance, and especially his general encouragement, with the preparation of this paper.

Index of Principal Persons and Places

Kings, queens and princes(ses) have been indexed by their Christian names, royal dukes by their titles, noblemen and women by their family names and bishops by their patronyms.